Praise for *Java 9 Modularity*

Modularity represents a truly deep and fundamental change to the way that Java applications are built and deployed. Java 9 Modularity is the guide you and your applications need to make the most of the potential of this new and uncharted world.

—*Ben Evans, Java Champion and Cofounder, jClarity*

Modularization is hard. Luckily I've been able to use Paul and Sander's book as my guide for writing my Java 9 tutorials, talks, and converting jClarity's applications to use Java's new modular system. I'm buying a copy for all the engineering team at jClarity, it's that good!

—*Martijn Verburg, CEO, jClarity and Sun/Oracle*
Java Champion

This book delivers the essential practical knowledge you need to create modular applications in Java 9. It's a must read for any developer or architect wanting to adopt one of the most significant features the JDK has seen in many years.

—*Simon Maple, Director of Developer Relations,*
ZeroTurnaround

Java 9 Modularity
Patterns and Practices for Developing Maintainable Applications

Sander Mak and Paul Bakker

Beijing · Boston · Farnham · Sebastopol · Tokyo

Java 9 Modularity

by Sander Mak and Paul Bakker

Printed in the United States of America.

Published by O'Reilly Media, Inc., 1005 Gravenstein Highway North, Sebastopol, CA 95472.

O'Reilly books may be purchased for educational, business, or sales promotional use. Online editions are also available for most titles (*http://oreilly.com/safari*). For more information, contact our corporate/institutional sales department: 800-998-9938 or *corporate@oreilly.com*.

Editors: Nan Barber and Brian Foster	**Indexer:** Ellen Troutman-Zaig
Production Editor: Nicholas Adams	**Interior Designer:** David Futato
Copyeditor: Sharon Wilkey	**Cover Designer:** Karen Montgomery
Proofreader: Charles Roumeliotis	**Illustrator:** Rebecca Demarest

September 2017:   First Edition

Revision History for the First Edition
2017-09-05:   First Release

See *http://oreilly.com/catalog/errata.csp?isbn=9781491954164* for release details.

978-1-491-95416-4

[LSI]

Table of Contents

Part II.   Migration

Foreword

What is modularity in Java? To some, it's a principle for development: programming to interfaces and hiding the details of implementations. This is the *school of encapsulation*. To others, it's about leaning hard on class loaders to provide dynamic execution environments. This is the *school of isolation*. To still others, it's about artifacts, repositories, and tooling. This is the *school of configuration*. Individually, these perspectives are valid, but they feel like pieces of a larger story that's not quite clear. If a developer knows that some portion of their code is for internal use only, why can't they hide a package as easily as hiding a class or a field? If code can be compiled and run only in the presence of its dependencies, why don't those dependencies flow smoothly from compilation to packaging to installation to execution? If tools work only when presented with pristine self-describing artifacts, how can anyone reuse older libraries that are just plain JAR files?

Java 9 offers a coherent story for modularity by introducing modules as a first-class feature of the Java platform. A module is a set of packages designed for reuse. This simple concept has a surprisingly powerful impact on how code is developed, deployed, and run. The longstanding mechanisms for promoting and controlling reuse in Java—interfaces, access control, JAR files, class loaders, dynamic linking—all work better when packages are placed into modules.

First, modules clarify the structure of a program in a way that other mechanisms cannot. Many developers will be surprised that their code is not as well structured as they thought. For example, a codebase spread across multiple JAR files has a good chance of cycles between classes in different JAR files, but cycles between classes in different modules are forbidden. One of the motivations for investing in the modularization of a codebase is the knowledge that, once complete, there won't be any backsliding into the ball of mud that cyclic dependencies allow. Developing with modules also leads to programming with services, which reduce coupling and increase abstraction even further.

Second, modules engender a sense of responsibility for code in a way that other mechanisms cannot. A developer who exports packages from a module is making a commitment to a stable API, and even the name of the module itself is part of the API. A developer who bundles too much functionality into a single module will cause that module to drag in a large number of dependencies that are irrelevant for any single task; anyone who reuses the module will realize its sprawling nature even if its internals are hidden. Developing with modules encourages every developer to think about the stability and cohesiveness of their code.

Most people are familiar with the tablecloth trick, where the cloth is whipped off the table without upsetting the plates and cups. For those of us who worked on Java 9, designing a module system that could slide into the Java Virtual Machine underneath the millions of classes developed since the 1990s felt rather like performing the trick in reverse. It turned out that modularizing the JDK caused the trick to fail, because some well-known libraries derived their power from trying to ignore the very encapsulation that the module system applied to the JDK's modules. This tension in the design of Java 9 had no easy academic answers. In the end, a strong cycle of feedback from the community led to the module system offering developers a variety of levers and dials, so that modularized platform code can enjoy truly strong encapsulation while modularized application code can enjoy "strong enough" encapsulation. Over time, we think the bold choices made in modularizing the JDK will make all code more reliable.

A module system works best when it works for everyone. The more developers who create modules today, the more developers who will create modules tomorrow. But what about developers who have not created their modules *yet*? It is no exaggeration to say that Java 9 is just as concerned about the code that is not in modules as about the code that is. The only developer who should modularize a codebase is its author, so until that happens, the module system has to provide a way for code in modules to reach out to code not in modules. This led to the design of automatic modules which are so well explained in this book.

Sander and Paul are expert practitioners of Java and trusted guides to the Java 9 ecosystem. They were on the front lines of Java 9's development, and in the vanguard of efforts to migrate popular open source libraries. *Java 9 Modularity* is the handbook for everyone interested in the core principles and best practices of modularity in Java: application developers looking to create maintainable components; library developers looking for advice on migration and reflection; and framework developers wishing to exploit the module system's advanced features. I hope this book will help you to create Java programs whose structure lets them stand the test of time.

— Alex Buckley
Java Platform Group, Oracle
Santa Clara, July 2017

Preface

Java 9 introduces a module system to the platform. This is a major leap, marking the start of a new era for modular software development on the Java platform. We're very excited about these changes, and we hope you are too after reading this book. You'll be ready to make the best use of the module system before you know it.

Who Should Read This Book

This book is for Java developers who want to improve the design and structure of their applications. The Java module system improves the way we can design and build Java applications. Even if you're not going to use modules right away, understanding the modularization of the JDK itself is an important first step. After you acquaint yourself with modules in the first part of the book, we expect you to also really appreciate the migration chapters that follow. Moving existing code to Java 9 and the module system will become an increasingly common task.

This book is by no means a general introduction to Java. We assume you have experience writing relatively large Java applications in a team setting. That's where modularity becomes more and more important. As an experienced Java developer, you will recognize the problems caused by the classpath, helping you appreciate the module system and its features.

There are many other changes in Java 9 besides the module system. This book, however, focuses on the module system and related features. Where appropriate, other Java 9 features are discussed in the context of the module system.

Why We Wrote This Book

We have been Java users since the early days of Java, when applets still were hot stuff. We've used and enjoyed many other platforms and languages over the years, but Java still remains our primary tool. When it comes to building maintainable software, modularity is a key principle. Pursuing modular application development has become somewhat of a passion for us, after spending a lot of energy building modular software over the years. We've used technology such as OSGi extensively to achieve this, without support in the Java platform itself. We've also learned from tools outside the Java space, such as module systems for JavaScript. When it became clear that Java 9 would feature the long-awaited module system, we decided we didn't want to just use this feature, but also help with onboarding other developers.

Maybe you have heard of Project Jigsaw at some point in the past decade. Project Jigsaw prototyped many possible implementations of a Java module system over the course of many years. A module system for Java has been on and off the table several times. Both Java 7 and 8 were originally going to include the results of Project Jigsaw.

With Java 9, this long period of experimentation culminates into an official module system implementation. Many changes have occurred in the scope and functionality of the various module system prototypes over the years. Even when you've been following this process closely, it's difficult to see what the final Java 9 module system really entails. Through this book, we want to provide a definitive overview of the module system. And, more important, what it can do for the design and architecture of your applications.

Navigating This Book

The book is split into three parts:

1. Introduction to the Java Module System

2. Migration

3. Modular Development Tooling

The first part teaches you how to use the module system. Starting with the modular JDK itself, it then goes into creating your own modules. Next we discuss services, which enable decoupling of modules. The first part ends with a discussion of modularity patterns, and how you use modules in a way to maximize maintainability and extensibility.

The second part of the book is about migration. You most likely have existing Java code, probably using Java libraries that were not designed for the module system. In this part of the book, you will learn how to migrate existing code to modules, and how to use existing libraries that are not modules yet. If you are the author or maintainer of a library, there is a chapter specifically about adding module support to libraries.

The third and last part of the book is about tooling. In this part, you will learn about the current state of IDEs and build tools. You will also learn how to test modules, because modules give some new challenges but also opportunities when it comes to (unit) testing. Finally, you will also learn about *linking*, another exciting feature of the module system. It enables the creation of highly optimized custom runtime images, changing the way you can ship Java applications by virtue of modules.

The book is designed to be read from cover to cover, but we kept in mind that this is not an option for every reader. We recommend to at least go over the first four chapters in detail. This will set you up with the basic knowledge to make good use of the rest of the book. If you are really short on time and have existing code to migrate, you can skip to the second part of the book after that. Once you're ready for it, you should be able to come back to the more advanced chapters.

Using Code Examples

The book contains many code examples. All code examples are available on GitHub at *https://github.com/java9-modularity/examples*. In this repository, the code examples are organized by chapter. Throughout the book we refer to specific code examples as follows: ➡ *chapter3/helloworld*. This means the example can be found in *https://github.com/java9-modularity/examples/chapter3/helloworld*.

We highly recommend having the code available when going through the book, because longer code sections just read better in a code editor. We also recommend playing with the code yourself—for example, to reproduce errors that we discuss in the book. Learning by doing beats just reading the words.

Conventions Used in This Book

The following typographical conventions are used in this book:

Italic
> Indicates new terms, URLs, email addresses, filenames, and file extensions.

`Constant width`
> Used for program listings, as well as within paragraphs to refer to program elements such as variable or function names, databases, data types, environment variables, statements, and keywords.

`Constant width bold`
> Shows commands or other text that should be typed literally by the user.

`Constant width italic`
> Shows text that should be replaced with user-supplied values or by values determined by context.

This icon signifies a general note.

 This icon signifies a tip or suggestion.

 This icon indicates a warning or caution.

O'Reilly Safari

 *Safari* (formerly Safari Books Online) is a membership-based training and reference platform for enterprise, government, educators, and individuals.

Members have access to thousands of books, training videos, Learning Paths, interactive tutorials, and curated playlists from over 250 publishers, including O'Reilly Media, Harvard Business Review, Prentice Hall Professional, Addison-Wesley Professional, Microsoft Press, Sams, Que, Peachpit Press, Adobe, Focal Press, Cisco Press, John Wiley & Sons, Syngress, Morgan Kaufmann, IBM Redbooks, Packt, Adobe Press, FT Press, Apress, Manning, New Riders, McGraw-Hill, Jones & Bartlett, and Course Technology, among others.

For more information, please visit *http://oreilly.com/safari*.

How to Contact Us

You can follow a Twitter account accompanying this book to keep up with developments around modular development in Java:

@javamodularity: *http://twitter.com/javamodularity*

You can also visit *https://javamodularity.com*

You can also contact the authors directly:

Sander Mak
  @sander_mak (*http://twitter.com/sander_mak*)

  sandermak@gmail.com

Paul Bakker
  @pbakker (*http://twitter.com/pbakker*)

  paul.bakker.nl@gmail.com

Please address comments and questions concerning this book to the publisher:

O'Reilly Media, Inc.
1005 Gravenstein Highway North
Sebastopol, CA 95472
800-998-9938 (in the United States or Canada)
707-829-0515 (international or local)
707-829-0104 (fax)

We have a web page for this book, where we list errata, examples, and any additional information. You can access this page at *http://bit.ly/java-9-modularity*.

To comment or ask technical questions about this book, send email to *bookquestions@oreilly.com*.

For more information about our books, courses, conferences, and news, see our website at *http://www.oreilly.com*.

Find us on Facebook: *http://facebook.com/oreilly*

Follow us on Twitter: *http://twitter.com/oreillymedia*

Watch us on YouTube: *http://www.youtube.com/oreillymedia*

Acknowledgments

The idea for this book originated during a conversation with Brian Foster from O'Reilly at JavaOne back in 2015. Thank you for entrusting us with this project. Since that moment, many people have helped us create *Java 9 Modularity*.

This book would not have been what it is today without the great technical reviews from Alex Buckley, Alan Bateman, and Simon Maple. Many thanks to them, as they contributed many improvements to the book. We're also grateful for the support of O'Reilly's editorial team. Nan Barber and Heather Scherer made sure all organizational details were taken care of.

Writing this book would not have been possible without the unwavering support of my wife, Suzanne. She and our three boys had to miss me on many evenings and weekends. Thank you for sticking with me to the end! I also want to thank Luminis (*http://luminis.eu/*) for graciously providing support to write this book. I'm glad to be part of a company that lives and breathes the mantra "Knowledge is the only treasure that increases on sharing."

Sander Mak

I would also like to thank my wife, Qiushi, for supporting me while writing my second book, even while we were moving to the other side of the world. Also thanks to both Netflix (*http://netflix.com/*) and Luminis (*http://luminis.eu/*), for giving me the time and opportunity to work on this book.

Paul Bakker

The comics in Chapters 1, 7, 13, and 14 were created by Oliver Widder (*http://geek-and-poke.com/*) and are licensed under Creative Commons Attribution 3.0 Unported (CC BY 3.0) (*https://creativecommons.org/licenses/by/3.0/deed.en_US*). The authors changed the comics to be horizontal and grayscale.

PART I

Introduction to the Java Module System

CHAPTER 1

Modularity Matters

Have you ever scratched your head in bewilderment, asking yourself, "Why is this code here? How does it relate to the rest of this gigantic codebase? Where do I even begin?" Or did your eyes glaze over after scanning the multitude of Java Archives (JARs) bundled with your application code? We certainly have.

The art of structuring large codebases is an undervalued one. This is neither a new problem, nor is it specific to Java. However, Java is one of the mainstream languages in which very large applications are built all the time—often making heavy use of many libraries from the Java ecosystem. Under these circumstances, systems can outgrow our capacity for understanding and efficient development. A lack of structure is dearly paid for in the long run, experience shows.

Modularity is one of the techniques you can employ to manage and reduce this complexity. Java 9 introduces a new module system that makes modularization easier and more accessible. It builds on top of abstractions Java already has for modular development. In a sense, it promotes existing best practices on large-scale Java development to be part of the Java language.

The Java module system will have a profound impact on Java development. It represents a fundamental shift to modularity as a first-class citizen for the whole Java platform. Modularization is addressed from the ground up, with changes to the language, Java Virtual Machine (JVM), and standard libraries. While this represents a monumental effort, it's not as flashy as, for example, the addition of streams and lambdas in Java 8. There's another fundamental difference between a feature like lambdas and the Java module system. A module system is concerned with the large-scale structure of whole applications. Turning an inner class into a lambda is a fairly small and localized change within a single class. Modularizing an application affects design, compilation, packaging, deployment, and so on. Clearly, it's much more than just another language feature.

With every new Java release, it's tempting to dive right in and start using the new features. To make the most out of the module system, we should first take a step back and focus on what modularity is. And, more important, why we should care.

What Is Modularity?

So far, we've touched upon the goal of modularity (managing and reducing complexity), but not what modularity entails. At its heart, *modularization* is the act of decomposing a system into self-contained but interconnected modules. *Modules* are identifiable artifacts containing code, with metadata describing the module and its relation to other modules. Ideally, these artifacts are recognizable from compile-time all the way through run-time. An application then consists of multiple modules working together.

So, modules group related code, but there's more to it than that. Modules must adhere to three core tenets:

Strong encapsulation
  A module must be able to conceal part of its code from other modules. By doing so, a clear line is drawn between code that is publicly usable and code that is deemed an internal implementation detail. This prevents accidental or unwanted coupling between modules: you simply cannot use what has been encapsulated. Consequently, encapsulated code may change freely without affecting users of the module.

Well-defined interfaces
  Encapsulation is fine, but if modules are to work together, not everything can be encapsulated. Code that is not encapsulated is, by definition, part of the public API of a module. Since other modules can use this public code, it must be managed with great care. A breaking change in nonencapsulated code can break other modules that depend on it. Therefore, modules should expose well-defined and stable interfaces to other modules.

Explicit dependencies
  Modules often need other modules to fulfill their obligations. Such dependencies must be part of the module definition, in order for modules to be self-contained. Explicit dependencies give rise to a *module graph*: nodes represent modules, and edges represent dependencies between modules. Having a module graph is important for both understanding an application and running it with all necessary modules. It provides the basis for a reliable configuration of modules.

Flexibility, understandability, and reusability all come together with modules. Modules can be flexibly composed into different configurations, making use of the explicit dependencies to ensure that everything works together. Encapsulation ensures that you never have to know implementation details and that you will never accidentally rely on them. To use a module, knowing its public API is enough. Also, a module exposing well-defined interfaces while encapsulating its implementation details can readily be swapped with alternative implementations conforming to the same API.

Modular applications have many advantages. Experienced developers know all too well what happens when codebases are nonmodular. Endearing terms like *spaghetti architecture*, *messy monolith*, or *big ball of mud* do not even begin to cover the associated pain. Modularity is not a silver bullet, though. It is an architectural principle that can *prevent* these problems to a high degree when applied correctly.

That being said, the definition of *modularity* provided in this section is deliberately abstract. It might make you think of component-based development (all the rage in the previous century), service-oriented architecture, or the current microservices hype. Indeed, these paradigms try to solve similar problems at various levels of abstraction.

What would it take to realize modules in Java? It's instructive to take a moment and think about how the core tenets of modularity are already present in Java as you know it (and where it is lacking).

Done? Then you're ready to proceed to the next section.

Before Java 9

Java is used for development of all sorts and sizes. Applications comprising millions of lines of code are no exception. Evidently, Java has done something right when it comes to building large-scale systems—even before Java 9 arrived on the scene. Let's examine the three core tenets of modularity again in the light of Java before the arrival of the Java 9 module system.

Encapsulation of types can be achieved by using a combination of *packages* and *access modifiers* (such as `private`, `protected`, or `public`). By making a class `protected`, for example, you can prevent other classes from accessing it unless they reside in the same package. That raises an interesting question: what if you want to access that class from another package in your component, but still want to prevent others from using it? There's no good way to do this. You can, of course, make the class public. But, public means public to every other type in the system, meaning no encapsulation. You can hint that using such a class is not smart by putting it in an `.impl` or `.internal` package. But really, who looks at that? People use it anyway, just because they can. There's no way to hide such an implementation package.

In the well-defined interfaces department, Java has been doing great since its inception. You guessed it, we're talking about Java's very own `interface` keyword. Exposing a public interface, while hiding the implementation class behind a factory or through dependency injection, is a tried-and-true method. As you will see throughout this book, interfaces play a central role in modular systems.

Explicit dependencies are where things start to fall apart. Yes, Java does have explicit import statements. Unfortunately, those imports are strictly a compile-time construct. Once you package your code into a JAR, there's no telling which other JARs contain the types your JAR needs to run. In fact, this problem is so bad, many external tools evolved alongside the Java language to solve this problem. The following sidebar provides more details.

External Tooling to Manage Dependencies: Maven and OSGi

Maven

One of the problems solved by the Maven build tool is compile-time dependency management. Dependencies between JARs are defined in an external Project Object Model (POM) file. Maven's great success is not the build tool per se, but the fact that it spawned a canonical repository called Maven Central. Virtually all Java libraries are published along with their POMs to Maven Central. Various other build tools such as Gradle or Ant (with Ivy) use the same repository and metadata. They all automatically resolve (transitive) dependencies for you at compile-time.

OSGi

What Maven does at compile-time, OSGi does at run-time. OSGi requires imported packages to be listed as metadata in JARs, which are then called *bundles*. You must also explicitly define which packages are exported, that is, visible to other bundles. At application start, all bundles are checked: can every importing bundle be wired to an exporting bundle? A clever setup of custom classloaders ensures that at run-time no types are loaded in a bundle besides what is allowed by the metadata. As with Maven, this requires the whole world to provide correct OSGi metadata in their JARs. However, where Maven has unequivocally succeeded with Maven Central and POMs, the proliferation of OSGi-capable JARs is less impressive.

Both Maven and OSGi are built on top of the JVM and Java language, which they do not control. Java 9 addresses some of the same problems in the core of the JVM and the language. The module system is not intended to completely replace those tools. Both Maven and OSGi (and similar tools) still have their place, only now they can build on a fully modular Java platform.

As it stands, Java offers solid constructs for creating large-scale modular applications. It's also clear there is definitely room for improvement.

JARs as Modules?

JAR files seem to be the closest we can get to modules pre-Java 9. They have a name, group related code, and can offer well-defined public interfaces. Let's look at an example of a typical Java application running on top of the JVM to explore the notion of JARs as modules; see Figure 1-1.

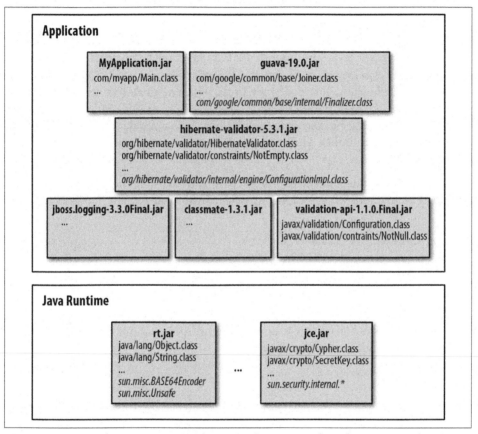

Figure 1-1. MyApplication is a typical Java application, packaged as a JAR and using other libraries

There's an application JAR called *MyApplication.jar* containing custom application code. Two libraries are used by the application: Google Guava and Hibernate Validator. There are three additional JARs as well. Those are transitive dependencies of Hibernate Validator, possibly resolved for us by a build tool like Maven. MyApplication runs on a pre-Java 9 runtime which itself exposes Java platform classes through several bundled JARs. The pre-Java 9 runtime may be a Java Runtime Environment (JRE) or a Java Development Kit (JDK), but in both cases it includes *rt.jar* (*runtime library*), which contains the classes of the Java standard library.

When you look closely at Figure 1-1, you can see that some of the JARs list classes in *italic*. These classes are supposed to be internal classes of the libraries. For example, com.google.common.base.internal.Finalizer is used in Guava itself, but is not part of the official API. It's a public class, since other Guava packages use Finalizer. Unfortunately, this also means there's no impediment for com.myapp.Main to use classes like Finalizer. In other words, there's no strong encapsulation.

The same holds for internal classes from the Java platform itself. Packages such as sun.misc have always been accessible to application code, even though documentation sternly warns they are unsupported APIs that should not be used. Despite this warning, utility classes such as sun.misc.BASE64Encoder are used in application code all the time. Technically, that code *may* break with any update of the Java runtime, since they are internal implementation classes. Lack of encapsulation essentially forced those classes to be considered semipublic APIs anyway, since Java highly values backward compatibility. This is an unfortunate situation, arising from the lack of true encapsulation.

What about explicit dependencies? As you've already learned, there is no dependency information anymore when looking strictly at JARs. You run MyApplication as follows:

```
java -classpath lib/guava-19.0.jar:\
                lib/hibernate-validator-5.3.1.jar:\
                lib/jboss-logging-3.3.0Final.jar:\
                lib/classmate-1.3.1.jar:\
                lib/validation-api-1.1.0.Final.jar \
        -jar MyApplication.jar
```

Setting up the correct classpath is up to the user. And, without explicit dependency information, it is not for the faint of heart.

Classpath Hell

The *classpath* is used by the Java runtime to locate classes. In our example, we run Main, and all classes that are directly or indirectly referenced from this class need to be loaded at some point. You can view the classpath as a list of all classes that *may* be loaded at runtime. While there is more to it behind the scenes, this view suffices to understand the issues with the classpath.

A condensed view of the resulting classpath for MyApplication looks like this:

```
java.lang.Object
java.lang.String
...
sun.misc.BASE64Encoder
sun.misc.Unsafe
...
javax.crypto.Cypher
```

```
javax.crypto.SecretKey
...
com.myapp.Main
...
com.google.common.base.Joiner
...
com.google.common.base.internal.Joiner
org.hibernate.validator.HibernateValidator
org.hibernate.validator.constraints.NotEmpty
...
org.hibernate.validator.internal.engine.ConfigurationImpl
...
javax.validation.Configuration
javax.validation.constraints.NotNull
```

There's no notion of JARs or logical grouping anymore. All classes are sequenced into a flat list, in the order defined by the -classpath argument. When the JVM loads a class, it reads the classpath in sequential order to find the right one. As soon as the class is found, the search ends and the class is loaded.

What if a class cannot be found on the classpath? Then you will get a run-time exception. Because classes are loaded lazily, this could be triggered when some unlucky user clicks a button in your application for the first time. The JVM cannot efficiently verify the completeness of the classpath upon starting. There is no way to tell in advance whether the classpath is complete, or whether you should add another JAR. Obviously, that's not good.

More insidious problems arise when duplicate classes are on the classpath. Let's say you try to circumvent the manual setup of the classpath. Instead, you let Maven construct the right set of JARs to put on the classpath, based on the explicit dependency information in POMs. Since Maven resolves dependencies transitively, it's not uncommon for two versions of the same library (say, Guava 19 and Guava 18) to end up in this set, through no fault of your own. Now both library JARs are flattened into the classpath, in an undefined order. Whichever version of the library classes comes first is loaded. However, other classes may expect a class from the (possibly incompatible) other version. Again, this leads to run-time exceptions. In general, whenever the classpath contains two classes with the same (fully qualified) name, even if they are completely unrelated, only one "wins."

It now becomes clear why the term *classpath hell* (also known as *JAR hell*) is so infamous in the Java world. Some people have perfected the art of tuning a classpath through trial-and-error—a rather sad occupation when you think about it. The fragile classpath remains a leading cause of problems and frustration. If only more information were available about the relations between JARs at run-time. It's as if a dependency graph is hiding in the classpath and is just waiting to come out and be exploited. Enter Java 9 modules!

Java 9 Modules

By now, you have a solid understanding of Java's current strengths and limitations when it comes to modularity. With Java 9, we get a new ally in the quest for well-structured applications: the *Java module system*. While designing the Java Platform Module System to overcome current limitations, two main goals were defined:

• Modularize the JDK itself.

• Offer a module system for applications to use.

These goals are closely related. Modularizing the JDK is done by using the same module system that we, as application developers, can use in Java 9.

The module system introduces a native concept of modules into the Java language and runtime. Modules can either export or strongly encapsulate packages. Furthermore, they express dependencies on other modules explicitly. As you can see, all three tenets of modularity are addressed by the Java module system.

Let's revisit the MyApplication example, now based on the Java 9 module system, in Figure 1-2.

Each JAR becomes a module, containing explicit references to other modules. The fact that `hibernate-validator` uses `jboss-logging`, `classmate`, and `validation-api` is part of its *module descriptor*. A module has a publicly accessible part (on the top) and an encapsulated part (on the bottom, indicated with the padlock). That's why MyApplication can no longer use Guava's `Finalizer` class. Through this diagram, we discover that MyApplication uses `validation-api`, as well, to annotate some of its classes. What's more, MyApplication has an explicit dependency on a module in the JDK called `java.sql`.

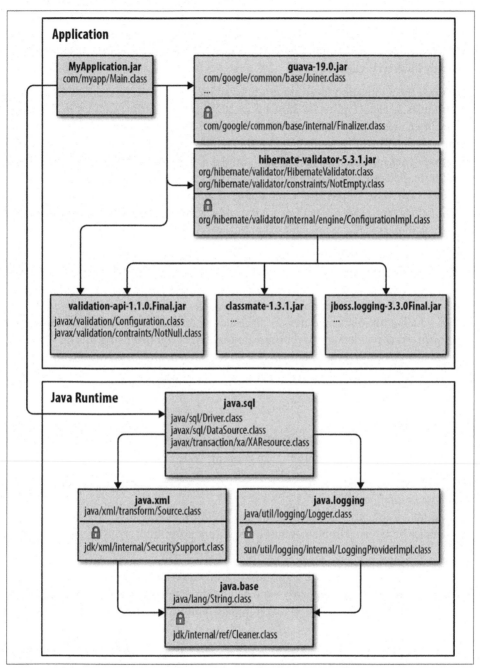

Figure 1-2. MyApplication as a modular application on top of modular Java 9

Figure 1-2 tells us much more about the application than in the classpath situation shown in Figure 1-1. All that could be said there is that MyApplication uses classes from *rt.jar*, like all Java applications—and that it runs with a bunch of JARs on the (possibly incorrect) classpath.

That's just the application layer. It's modules all the way down. At the JDK layer, there are modules as well (Figure 1-2 shows a small subset). Like the modules in the application layer, they have explicit dependencies and expose some packages while concealing others. The most essential *platform module* in the modular JDK is `java.base`. It exposes packages such as `java.lang` and `java.util`, which no other module can do without. Because you cannot avoid using types from these packages, every module requires `java.base` implicitly. If the application modules require any functionality from platform modules other than what's in `java.base`, these dependencies must be explicit as well, as is the case with MyApplication's dependency on `java.sql`.

Finally, there's a way to express dependencies between separate parts of the code at a higher level of granularity in the Java language. Now imagine the advantages of having all this information available at compile-time and run-time. Accidental dependencies on code from other nonreferenced modules can be prevented. The toolchain knows which additional modules are necessary for running a module by inspecting its (transitive) dependencies, and optimizations can be applied using this knowledge.

Strong encapsulation, well-defined interfaces, and explicit dependencies are now part of the Java platform. In short, these are the most important benefits of the Java Platform Module System:

Reliable configuration
> The module system checks whether a given combination of modules satisfies all dependencies before compiling or running code. This leads to fewer run-time errors.

Strong encapsulation
> Modules explicitly choose what to expose to other modules. Accidental dependencies on internal implementation details are prevented.

Scalable development
> Explicit boundaries enable teams to work in parallel while still creating maintainable codebases. Only explicitly exported public types are shared, creating boundaries that are automatically enforced by the module system.

Security
> Strong encapsulation is enforced at the deepest layers inside the JVM. This limits the attack surface of the Java runtime. Gaining reflective access to sensitive internal classes is not possible anymore.

Optimization

Because the module system knows which modules belong together, including platform modules, no other code needs to be considered during JVM startup. It also opens up the possibility to create a minimal configuration of modules for distribution. Furthermore, whole-program optimizations can be applied to such a set of modules. Before modules, this was much harder, because explicit dependency information was not available and a class could reference any other class from the classpath.

In the next chapter, we explore how modules are defined and what concepts govern their interactions. We do this by looking at modules in the JDK itself. There are many more platform modules than shown in Figure 1-2.

Exploring the modular JDK in Chapter 2 is a great way to get to know the module system concepts, while at the same time familiarizing yourself with the modules in the JDK. These are, after all, the modules you'll be using first and foremost in your modular Java 9 applications. After that, you'll be ready to start writing your own modules in Chapter 3.

Modules and the Modular JDK

Java is over 20 years old. As a language, it's still popular, proving that Java has held up well. The platform's long evolution becomes especially apparent when looking at the standard libraries. Prior to the Java module system, the runtime library of the JDK consisted of a hefty *rt.jar* (as shown previously in Figure 1-1), weighing in at more than 60 megabytes. It contains most of the runtime classes for Java: the ultimate monolith of the Java platform. In order to regain a flexible and future-proof platform, the JDK team set out to modularize the JDK—an ambitious goal, given the size and structure of the JDK. Over the course of the past 20 years, many APIs have been added. Virtually none have been removed.

Take CORBA—once considered the future of enterprise computing, and now a mostly forgotten technology. (To those who are still using it: we feel for you.) The classes supporting CORBA in the JDK are still present in *rt.jar* to this day. Each and every distribution of Java, regardless of the applications it runs, includes those CORBA classes. No matter whether you use CORBA or not, the classes are there. Carrying this legacy in the JDK results in unnecessary use of disk space, memory, and CPU time. In the context of using resource-constrained devices, or creating small containers for the cloud, these resources are in short supply. Not to mention the cognitive overhead of obsolete classes showing up in IDE autocompletions and documentation during development.

Simply removing these technologies from the JDK isn't a viable option, though. Backward compatibility is one of the most important guiding principles for Java. Removal of APIs would break a long streak of backward compatibility. Although it may affect only a small percentage of users, plenty of people are still using technologies like CORBA. In a modular JDK, people who aren't using CORBA can choose to ignore the module containing CORBA.

Alternatively, an aggressive deprecation schedule for truly obsolete technologies could work. Still, it would take several major releases before the JDK sheds the excess weight. Also, deciding what technology is truly obsolete would be at the discretion of the JDK team, which is a difficult position to be in.

 In the specific case of CORBA, the module is marked as deprecated, meaning it will likely be removed in a subsequent major Java release.

But the desire to break up the monolithic JDK is not just about removing obsolete technology. A vast array of technologies are useful to certain types of applications, while useless for others. JavaFX is the latest user-interface technology in Java, after AWT and Swing. This is certainly not something to be removed, but clearly it's not required in every application either. Web applications, for example, use none of the GUI toolkits in Java. Yet there is no way to deploy and run them without all three GUI toolkits being carried along.

Aside from convenience and waste, consider the security perspective. Java has experienced a considerable number of security exploits in the past. Many of these exploits share a common trait: somehow attackers gain access to sensitive classes inside the JDK to bypass the JVM's security sandbox. Strongly encapsulating dangerous internal classes within the JDK is a big improvement from a security standpoint. Also, decreasing the number of available classes in the runtime decreases the attack surface. Having tons of unused classes around in your application runtime only for them to be exploited later is an unfortunate trade-off. With a modular JDK, only those modules your application needs are resolved.

By now, it's abundantly clear that a modular approach for the JDK itself is sorely needed.

The Modular JDK

The first step toward a more modular JDK was taken in Java 8 with the introduction of *compact profiles*. A profile defines a subset of packages from the standard library available to applications targeting that profile. Three profiles are defined, imaginatively called *compact1*, *compact2*, and *compact3*. Each profile is a superset of the previous, adding more packages that can be used. The Java compiler and runtime were updated with knowledge of these predefined profiles. Java SE Embedded 8 (Linux only) offers low-footprint runtimes matching the compact profiles.

If your application fits one of the profiles described in Table 2-1, this is a good way to target a smaller runtime. But if you require even so much as a single class outside of the predefined profiles, you're out of luck. In that sense, compact profiles are far from flexible. They also don't address strong encapsulation. As an intermediate solution, compact profiles fulfilled their purpose. Ultimately, a more flexible approach is needed.

Table 2-1. Profiles defined for Java 8

Profile	Description
compact1	Smallest profile with Java core classes and logging and scripting APIs
compact2	Extends compact1 with XML, JDBC, and RMI APIs
compact3	Extends compact2 with security and management APIs

You already saw a glimpse of how JDK 9 is split into modules in Figure 1-2. The JDK now consists of about 90 *platform modules*, instead of a monolithic library. A platform module is part of the JDK, unlike application modules, which you can create yourself. There is no technical distinction between platform modules and application modules. Every platform module constitutes a well-defined piece of functionality of the JDK, ranging from logging to XML support. All modules explicitly define their dependencies on other modules.

A subset of these platform modules and their dependencies is shown in Figure 2-1. Every edge indicates a unidirectional dependency between modules (we'll get to the difference between solid and dashed edges later). For example, java.xml depends on java.base. As stated in "Java 9 Modules" on page 10, every module implicitly depends on java.base. In Figure 2-1 this implicit dependency is shown only when java.base is the sole dependency for a given module, as is the case with, for example, java.xml.

Even though the dependency graph may look a little overwhelming, we can glean a lot of information from it. Just by looking at the graph, you can get a decent overview of what the Java standard libraries offer and how the functionalities are related. For example, java.logging has many *incoming dependencies*, meaning it is used by many other platform modules. That makes sense for a central functionality such as logging. Module java.xml.bind (containing the JAXB API for XML binding) has many *outgoing dependencies*, including an unexpected one on java.desktop. The fact that we can notice this oddity by looking at a generated dependency graph and talk about it is a huge improvement. Because of the modularization of the JDK, there are clean module boundaries and explicit dependencies to reason about. Having an overview of a large codebase like the JDK, based on explicit module information, is invaluable.

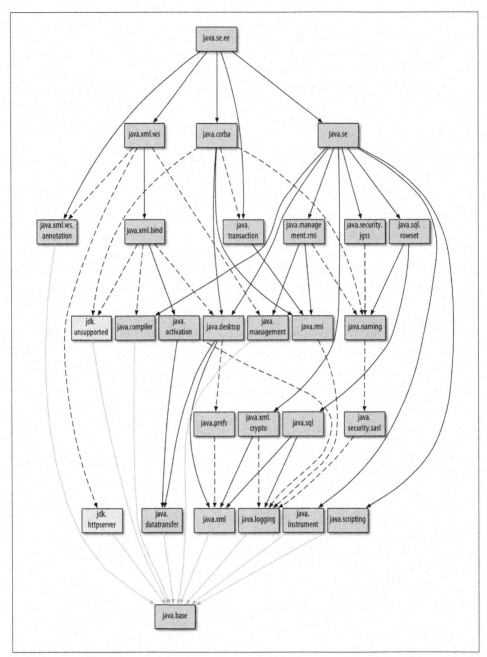

Figure 2-1. Subset of platform modules in the JDK

Another thing to note is how all arrows in the dependency graph point downward. There are no cycles in this graph. That's not by accident: the Java module system does not allow compile-time circular dependencies between modules.

 Circular dependencies are generally an indication of bad design. In "Breaking Cycles" on page 96, we discuss how to identify and resolve circular dependencies in your codebase.

All modules in Figure 2-1, except `jdk.httpserver` and `jdk.unsupported`, are part of the Java SE specification. They share the `java.*` prefix for module names. Every certified Java implementation must contain these modules. Modules such as `jdk.httpserver` contain *implementations* of tools and APIs. Where such implementations live is not mandated by the Java SE specification, but of course such modules are essential to a fully functioning Java platform. There are many more modules in the JDK, most of them in the `jdk.*` namespace.

 You can get the full list of platform modules by running `java --list-modules`.

Two important modules can be found at the top of Figure 2-1: `java.se` and `java.se.ee`. These are so-called *aggregator modules*, and they serve to logically group several other modules. We'll see how aggregator modules work later in this chapter.

Decomposing the JDK into modules has been a tremendous amount of work. Splitting up an entangled, organically grown codebase containing tens of thousands of classes into well-defined modules with clear boundaries, while retaining backward compatibility, takes time. This is one of the reasons it took a long time to get a module system into Java. With over 20 years of legacy accumulated, many dubious dependencies had to be untangled. Going forward, this effort will definitely pay off in terms of development speed and increased flexibility for the JDK.

Incubator Modules

Another example of the improved evolvability afforded by modules is the concept of *incubator modules*, described in JEP 11 (*http://openjdk.java.net/jeps/11*) (*JEP* stands for *Java Enhancement Proposal*). Incubator modules are a means to ship experimental APIs with the JDK. With Java 9, for example, a new HttpClient API is shipped in the `jdk.incubator.httpclient` module (all incubator modules have the `jdk.incubator` prefix). You can depend on such incubator modules if you want to, with the explicit expectation that their APIs may still change. This allows the APIs to mature and harden in a real-world environment, so they can be shipped as a fully supported module in a later JDK release—or be removed, if the API isn't successful in practice.

Module Descriptors

Now that we have a high-level overview of the JDK module structure, let's explore how modules work. What is a module, and how is it defined? A module has a name, it groups related code and possibly other resources, and is described by a module descriptor. The module descriptor lives in a file called *module-info.java*. Example 2-1 shows the module descriptor for the `java.prefs` platform module.

Example 2-1. module-info.java

```
module java.prefs {
    requires java.xml; ❶

    exports java.util.prefs; ❷
}
```

❶ The `requires` keyword indicates a dependency, in this case on module `java.xml`.

❷ A single package from the `java.prefs` module is exported to other modules.

Modules live in a global namespace; therefore, module names must be unique. As with package names, you can use conventions such as reverse DNS notation (e.g., `com.mycompany.project.somemodule`) to ensure uniqueness for your own modules. A module descriptor always starts with the `module` keyword, followed by the name of the module. Then, the body of *module-info.java* describes other characteristics of the module, if any.

Let's move on to the body of the module descriptor for `java.prefs`. Code in `java.prefs` uses code from `java.xml` to load preferences from XML files. This dependency must be expressed in the module descriptor. Without this dependency declaration, the `java.prefs` module would not compile (or run), as enforced by the module system. A dependency is declared with the `requires` keyword followed by a module name, in this case `java.xml`. The implicit dependency on `java.base` may be added to a module descriptor. Doing so adds no value, similar to how you can (but generally don't) add `"import java.lang.String"` to a class using strings.

A module descriptor can also contain `exports` statements. Strong encapsulation is the default for modules. Only when a package is explicitly exported, like `java.util.prefs` in this example, can it be accessed from other modules. Packages inside a module that are not exported are inaccessible from other modules by default. Other modules cannot refer to types in encapsulated packages, even if they have a dependency on the module. When you look at Figure 2-1, you see that java.desktop has a dependency on java.prefs. That means java.desktop is able to access only types in package java.util.prefs of the java.prefs module.

Readability

An important new concept when reasoning about dependencies between modules is *readability*. Reading another module means you can access types from its exported packages. You set up readability relations between modules through requires clauses in the module descriptor. By definition, every module reads itself. A module that requires another module *reads* the other module.

Let's explore the effects of readability by revisiting the java.prefs module. In this JDK module in Example 2-2, the following class imports and uses classes from the java.xml module.

Example 2-2. Small excerpt from the class java.util.prefs.XmlSupport

```
import org.w3c.dom.Document;
// ...

class XmlSupport {

    static void importPreferences(InputStream is)
        throws IOException, InvalidPreferencesFormatException
    {
        try {
            Document doc = loadPrefsDoc(is);
            // ...
        }
    }

    // ...
}
```

Here, org.w3c.dom.Document (among other classes) is imported. It comes from the java.xml module. Because the java.prefs module descriptor contains requires java.xml, as you saw in Example 2-1, this code compiles without issue. Had the author of the java.prefs module left out the requires clause, the Java compiler would report an error. Using code from java.xml in module java.prefs is a deliberate and explicitly recorded choice.

Accessibility

Readability relations are about which modules read other modules. However, if you read a module, this doesn't mean you can *access* everything from its exported packages. Normal Java accessibility rules are still in play after readability has been established.

Java has had accessibility rules built into the language since the beginning. Table 2-2 provides a refresher on the existing access modifiers and their impact.

Table 2-2. Access modifiers and their associated scopes

Access modifier	Class	Package	Subclass	Unrestricted
public	✓	✓	✓	✓
protected	✓	✓	✓	
- (default)	✓	✓		
private	✓			

Accessibility is enforced at compile- and run-time. Combining accessibility and readability provides the strong encapsulation guarantees we so desire in a module system. The question of whether you can access a type from module M2 in module M1 becomes twofold:

1. Does M1 read M2?
2. If yes, is the type accessible in the package exported by M2?

Only public types in exported packages are accessible in other modules. If a type is in an exported package but not public, traditional accessibility rules block its use. If it is public but not exported, the module system's readability rules prevent its use. Violations at compile-time result in a compiler error, whereas violations at run-time result in IllegalAccessError.

Is Public Still Public?

No types from a nonexported package can be used by other modules—even if types inside that package are public. This is a fundamental change to the accessibility rules of the Java language.

Until Java 9, things were quite straightforward. If you had a public class or interface, it could be used by every other class. As of Java 9, public means public only to all other packages inside that module. Only when the package containing the public type is exported can it be used by other modules. This is what strong encapsulation is all about. It forces developers to carefully design a package structure where types meant

---

for external consumption are clearly separated from internal implementation concerns.

Before modules, the only way to strongly encapsulate implementation classes was to keep them all in a single package and mark them package-private. Since this leads to unwieldy packages, in practice classes were made public just for access across different packages. With modules, you can structure packages any way you like and export only those that really must be accessible to the consumers of the module. Exported packages form the API of a module, if you will.

Another elephant in the room with regards to accessibility rules is *reflection*. Before the module system, an interesting but dangerous method called `setAccessible` was available on all reflected objects. By calling `setAccessible(true)`, any element (regardless of whether it is public or private) becomes accessible. This method is still available but now abides by the same rules as discussed previously. It is no longer possible to invoke `setAccessible` on an arbitrary element exported from another module and expect it to work as before. Even reflection cannot break strong encapsulation.

There are ways around the new accessibility rules imposed by the module system. Most of these workarounds should be viewed as migration aids and are discussed in Part II.

Implied Readability

Readability is not transitive by default. We can illustrate this by looking at the incoming and outgoing read edges of `java.prefs`, as shown in Figure 2-2.

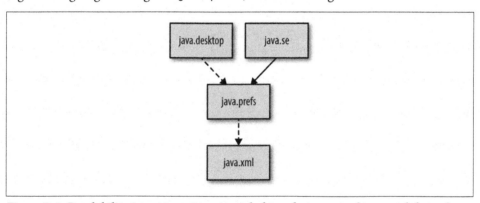

Figure 2-2. Readability is not transitive: java.desktop does not read java.xml through java.prefs

Here, java.desktop reads java.prefs (among other modules, left out for clarity). We've already established that this means java.desktop can access public types from the java.util.prefs package. However, java.desktop cannot access types from java.xml through its dependency on java.prefs. It just so happens that java.desktop *does use* types from java.xml as well. That's why java.desktop has its own requires java.xml clause in its module descriptor. In Figure 2-1, this dependency is also visible.

Sometimes you do want read relations to be transitive—for example, when a type in an exported package of module M1 refers to a type from another module M2. In that case, modules requiring M1 and thereby referencing types from M2 cannot be used without reading M2 as well.

That sounds completely abstract, so an illustration is in order. A good example of this phenomenon can be found in the JDK's java.sql module. It contains two interfaces (Driver, shown in Example 2-3, and SQLXML, shown in Example 2-4) defining method signatures whose result types come from other modules.

Example 2-3. Driver interface (partially shown), allowing a Logger from the java.logging module to be retrieved

```
package java.sql;

import java.util.logging.Logger;

public interface Driver {
  public Logger getParentLogger();
  // ..
}
```

Example 2-4. SQLXML interface (partially shown), with Source from module java.xml representing XML coming back from the database

```
package java.sql;

import javax.xml.transform.Source;

public interface SQLXML {
  <T extends Source> T getSource(Class<T> sourceClass);
  // ..
}
```

If you add a dependency on java.sql to your module descriptor, you can program to these interfaces, since they are in exported packages. But whenever you call get ParentLogger or getSource, you get back values of a type not exported by java.sql. In the first case, you get a java.util.logging.Logger from java.logging, and in the second case, you get a `javax.xml.transform.Source` from `java.xml`. In order to do anything useful with these return values (assign to a local variable, call methods on them), you need to read those other modules as well.

Of course, you can manually add dependencies on `java.logging` or `java.xml`, respectively, to your own module descriptor. But that's hardly satisfying, especially since the `java.sql` author already knew the interfaces are unusable without readability on those other modules. Implied readability allows module authors to express this transitive readability relation in module descriptors.

For `java.sql`, it looks like this:

```
module java.sql {
    requires transitive java.logging;
    requires transitive java.xml;

    exports java.sql;
    exports javax.sql;
    exports javax.transaction.xa;
}
```

The `requires` keyword is now followed by the `transitive` modifier, slightly changing the semantics. A normal `requires` allows a module to access types in exported packages from the required module only. `requires transitive` means the same and more. In addition, any module requiring `java.sql` will now automatically be requiring `java.logging` and `java.xml`. That means you get access to the exported packages of those modules as well by virtue of these implied readability relations. With `requires transitive`, module authors can set up additional readability relations for users of the module.

From the consumer side, this makes it easier to use `java.sql`. When you require `java.sql`, you get access to the exported packages `java.sql`, `javax.sql`, and `javax.transaction.xa` (which are all exported by `java.sql` directly), but also to all packages exported by modules `java.logging` and `java.xml`. It's as if `java.sql` re-exports those packages for you, courtesy of the implied readability relations it sets up with `requires transitive`. To be clear, there's no such thing as re-exporting packages from other modules, but thinking about it this way may help you understand the effects of implied readability.

For an application module `app` using `java.sql`, this module definition suffices:

```
module app {
    requires java.sql;
}
```

With this module descriptor, the implied readability edges in Figure 2-3 are in effect.

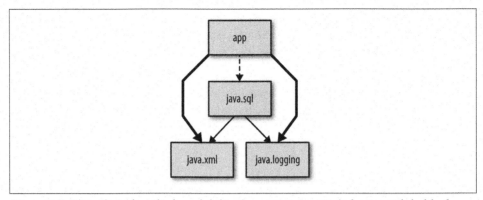

Figure 2-3. The effect of implied readability (requires transitive) shown with bold edges

Implied readability on `java.xml` and `java.logging` (the bold edges in Figure 2-3) is granted to `app` because `java.sql` uses `requires transitive` (solid edges in Figure 2-3) for those modules. Because `app` does not export anything and uses only `java.sql` for its encapsulated implementation, a normal `requires` clause is enough (dashed edge in Figure 2-3). When you need another module for internal uses, a normal `requires` suffices. If, on the other hand, types from another module are used in exported types, `requires transitive` is in order. In "API Modules" on page 83, we'll discuss how and when implied readability is important for your own modules in more detail.

Now's a good time to take another look at Figure 2-1. All solid edges in that graph are `requires transitive` dependencies too. The dashed edges, on the other hand, are normal `requires` dependencies. A *nontransitive dependency* means the dependency is necessary to support the internal implementation of that module. A *transitive dependency* means the dependency is necessary to support the API of the module. These latter dependencies are more significant; hence they are depicted by solid lines in the diagrams in this book.

Looking at Figure 2-1 with these new insights, we can highlight another use case for implied readability: it can be used to aggregate several modules into a single new module. Take, for example, `java.se`. It's a module that doesn't contain any code and consists of just a module descriptor. In this module descriptor, a `requires transitive` clause is listed for each module that is part of the Java SE specification. When you require `java.se` in a module, you get access to all exported APIs of every module aggregated by `java.se` by virtue of implied readability:

```
module java.se {
    requires transitive java.desktop;
    requires transitive java.sql;
    requires transitive java.xml;
    requires transitive java.prefs;
```

```
    // .. many more
}
```

Implied readability itself is transitive as well. Take another aggregator module in the platform, `java.se.ee`. Figure 2-1 shows that `java.se.ee` aggregates even more modules than `java.se`. It does so by using `requires transitive java.se` and adding several modules containing parts of the Java Enterprise Edition (EE) specification. Here's what the `java.se.ee` aggregator module descriptor looks like:

```
module java.se.ee {
    requires transitive java.se;
    requires transitive java.xml.ws;
    requires transitive java.xml.bind;
    // .. many more
}
```

The `requires transitive` on `java.se` ensures that if `java.se.ee` is required, implied readability is also established to all modules aggregated by `java.se`. Furthermore, `java.se.ee` sets up implied readability to several EE modules.

In the end, `java.se` and `java.se.ee` provide implied readability on a huge number of modules reachable through these transitive dependencies.

 Requiring `java.se.ee` or `java.se` in application modules is rarely the right thing to do. It means you're effectively replicating the pre-Java 9 behavior of having all of *rt.jar* accessible in your module. Dependencies should be defined as fine-grained as possible. It pays to be more precise in your module descriptor and require only modules you actually use.

In "Aggregator Modules" on page 90, we'll explore how the aggregator module pattern helps in modular library design.

Qualified Exports

In some cases, you'll want to expose a package only to certain other modules. You can do this by using *qualified exports* in the module descriptor. An example of a qualified export can be found in the `java.xml` module:

```
module java.xml {
    ...
    exports com.sun.xml.internal.stream.writers to java.xml.ws
    ...
}
```

Here we see a platform module sharing useful internals with another platform module. The exported package is accessible only by the modules specified after to. Multiple module names, separated by a comma, can be provided as targets for a qualified export. Any module not mentioned in this to clause cannot access types in this package, even when they read the module.

The fact that qualified exports exist doesn't unequivocally mean you should use them. In general, avoid using qualified exports between modules in an application. Using them creates an intimate bond between the exporting module and its allowable consumers. From a modularity perspective, this is undesirable. One of the great things about modules is that you effectively decouple producers from consumers of APIs. Qualified exports break this property because now the names of consumer modules are part of the provider module's descriptor.

For modularizing the JDK, however, this is a lesser concern. Qualified exports have been indispensable to modularizing the platform with all of its legacy. Many platform modules encapsulate part of their code, expose some internal APIs through qualified exports to select other platform modules, and use the normal export mechanism for public APIs used in applications. By using qualified exports, platform modules could be made more fine-grained without duplicating code.

Module Resolution and the Module Path

Having explicit dependencies between modules is not just useful to generate pretty diagrams. The Java compiler and runtime use module descriptors to resolve the right modules when compiling and running modules. Modules are resolved from the *module path*, as opposed to the classpath. Whereas the classpath is a flat list of types (even when using JAR files), the module path contains only modules. As you've learned, these modules carry explicit information on what packages they export, making the module path efficiently indexable. The Java runtime and compiler know exactly which module to resolve from the module path when looking for types from a given package. Previously, a scan through the whole classpath was the only way to locate an arbitrary type.

When you want to run an application packaged as a module, you need all of its dependencies as well. Module resolution is the process of computing a minimal required set of modules given a dependency graph and a *root module* chosen from that graph. Every module reachable from the root module ends up in the set of *resolved modules*. Mathematically speaking, this amounts to computing the *transitive closure* of the dependency graph. As intimidating as it may sound, the process is quite intuitive:

1. Start with a single root module and add it to the resolved set.

2. Add each required module (requires or requires transitive in *module-info.java*) to the resolved set.

3. Repeat step 2 for each new module added to the resolved set in step 2.

This process is guaranteed to terminate because we repeat the process only for newly discovered modules. Also, the dependency graph must be acyclic. If you want to resolve modules for multiple root modules, apply the algorithm to each root module, and then take the union of the resulting sets.

Let's try this with an example. We have an application module `app` that will be the root module in the resolution process. It uses only `java.sql` from the modular JDK:

```
module app {
    requires java.sql;
}
```

Now we run through the steps of module resolution. We omit `java.base` when considering the dependencies of modules and assume it always is part of the resolved modules. You can follow along by looking at the edges in Figure 2-1:

1. Add `app` to the resolved set; observe that it requires `java.sql`.

2. Add `java.sql` to the resolved set; observe that it requires `java.xml` and `java.logging`.

3. Add `java.xml` to the resolved set; observe that it requires nothing else.

4. Add `java.logging` to the resolved set; observe that it requires nothing else.

5. No new modules have been added; resolution is complete.

The result of this resolution process is a set containing `app`, `java.sql`, `java.xml`, `java.logging`, and `java.base`. When running `app`, the modules are resolved in this way, and the module system gets the modules from the module path.

Additional checks are performed during this process. For example, two modules with the same name lead to an error at startup (rather than at run-time during inevitable classloading failures). Another check is for uniqueness of exported packages. Only one module on the module path may expose a given package. "Split Packages" on page 94 discusses problems with multiple modules exporting the same packages.

Versions

So far, we've discussed module resolution without mentioning versions. That may seem odd, since we're used to specifying versions with dependencies in, for example, Maven POMs. It is a deliberate design decision to leave *version selection* outside the scope of the Java module system. Versions do not play a role during module resolution. In "Versioned Modules" on page 106 we discuss this decision in greater depth.

The module resolution process and additional checks ensure that the application runs in a reliable environment and is less likely to fail at run-time. In Chapter 3, you'll learn how to construct a module path when compiling and running your own modules.

Using the Modular JDK Without Modules

You've learned about many new concepts the module system introduces. At this point, you may be wondering how this all affects existing code, which obviously is not modularized yet. Do you really need to convert your code to modules to start using Java 9? Fortunately not. Java 9 can be used like previous versions of Java, without moving your code into modules. The module system is completely opt-in for application code, and the classpath is still alive and kicking.

Still, the JDK itself does consist of modules. How are these two worlds reconciled? Say you have the piece of code in Example 2-5.

Example 2-5. NotInModule.java

```
import java.util.logging.Level;
import java.util.logging.Logger;
import java.util.logging.LogRecord;


public class NotInModule {

  public static void main(String... args) {
    Logger logger = Logger.getGlobal();
    LogRecord message = new LogRecord(Level.INFO, "This still works!");
    logger.log(message);
  }

}
```

It's just a class, not put into any module. The code clearly uses types from the `java.logging` module in the JDK. However, there is no module descriptor to express this dependency. Still, when you compile this code without a module descriptor, put it on the classpath, and run it, it will just work. How can this be? Code compiled and loaded outside a module ends up in the *unnamed module*. In contrast, all modules you've seen so far are *explicit modules*, defining their name in *module-info.java*. The unnamed module is special: it reads all other modules, including the `java.logging` module in this case.

Through the unnamed module, code that is not yet modularized continues to run on JDK 9. Using the unnamed module happens automatically when you put your code on the classpath. That also means you are still responsible for constructing a correct classpath yourself. Almost all guarantees and benefits of the module system we have discussed so far are voided when working through the unnamed module.

You need to be aware of two more things when using the classpath in Java 9. First, because the platform is modularized, it strongly encapsulates internal implementation classes. In Java 8 and earlier, you could use these unsupported internal APIs without repercussions. With Java 9, you cannot compile against encapsulated types in platform modules. To aid migration, code compiled on earlier versions of Java using these internal APIs continues to run on the JDK 9 classpath for now.

 When running (as opposed to compiling) an application on the JDK 9 classpath, a more lenient form of strong encapsulation is activated. All internal classes that were accessible on JDK 8 and earlier remain accessible at run-time on JDK 9. A warning is printed when these encapsulated types are accessed through reflection.

The second thing to be aware of when compiling code in the unnamed module is that java.se is taken as the root module during compilation. You can access types from any module reachable through java.se and it will work, as shown in Example 2-5. Conversely, this means modules under java.se.ee but not under java.se (such as java.corba and java.xml.ws) are not resolved and therefore not accessible. One of the most prominent examples of this policy is the JAXB API. The rationale behind both restrictions, and how to approach them, is discussed in more detail in Chapter 7.

In this chapter, you've seen how the JDK has been modularized. Even though modules play a central role in JDK 9, they are optional for applications. Care has been taken to ensure that applications running on the classpath before JDK 9 continue to work, but there are some caveats, as you've seen. In the next chapter, we'll take the module concepts discussed so far and use them to build our own modules.

CHAPTER 3

Working with Modules

In this chapter, we take the first steps towards modular development using Java 9. Instead of looking at existing modules in the JDK, it's time to get your hands dirty by writing your first module. To start things off easily, we turn our attention to the simplest possible module. Let's call it our *Modular Hello World*. Armed with this experience, we'll then be ready to take on a more ambitious example with multiple modules. At that point, we'll introduce the running example to be used throughout this book, called EasyText. It's designed to gradually grow with you, as you learn more about the module system.

Your First Module

You've seen examples of module descriptors in the previous chapter. A module is generally more than just a descriptor, though. The Modular Hello World therefore transcends the level of a single source file: we need to examine it in context. We'll start by compiling, packaging, and running a single module to get acquainted with the new tooling options for modules.

Anatomy of a Module

Our goal for this first example is to compile the following class into a module and run it (Example 3-1). We start out with a single class in a package, leading to a single module. Modules may contain only types that are inside packages, so a package definition is required.

Example 3-1. HelloWorld.java (➡ chapter3/helloworld)

```java
package com.javamodularity.helloworld;

public class HelloWorld {

    public static void main(String... args) {
        System.out.println("Hello Modular World!");
    }

}
```

The layout of the sources on the filesystem looks as follows:

```
src
└── helloworld ❶
    ├── com
    │   └── javamodularity
    │       └── helloworld
    │           └── HelloWorld.java
    └── module-info.java ❷
```

❶ Module directory

❷ Module descriptor

Compared to the traditional layout of Java source files, there are two major differences. First, there is an extra level of indirection: below *src* we introduce another directory, *helloworld*. The directory is named after the name of the module we're creating. Second, inside this module directory we find both the source file (nested in its package structure as usual) and a *module descriptor*. A module descriptor lives in *module-info.java* and is the key ingredient to Java modules. Its presence signals to the Java compiler that we are working with a module rather than plain Java sources. Compiler behavior is quite different when working with modules as compared to plain Java source files, as you will see in the remainder of this chapter. The module descriptor must be present in the root of the module directory. It is compiled along with the other source files into a binary class-file called *module-info.class*.

So what's inside the module descriptor? Our *Modular Hello World* example is quite minimalistic:

```
module helloworld {

}
```

We declare a module by using the new `module` keyword, followed by the module name. The name *must* match the name of the directory containing the module descriptor. Otherwise, the compiler refuses to compile and reports the mismatch.

This name-matching requirement is true only when running the compiler in multimodule mode, which is a common scenario. For the single-module scenario discussed in "Compilation" on page 36, the directory name does not matter. In any case, it's still a good idea to use the name of the module as the directory name.

Because of the empty module declaration body, nothing from the helloworld module is exported to other modules. By default, all packages are strongly encapsulated. Even though there's no dependency information (yet) in this declaration, remember that this module implicitly depends on the java.base platform module.

You may be wondering whether adding a new keyword to the language breaks existing code that uses module as an identifier. Fortunately, that's not the case. You can still use identifiers called module in your other source files, because the module keyword is a *restricted keyword*. It is treated as a keyword only inside *module-info.java*. The same holds for the requires keyword and other new keywords you've seen so far in module descriptors.

The module-info Name

Normally, the name of a Java source file corresponds to the (public) type it contains. For example, our file containing the HelloWorld class must be in a file named *Hello-World.java*. The module-info name breaks this correspondence. Moreover, module-info is not even a legal Java identifier, because it contains a dash. This is done on purpose, to prevent non-module-aware tools from blindly processing *module-info.java* or *module-info.class* as if it were a normal Java class.

Reserving a name for special source files is not unprecedented in the Java language. Before *module-info.java*, there was *package-info.java*. Although it is relatively unknown, it's been around since Java 5. In *package-info.java*, you can add documentation and annotations to a package declaration. Like *module-info.java*, it is compiled to a class file by the Java compiler.

We now have a module descriptor containing nothing but a module declaration, and a single source file. Enough to compile our first module!

Naming Modules

Naming things, while hard, is important. Especially for modules, since they will convey the high-level structure of your application.

Module names live in a global namespace separate from other namespaces in Java. So, theoretically, you could give a module the same name as a class, interface, or package. In practice, this might lead to confusion.

Module names must be unique: an application can have only a single module for any given name. In Java it's customary to make package names globally unique by using *reverse DNS* notation. You could apply the same reasoning to modules. For example, you could rename the `helloworld` module to `com.javamodularity.helloworld`. However, this leads to long and somewhat clunky module names.

Is it really necessary for module names in *applications* to be globally unique? Certainly, when your module is a published library, used in many applications, it makes sense to choose a globally unique module name. In "Choosing a Library Module Name" on page 209, we discuss this notion further. For application modules, there's no shame in choosing shorter and more memorable names.

In this book we prefer shorter module names to increase the readability of examples.

Compilation

Having a module in source format is one thing, but we can't run it without compiling first. Prior to Java 9, the Java compiler is invoked with a destination directory and a set of sources to compile:

```
javac -d out src/com/foo/Class1.java src/com/foo/Class2.java
```

In practice, this is often done under the hood by build tools such as Maven or Gradle, but the principle remains the same. Classes are emitted in the target directory (out in this case) with nested folders representing the input (package) structure. Following the same pattern, we can compile our Modular Hello World example:

```
javac -d out/helloworld \
    src/helloworld/com/javamodularity/helloworld/HelloWorld.java \
    src/helloworld/module-info.java
```

There are two notable differences:

- We output into a *helloworld* directory, reflecting the module name.
- We add *module-info.java* as an additional source file to compile.

The presence of *module-info.java* in the set of files to be compiled triggers the module-aware mode of javac. Running the compilation results in the following output, also known as the *exploded module* format:

```
out
└── helloworld
    ├── com
    │   └── javamodularity
    │       └── helloworld
    │           └── HelloWorld.class
    └── module-info.class
```

It's best to name the directory containing the exploded module after the module, but not required. Ultimately, the module system takes the name of the module from the descriptor, not from the directory name. In "Running Modules" on page 38, we'll take this exploded module and run it.

Compiling multiple modules

What you've seen so far is the so-called *single-module mode* of the Java compiler. Typically, the project you want to compile consists of multiple modules. These modules may or may not refer to each other. Or the project might be a single module but uses other (already compiled) modules. For these cases, additional compiler flags have been introduced: `--module-source-path` and `--module-path`. These are the module-aware counterparts of the `-sourcepath` and `-classpath` flags that have been part of javac for a long time. Their semantics are explained when we start looking at multi-module examples in "A Tale of Two Modules" on page 44. Keep in mind, the name of the module source directories *must* match the name declared in *module-info.java* in this multimodule mode.

Build tools

It is not common practice to use the Java compiler directly from the command line, manipulating its flags and listing all source files manually. More often, build tools such as Maven or Gradle are used to abstract away these details. For this reason, we won't cover all the nitty-gritty details of every new option added to the Java compiler and runtime in this book. You can find comprehensive coverage of these in the official documentation (*http://bit.ly/tools-comm-ref*). Of course, build tools need to adapt to the new modular reality as well. In Chapter 11, we show how some of the most popular build tools can be used with Java 9.

Packaging

So far, we've created a single module and compiled it into the exploded module format. In the next section, we show you how to run such an exploded module as is. This works in a development situation, but in production scenarios you want to distribute your module in a more convenient format. To this end, modules can be packaged and used in JAR files. This results in *modular JAR* files. A modular JAR file is similar to a regular JAR file, except it also contains a *module-info.class*.

The JAR tool has been updated to work with modules in Java 9. To package up the Modular Hello World example, execute the following command:

```
jar -cfe mods/helloworld.jar com.javamodularity.helloworld.HelloWorld \
    -C out/helloworld .
```

With this command, we're creating a new archive (`-cf`) called *helloworld.jar* in the *mods* directory (make sure the directory exists, though). Furthermore, we want the entry point (-e) for this module to be the HelloWorld class; whenever the module is started without specifying another main class to run, this is the default. We provide the fully qualified classname as an argument for the entry point. Finally, we instruct the jar tool to change (-C) to the *out/helloworld* directory and put all compiled files from this directory in the JAR file. The contents of the JAR are now similar to the exploded module, with the addition of a *MANIFEST.MF* file:

```
helloworld.jar
├── META-INF
│   └── MANIFEST.MF
├── com
│   └── javamodularity
│       └── helloworld
│           └── HelloWorld.class
└── module-info.class
```

The filename of the modular JAR file is not significant, unlike the situation with the module directory name during compilation. You can use any filename you like, since the module is identified by the name declared in the bundled *module-info.class*.

Running Modules

Let's recap what we did so far. We started our Modular Hello World example by creating a helloworld module with a single *HelloWorld.java* source file and a module descriptor. Then we compiled the module into the exploded module format. Finally, we took the exploded module and packaged it as a modular JAR file. This JAR file contains our compiled class and the module descriptor, and knows about the main class to execute.

Now let's try to run the module. Both the exploded module format and modular JAR file can be run. The exploded module format can be started with the following command:

```
$ java --module-path out \
       --module helloworld/com.javamodularity.helloworld.HelloWorld
Hello Modular World!
```

 You can also use the short-form -p flag instead of --module-path. The --module flag can be shortened to -m.

The java command has gained new flags to work with modules in addition to classpath-based applications. Notice we put the *out* directory (containing the exploded helloworld module) on the module path. The module path is the module-aware counterpart of the original classpath.

Next, we provide the module to be run with the --module flag. In this case, it consists of the module name followed by a slash and then the class to be run. On the other hand, if we run our modular JAR, providing just the module name is enough:

```
$ java --module-path mods --module helloworld
Hello Modular World!
```

This makes sense, because the modular JAR knows the class to execute from its metadata. We explicitly set the entry point to com.javamodularity.helloworld.Hello World when constructing the modular JAR.

 The --module or -m flag with corresponding module name (and optional main class) must always come last. Any subsequent arguments are passed to the main class being started from the given module.

Launching in either of these two ways makes helloworld the *root module* for execution. The JVM starts from this root module, and resolves any other modules necessary to run the root module from the module path. Resolving modules is a recursive process: if a newly resolved module requires other modules, the module system automatically takes this into account, as discussed earlier in "Module Resolution and the Module Path" on page 28.

In our simple helloworld example, there is not too much to resolve. You can trace the actions taken by the module system by adding --show-module-resolution to the java command:

```
$ java --show-module-resolution --limit-modules java.base \
       --module-path mods --module helloworld
root helloworld file:///chapter3/helloworld/mods/helloworld.jar
Hello Modular World!
```

(The --limit-modules java.base flag is added to prevent other platform modules from being resolved through service binding. Service binding is discussed in the next chapter.)

In this case, no other modules are required (besides the implicitly required platform module java.base) to run helloworld. Only the root module, helloworld, is shown in the module resolution output. This means running the Modular Hello World example involves just two modules at run-time: helloworld and java.base. Other platform modules, or modules on the module path, are not resolved. During classloading, no resources are wasted searching through classes that aren't relevant to the application.

Even more diagnostic information about module resolution can be shown with `-Xlog:module=debug`. Options starting with `-X` are nonstandard, and may not be supported on Java implementations that are not based on OpenJDK.

An error would be encountered at startup if another module were necessary to run `helloworld` and it's not present on the module path (or part of the JDK platform modules). This form of reliable configuration is a huge improvement over the old classpath situation. Before the module system, a missing dependency is noticed only when the JVM tries to load a nonexistent class at run-time. Using the explicit dependency information of module descriptors, module resolution ensures a working configuration of modules before running any code.

Module Path

Even though *module path* sounds quite similar to *classpath*, they behave differently. The module path is a list of paths to individual modules and directories containing modules. Each directory on the module path can contain zero or more module definitions, where a module definition can be an exploded module or a modular JAR file. An example module path containing all three options looks like this: `out/:myexplo dedmodule/:mypackagedmodule.jar`. All modules inside the *out* directory are on the module path, in conjunction with the module `myexplodedmodule` (a directory) and `mypackagedmodule` (a modular JAR file).

Entries on the module path are separated by the default platform separator. On Linux/macOS, that's a colon (`java -p dir1:dir2`); on Windows, use a semicolon (`java -p dir1;dir2`). The `-p` flag is short for `--module-path`.

Most important, all artifacts on the module path have module descriptors (possibly synthesized on the fly, as we will learn in "Automatic Modules" on page 173). The resolver relies on this information to find the right modules on the module path. When multiple modules with the same name are in the same directory on the module path, the resolver shows an error and won't start the application. Again, this prevents scenarios with conflicting JAR files that were previously possible on the classpath.

When multiple modules with the same name are in different directories on the module path, no error is produced. Instead, the first module is selected and subsequent modules with the same name are ignored.

Linking Modules

In the previous section, you saw that the module system resolved only two modules: helloworld and java.base. Wouldn't it be great if we could take advantage of this up-front knowledge by creating a special distribution of the Java runtime containing the bare minimum to run our application? That's exactly what you can do in Java 9 with *custom runtime images*.

An optional linking phase is introduced with Java 9, between the compilation and run-time phases. With a new tool called jlink, you can create a runtime image containing only the necessary modules to run an application. Using the following command, we create a new runtime image with the helloworld module as root:

```
$ jlink --module-path mods/:$JAVA_HOME/jmods \
        --add-modules helloworld \
        --launcher hello=helloworld \
        --output helloworld-image
```

 The jlink tool lives in the *bin* directory of the JDK installation. It is not added to the system path by default, so in order to use it as in the preceding example, you must add it to the path first.

The first option constructs a module path containing the *mods* directory (where helloworld lives) and the directory of the JDK installation containing the platform modules we want to link into the image. Unlike with javac and java, you have to explicitly add platform modules to the jlink module path. Then, --add-modules indicates helloworld is the root module that needs to be runnable in the runtime image. With --launcher, we define an entry point to directly run the module in the image. Last, --output indicates a directory name for the runtime image.

The result of running this command is a new directory containing essentially a Java runtime completely tailored to running helloworld:

```
helloworld-image
├── bin
│   ├── hello ❶
│   ├── java ❷
│   └── keytool
├── conf
│   └── ...
├── include
│   └── ...
├── legal
│   └── ...
├── lib
```

```
|   └─ ...
└─ release
```

❶ An executable script directly launching the `helloworld` module

❷ The Java runtime, capable of resolving only `helloworld` and its dependencies

Since the resolver knows that only `java.base` is necessary in addition to `helloworld`, nothing more is added to the runtime image. Therefore, the resulting runtime image is many times smaller than a full JDK. A custom runtime image can be used on resource-constrained devices, or serve as the basis for a container image for running an application in the cloud. Linking is optional, but can substantially reduce the footprint of your application. In Chapter 13, the advantages of custom runtime images and the use of jlink are discussed in greater detail.

No Module Is an Island

So far, we've purposely kept things small and simple in order to understand the mechanics of module creation and the associated tooling. However, the real magic happens when you compose multiple modules. Only then the advantages of the module system become apparent.

It would be rather boring to extend our Modular Hello World example. Therefore, we continue with a more interesting example application called *EasyText*. Starting from a single monolithic module, we gradually create a multimodule application. EasyText may not be as big as your typical enterprise application (fortunately), but it touches enough real-world concerns to serve as a learning vehicle.

Introducing the EasyText Example

EasyText is an application for analyzing text complexity. It turns out there are some quite interesting algorithms you can apply to text to determine its complexity. Read "Text Complexity in a Nutshell" on page 43 if you're interested in the details.

Of course, our focus is not on the text analysis algorithms, but rather on the composability of the modules making up EasyText. The goal is to use Java modules to create a flexible and maintainable application. Here are the requirements we want to fulfill through a modular implementation of EasyText:

- It must have the ability to add new analysis algorithms without modifying or recompiling existing modules.

- Different frontends (for example, GUI and command line) must be able to reuse the same analysis logic.

- It must support different configurations, without recompilation and without deploying all code for each configuration.

Granted, all of these requirements *can* be met without modules. It's not an easy job, though. Using the Java module system helps us to meet these requirements.

Text Complexity in a Nutshell

Even though the focus of the EasyText example is on the structure of the solution, it never hurts to learn something new along the way. Text analysis is a field with a long history. The EasyText application applies *readability formulas* to texts. One of the most popular readability formulas is the Flesch-Kincaid score:

$$complexity_{flesch\_kincaid} = 206.835 - 1.015\ \frac{totalwords}{totalsentences} - 84.6\ \frac{totalsyllables}{totalwords}$$

Given some relatively easily derivable metrics from a text, a score is calculated. If a text scores between 90 and 100, it is easily understood by an average 11-year-old student. Texts scoring in the range of 0 to 30, on the other hand, are best suited to graduate-level students.

There are numerous other readability formulas, such as Coleman-Liau and Fry readability, not to mention the many localized formulas. Each formula has its own scope, and there is no single best one. Of course, this is one of the reasons to make EasyText as flexible as possible.

Throughout this chapter and the subsequent chapters, each of these requirements is addressed. From a functional perspective, analyzing a text comprises several steps:

1. Read the input text (either from a file, GUI, or otherwise).

2. Split the text into sentences and words (since many readability formulas work with sentence- or word-level metrics).

3. Run one or more analyses on the text.

4. Show the result to the user.

Initially, our implementation consists of a single module, `easytext`. With this starting point, there is no separation of concerns. There's just a single package inside a module, which by now we are familiar with, as shown in Example 3-2.

Example 3-2. EasyText as single module (➡ chapter3/easytext-singlemodule)

```
src
└── easytext
    ├── javamodularity
    │   └── easytext
    │       └── Main.java
    └── module-info.java
```

The module descriptor is an empty one. The `Main` class reads a file, applies a single readability formula (Flesch-Kincaid) and prints the results to the console. After compiling and packaging the module, it works like this:

```
$ java --module-path mods -m easytext input.txt
Reading input.txt
Flesh-Kincaid: 83.42468299865723
```

Obviously, the single-module setup ticks none of the boxes as far as our requirements are concerned. It's time to add more modules into the mix.

A Tale of Two Modules

As a first step, we separate the text-analysis algorithm and the main program into two modules. This opens up the possibility to reuse the analysis module with different frontend modules later. The main module uses the analysis module, as shown in Figure 3-1.

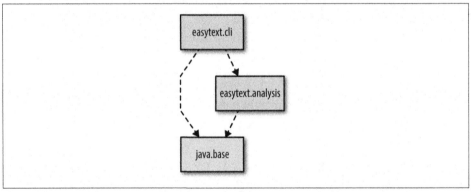

Figure 3-1. EasyText in two modules

The `easytext.cli` module contains the command-line handling logic and file-parsing code. The `easytext.analysis` module contains the implementation of the Flesch-Kincaid algorithm. During the split of the single `easytext` module, we create two new modules with two different packages, as shown in Example 3-3.

Example 3-3. EasyText as two modules (➡ chapter3/easytext-twomodules)

```
src
├── easytext.analysis
│   ├── javamodularity
│   │   └── easytext
│   │       └── analysis
│   │           └── FleschKincaid.java
│   └── module-info.java
└── easytext.cli
    ├── javamodularity
    │   └── easytext
    │       └── cli
    │           └── Main.java
    └── module-info.java
```

The difference is that the `Main` class now delegates the algorithmic analysis to the `FleschKincaid` class. Since we have two interdependent modules, we need to compile them using the multimodule mode of javac:

```
javac -d out --module-source-path src -m easytext.cli
```

From this point onward, we assume all modules of our examples are always compiled together. Instead of listing all source files as input to the compiler, we specify the actual modules to be compiled with `-m`. In this case, providing the `easytext.cli` module is enough. The compiler knows through the module descriptor that `easy text.cli` also needs `easytext.analysis`, which it then compiles from the module source path as well. Just providing a list of all source files[1] (not using `-m`), as we saw in the Hello World example, also works.

The `--module-source-path` flag tells javac where to look for other modules in source format during compilation. It is mandatory to provide a destination directory with `-d` when compiling in multimodule mode. After compilation, the destination directory contains the compiled modules in exploded module format. This output directory can then be used as an element on the module path when running modules.

In this example, javac looks up *FleschKincaid.java* on the module source path when compiling *Main.java*. But how does the compiler know to look in the `easytext.anal ysis` module for this class? In the old classpath situation, it might have been in any JAR that is put on the compilation classpath. Remember, the classpath is a flat list of types. Not so for the module path; it deals only with modules. Of course, the missing piece of the puzzle is in the content of the module descriptors. They provide the nec-

---

1 On a Linux/macOS system, you can easily provide `$(find . -name '*.java')` as the last argument to the compiler to achieve this.

essary information for locating the right module exporting a given package. No more aimless scanning of all available classes wherever they live.

In order for the example to work, we need to express the dependencies we've already seen in Figure 3-1. The analysis module needs to export the package containing the FleschKincaid class:

```
module easytext.analysis {
    exports javamodularity.easytext.analysis;
}
```

With the exports keyword, packages in the module are exposed for use by other modules. By declaring that package javamodularity.easytext.analysis is exported, all its public types can now be used by other modules. A module can export multiple packages. In this case, only the FleschKincaid class is exported to other modules. Conversely, every package inside a module that is *not* exported is private to the module.

You've seen how the analysis module exports the package containing the FleschKincaid class. The module descriptor for easytext.cli, on the other hand, needs to express its dependency on the analysis module:

```
module easytext.cli {
    requires easytext.analysis;
}
```

We require the module easytext.analysis because the Main class imports the FleschKincaid class, originating from that module. With both these module descriptors in place, the code compiles and can be run.

What happens if we omit the requires statement from the module descriptor? In that case, the compiler produces the following error:

```
src/easytext.cli/javamodularity/easytext/cli/Main.java:11:
    error: package javamodularity.easytext.analysis is not visible
import javamodularity.easytext.analysis.FleschKincaid;
                                       ^
    (package javamodularity.easytext.analysis is declared in module
    easytext.analysis, but module easytext.cli does not read it)
```

Even though the *FleschKincaid.java* source file is still available to the compiler (assuming we compile with -m easytext.analysis,easytext.cli to compensate for the missing requires easytext.analysis), it throws this error. A similar error is produced when we omit the exports statement from the analysis module's descriptor. Here we see the major advantage of making dependencies explicit in every step of the software development process. A module can use only what it requires, and the compiler enforces this. At run-time, the same information is used by the resolver to ensure that all modules are present before starting the application. No more accidental compile-time dependencies on libraries, only to find out at run-time this library isn't available on the classpath.

Another check the module system enforces is for cyclic dependencies. In the previous chapter, you learned that readability relations between modules must be acyclic at compile-time. Within modules, you can still create cyclic relations between classes, as has always been the case. It's debatable whether you really want to do so from a software engineering perspective, but you can. However, at the module level, there is no choice. Dependencies between modules must form an acyclic, directed graph. By extension, there can never be cyclic dependencies between classes in different modules. If you do introduce a cyclic dependency, the compiler won't accept it. Adding `requires easytext.cli` to the analysis module descriptor introduces a cycle, as shown in Figure 3-2.

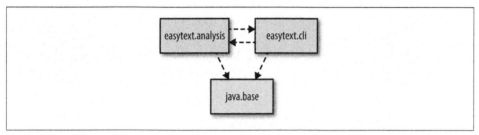

Figure 3-2. EasyText modules with an illegal cyclic dependency

If you try to compile this, you run into the following error:

```
src/easytext.analysis/module-info.java:3:
    error: cyclic dependence involving easytext.cli
    requires easytext.cli;
             ^
```

Note that cycles can be indirect as well, as illustrated in Figure 3-3. These cases are less obvious in practice, but are treated the same as direct cycles: they result in an error from the Java module system.

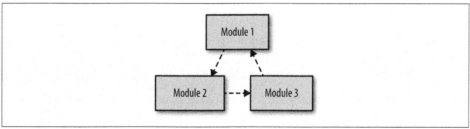

Figure 3-3. Cycles can be indirect as well

Many real-world applications do have cyclic dependencies between their components. In "Breaking Cycles" on page 96, we discuss how to prevent and break cycles in your application's module graph.

Working with Platform Modules

Platform modules come with the Java runtime and provide functionality including XML parsers, GUI toolkits, and other functionality that you expect to see in a standard library. In Figure 2-1, you already saw a subset of the platform modules. From a developer's perspective, they behave the same as application modules. Platform modules encapsulate certain code, possibly export packages, and can have dependencies on other (platform) modules. Having a modular JDK means you need to be aware of what platform modules you're using in application modules.

In this section, we extend the EasyText application with a new module. It's going to use platform modules, unlike the modules we've created thus far. Technically we did use a platform module already: the `java.base` module. However, this is an implicit dependency. The new module we are going to create has explicit dependencies on other platform modules.

Finding the Right Platform Module

If you need to be aware of the platform modules you use, how do you find out which platform modules exist? You can depend on a (platform) module only if you know its name. When you run `java --list-modules`, the runtime outputs all available platform modules:

```
$ java --list-modules
java.base@9
java.xml@9
javafx.base@9
jdk.compiler@9
jdk.management@9
```

This abbreviated output shows there are several types of platform modules. Platform modules prefixed with `java.` are part of the Java SE specification. They export APIs as standardized through the Java Community Process for Java SE. The JavaFX APIs are distributed in modules sharing the `javafx.` prefix. Modules starting with `jdk.` contain JDK-specific code, which may be different across JDK implementations.

Even though the `--list-modules` functionality is a good starting point for discovering platform modules, you need more. Whenever you import from a package that's not exported by `java.base`, you need to know which platform module provides this package. That module must be added to *module-info.java* with a `requires` clause. So let's return to our example application to find out what working with platform modules entails.

Creating a GUI Module

EasyText so far has two application modules working together. The command-line main application has been separated from the analysis logic. In the requirements, we stated that we want to support multiple frontends on top of the same analysis logic. So let's try to create a GUI frontend in addition to the command-line version. Obviously, it should reuse the analysis module that is already in place.

We'll use JavaFX to create a modest GUI for EasyText. As of Java 8, the JavaFX GUI framework has been part of the Java platform and is intended to replace the older Swing framework. The GUI looks like Figure 3-4.

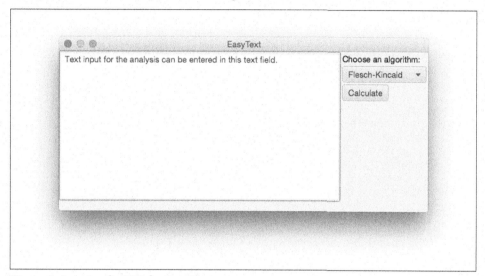

Figure 3-4. A simple GUI for EasyText

When you click Calculate, the analysis logic is run on the text from the text field and the resulting value is shown in the GUI. Currently, we have only a single analysis algorithm that can be selected in the drop-down, but that will change later, given our extensibility requirements. For now, we'll keep it simple and assume that the Flesch-Kincaid analysis is the only available algorithm. The code for the GUI `Main` class is quite straightforward, as shown in Example 3-4.

Example 3-4. EasyText GUI implementation (➥ chapter3/easytext-threemodules)

```
package javamodularity.easytext.gui;

import java.util.ArrayList;
import java.util.List;

import javafx.application.Application;
```

```java
import javafx.event.*;
import javafx.geometry.*;
import javafx.scene.*;
import javafx.scene.control.*;
import javafx.scene.layout.*;
import javafx.scene.text.Text;
import javafx.stage.Stage;

import javamodularity.easytext.analysis.FleschKincaid;

public class Main extends Application {

    private static ComboBox<String> algorithm;
    private static TextArea input;
    private static Text output;

    public static void main(String[] args) {
        Application.launch(args);
    }

    @Override
    public void start(Stage primaryStage) {
        primaryStage.setTitle("EasyText");
        Button btn = new Button();
        btn.setText("Calculate");
        btn.setOnAction(event ->
          output.setText(analyze(input.getText(), (String) algorithm.getValue()))
        );

        VBox vbox = new VBox();
        vbox.setPadding(new Insets(3));
        vbox.setSpacing(3);
        Text title = new Text("Choose an algorithm:");
        algorithm = new ComboBox<>();
        algorithm.getItems().add("Flesch-Kincaid");

        vbox.getChildren().add(title);
        vbox.getChildren().add(algorithm);
        vbox.getChildren().add(btn);

        input = new TextArea();
        output = new Text();
        BorderPane pane = new BorderPane();
        pane.setRight(vbox);
        pane.setCenter(input);
        pane.setBottom(output);
        primaryStage.setScene(new Scene(pane, 300, 250));
        primaryStage.show();
    }

    private String analyze(String input, String algorithm) {
        List<List<String>> sentences = toSentences(input);
```

```
        return "Flesch-Kincaid: " + new FleschKincaid().analyze(sentences);
    }

    // implementation of toSentences() omitted for brevity
}
```

There are imports from eight JavaFX packages in the Main class. How do we know which platform modules to require in *module-info.java*? One way to find out in which module a package lives is through JavaDoc. For Java 9, JavaDoc has been updated to include the module name that each type is part of.

Another approach is to inspect the JavaFX modules available by using java --list-modules. After running this command, we see eight modules containing javafx in the name:

```
javafx.base@9
javafx.controls@9
javafx.deploy@9
javafx.fxml@9
javafx.graphics@9
javafx.media@9
javafx.swing@9
javafx.web@9
```

Because there is not always a one-to-one correspondence between the module name and the packages it contains, choosing the right module is somewhat of a guessing game from this list. You can inspect the module declarations of platform modules with --describe-module to verify assumptions. If, for example, we think javafx.con trols might contain the javafx.scene.control package, we can verify that with the following:

```
$ java --describe-module javafx.controls
javafx.controls@9
exports javafx.scene.chart
exports javafx.scene.control ❶
exports javafx.scene.control.cell
exports javafx.scene.control.skin
requires javafx.base transitive
requires javafx.graphics transitive
...
```

❶ Module javafx.controls exports the javafx.scene.control package.

Indeed, the package we want is contained in this package. This process of manually finding the right platform module this way is a bit tedious. It's expected that IDEs will support the developer with this task after Java 9 support is in place. For the EasyText GUI, it turns out we need to require two JavaFX platform modules:

```
module easytext.gui {
    requires javafx.graphics;
    requires javafx.controls;
    requires easytext.analysis;
}
```

Given this module descriptor, the GUI module compiles correctly. However, when trying to run it, the following curious error comes up:

```
Exception in Application constructor
Exception in thread "main" java.lang.reflect.InvocationTargetException
        ...
Caused by: java.lang.RuntimeException: Unable to construct Application instance:
        class javamodularity.easytext.gui.Main
    at javafx.graphics/..LauncherImpl.launchApplication1(LauncherImpl.java:963)
    at javafx.graphics/..LauncherImpl.lambda$launchApplication$2(LauncherImpl.java)
    at java.base/java.lang.Thread.run(Thread.java:844)
Caused by: java.lang.IllegalAccessException: class ..application.LauncherImpl
        (in module javafx.graphics) cannot access class
                                javamodularity.easytext.gui.Main
        (in module easytext.gui) because module easytext.gui does not export
        javamodularity.easytext.gui to module javafx.graphics
    at java.base/..Reflection.newIllegalAccessException(Reflection.java:361)
    at java.base/..AccessibleObject.checkAccess(AccessibleObject.java:589)
```

 Another change in Java 9 is that stacktraces now also show which module a class comes from. The name before the slash (/) is the module containing the class given after the slash.

What is going on here? The root cause is an IllegalAccessException because class Main cannot be loaded. Main extends javafx.application.Application (which lives in the javafx.graphics module) and calls Application::launch from the main method. That's a typical way to bootstrap a JavaFX application, delegating the UI creation to the JavaFX framework. JavaFX then uses reflection to instantiate Main, subsequently invoking the start method. That means the javafx.graphics module must have access to the Main class in easytext.gui. As you learned in "Accessibility" on page 22, accessibility to a class in another module calls for two things: readability to the target module, and the target module must export the given class.

In this case, javafx.graphics must have a readability relation to easytext.gui. Fortunately, the module system is smart enough to dynamically establish a readability relation to the GUI module. This happens transparently whenever reflection is used to load a class from another module. The problem is, the package containing Main is never exposed from the GUI module. Main is not accessible for the javafx.graphics module because it is not exported. This is exactly what the preceding error message tells us.

One solution would be adding an `exports` clause for the `javamodularity.easy text.gui` package to the module descriptor. Only that would expose the `Main` class to any module requiring the GUI module. Is that really what we want? Is the `Main` class really part of a public API we want to support? Not really. The only reason we need it to be accessible is that JavaFX needs to instantiate it. This is a perfect use case for qualified exports:

```
module easytext.gui {

    exports javamodularity.easytext.gui to javafx.graphics;

    requires javafx.graphics;
    requires javafx.controls;
    requires easytext.analysis;
}
```

 During compilation, the target modules of a qualified export must be on the module path or be compiled at the same time. Obviously this is not an issue for platform modules, but it is something to be aware of when using qualified exports to nonplatform modules.

Through the qualified exports, only `javafx.graphics` is able to access our `Main` class. Now we can run the application, and JavaFX is able to instantiate `Main`. In "Open Modules and Packages" on page 118, you'll learn about another way to deal with reflective access to module internals at run-time.

An interesting situation arises at run-time. As discussed, the `javax.graphics` module dynamically establishes a readability relation with `easytext.gui` at run-time (depicted by the bold edge in Figure 3-5).

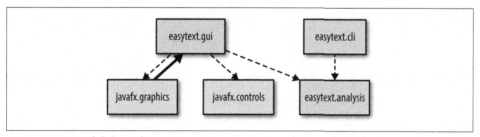

Figure 3-5. Readability edges at run-time

But that means there is a cycle in the readability graph! How can this be? Cycles were supposed to be impossible. They are, *at compile-time*. In this case, we compile `easy text.gui` with a dependency on (and thus readability relation to) `javafx.graphics`. At run-time, `javax.graphics` automatically establishes a readability relation to `easy text.gui` when it reflectively instantiates `Main`. Readability relations can be cyclic *at run-time*. Because the export is qualified, only `javafx.graphics` can access our `Main` class. Any other module establishing a readability relation with `easytext.gui` won't be able to access the `javamodularity.easytext.gui` package.

The Limits of Encapsulation

Looking back, we have come a long way in this chapter. You learned how to create modules, run them, and use them in conjunction with platform modules. Our example application, EasyText, has grown from a *mini-monolith* to a multimodule Java application. Meanwhile, it achieves two of the stated requirements: it supports multiple frontends while reusing the same analysis module, and we can create different configurations of our modules targeting the command line or a GUI.

Looking at the other requirements, however, there's still a lot to be desired. As things stand, both frontend modules instantiate a specific implementation class (`FleschKin caid`) from the analysis module to do their work. Even though the code lives in separate modules, tight coupling is going on here. What if we want to extend the application with different analyses? Should every frontend module be changed to know about new implementation classes? That sounds like poor encapsulation. Should the frontend modules be updated with dependencies on newly introduced analysis modules? That sounds distinctly nonmodular. It also runs counter to our requirement of adding new analysis algorithms without modifying or recompiling existing modules. Figure 3-6 already shows how messy this gets with two frontends and two analyses. (Coleman-Liau is another well-known complexity metric.)

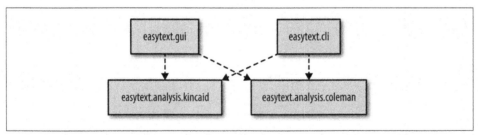

Figure 3-6. Every frontend module needs to depend on all analysis modules in order to instantiate their exported implementation classes

In summary, we have two issues to address:

- The frontends need to be decoupled from concrete analysis implementation types and modules. Analysis modules should not export these types either to avoid tight coupling.

- Frontends should be able to *discover* new analysis implementations in new modules without any code changes.

By solving these two problems, we satisfy the requirement that new analyses can be introduced by adding them on the module path, without touching the frontends.

Interfaces and Instantiation

Ideally, we'd abstract away the different analyses behind an interface. After all, we're just passing in sentences and getting back a score for each algorithm:

```java
public interface Analyzer {

    String getName();

    double analyze(List<List<String>> text);

}
```

As long as we can find out the name of an algorithm (for display purposes) and get it to calculate the complexity, we're good. This type of abstraction is what interfaces were made for. The `Analyzer` interface is stable and can live in its own module—say, `easytext.analysis.api`. That's what the frontend modules should know and care about. The analysis implementation modules then require this API module as well and implement the `Analyzer` interface. So far, so good.

However, there's a problem. Even though the frontend modules care only about calling the `analyze` method through the `Analyzer` interface, they still need a concrete instance to call this method on:

```java
Analyzer analyzer = ???
```

How can we get ahold of an instance that implements `Analyzer` without relying on a specific implementation class? You could say this:

```java
Analyzer analyzer = new FleschKincaid();
```

Unfortunately, the `FleschKincaid` class still needs to be exported for this to work, bringing us right back to square one. Instead, we need a way to obtain instances without referring to concrete implementation classes.

As with all problems in computer science, we can try to solve this by adding a new layer of indirection. We will look at solutions for this problem in the next chapter, which details the factory pattern and how it leads to services.

CHAPTER 4

Services

In this chapter, you will learn how to use *services*, an important feature for creating modular codebases. After learning the basics of providing and consuming services, we will apply them to EasyText, making it more extensible.

Factory Pattern

In the previous chapter, you saw that encapsulation alone doesn't get us very far when we want to create truly decoupled modules. If we still write

```
MyInterface i = new MyImpl();
```

every time we need to use an implementation class, it means the implementation class must be exported. Consequently, strong coupling still remains between the consumer and provider of the implementation: the consumer requires the provider module directly to use its exported implementation class. Changes in the implementation directly affect all consumers. As you will soon see, services are an excellent solution to this problem. But before diving into services, let's see if we can fix this problem by using an existing pattern, building on our knowledge of the module system so far.

The *factory pattern* is a well-known *creational design pattern* that seems to address the very problem we are dealing with. Its goal is to decouple a consumer of objects from the instantiation of specific classes. Many variations on the factory pattern have emerged since it was first described in the iconic Gang of Four *Design Patterns* book by Gamma et al. (Addison-Wesley). Let's try to implement a simple variation of this pattern and see how far it gets us with decoupling modules.

We will use the EasyText application again to illustrate the example, by implementing a factory for `Analyzer` instances. Getting an implementation for a given algorithm name is quite straightforward, as shown in Example 4-1.

Example 4-1. A factory class for Analyzer instances (➡ chapter4/easytext-factory)

```java
public class AnalyzerFactory {

  public static List<String> getSupportedAnalyses() {
    return List.of(FleschKincaid.NAME, Coleman.NAME);
  }

  public static Analyzer getAnalyzer(String name) {
    switch (name) {
      case FleschKincaid.NAME: return new FleschKincaid();
      case Coleman.NAME: return new Coleman();
      default: throw new IllegalArgumentException("No such analyzer!");
    }
  }

}
```

You can retrieve a list of supported algorithms from the factory, and request an Ana
lyzer instance for an algorithm name. Callers of the AnalyzerFactory are now
oblivious to any underlying implementation classes for the analyzers.

But where do we place this factory? For one, the factory itself still needs access to
multiple analysis modules with their implementation classes. Otherwise, the instantiation of the various implementation classes in getAnalyzer would not be possible.
We could put the factory in the API module, but then the API module would have a
compile-time dependency on all implementation modules, which is unsatisfactory.
An API should not be tightly coupled to its implementations.

Let's put the factory in its own module for now, as shown in Figure 4-1.

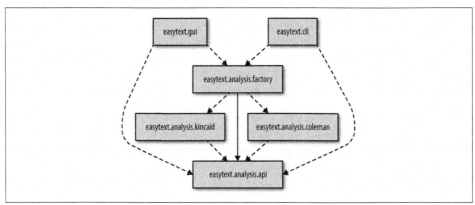

*Figure 4-1. The factory module decouples the frontends from the analysis implementa-
tion modules. There is no requires relation from the frontend modules to the analysis
implementation modules.*

Now, the frontend modules know about only the API and the factory:

```
module easytext.cli {
    requires easytext.analysis.api;
    requires easytext.analysis.factory;
}
```

Getting an `Analyzer` instance becomes trivial:

```
Analyzer analyzer = AnalyzerFactory.getAnalyzer("Flesch-Kincaid");
```

Did we gain anything with this factory approach, besides increased complexity?

On the one hand, yes, the frontend modules are now blissfully unaware of the analysis modules and implementation classes. There is no direct `requires` relation anymore between the consumer and providers of analyses. Frontend modules can be compiled independently from analysis implementation modules. When the factory offers additional analyses, the frontends will happily use them without any modification. (Remember, with `AnalyzerFactory::getSupportedAnalyses`, they can discover algorithm names to request instances.)

On the other hand, the same tight coupling issues are still present at the factory module level and below. Whenever a new analysis module comes along, the factory needs to get a dependency on it and expand the `getAnalyzer` implementation. And the analysis modules still need to export their implementation classes for the factory to use. They could do so through a qualified export (as discussed in "Qualified Exports" on page 27) toward the factory module to limit the scope of exposure. But that presumes the analysis modules know about the factory module, which is another form of unwanted coupling.

So the factory pattern provides only a partial solution. We are running into a fundamental limitation of what you can do with modules through `requires` and `exports` relations. Programming to interfaces is all well and good, but we have to sacrifice encapsulation to create instances. Fortunately, there is a solution in the Java module system. In the next section, we'll explore how *services* provide a way out of this tough spot.

Dependency Injection

Many Java applications use a *dependency injection* (DI) framework to solve the issue of programming to interfaces without tight coupling to implementation classes. A DI framework takes care of creating implementation instances based on metadata such as annotations or (more traditionally) XML descriptors. The DI framework then injects instances into code depending on the defined interfaces. This principle is more generally known as *Inversion of Control* (IoC) because the framework is in control of instantiating classes rather than the application code itself.

DI is an excellent way to decouple code, but there are several caveats in the context of modules. This chapter focuses on the module system's solution for decoupling in the form of services. Services provide IoC through other means than dependency injection. Later, in "Dependency Injection" on page 121, you will see how to use DI frameworks in combination with modules for another way to achieve the same level of decoupling.

Services for Implementation Hiding

We tried hiding the implementation classes by using the factory pattern and succeeded only partially. The main problem is that the factory still has to know about all available implementations at compile-time, and the implementation classes must be exported. A solution similar to traditional classpath scanning to discover implementations is not going to solve this, because this would still require readability to all implementation classes in all modules. It still wouldn't be possible to extend the application with another implementation (new algorithms in the case of EasyText) without changing code and recompiling. This doesn't sound like seamless extensibility at all!

The decoupling story can be improved a lot by the services mechanism in the Java module system. Using services, we can truly just share public interfaces, and strongly encapsulate implementation code in packages that are not exported. Keep in mind, using services in the module system is completely optional, unlike strong encapsulation (with explicit exports) and explicit dependencies (with requires). You don't have to use services, but they offer a compelling way of decoupling modules.

Services are expressed both in module descriptors and in code by using the Service Loader API. In that sense, using services is intrusive: you need to design your application to use them. As discussed in "Dependency Injection" on page 59, there are alternative ways to achieve inversion of control besides using services. In the remainder of this chapter, you will learn how services bring better decoupling and extensibility.

We will refactor the EasyText application to start using services. Our goal is to have several modules provide an analysis implementation. The frontend modules can consume those analysis implementations without knowing the provider modules at compile-time.

Providing Services

Exposing service implementations to another module without exporting implementation classes is not possible without special support from the module system. The Java module system allows for a declarative description of providing and consuming services in *module-info.java*.

In the EasyText code, we already defined the `Analyzer` interface, which will be our service interface type. The interface is exported by the `easytext.analysis.api` module, which is strictly an API-only module.

```
package javamodularity.easytext.analysis.api;

import java.util.List;

public interface Analyzer {

    String getName();

    double analyze(List<List<String>> text);

}
```

Typically, the service type is an interface, as is the case here. However, it could also be an abstract or even concrete class; there is no inherent technical limitation. Also, the `Analyzer` type is meant to be used by service consumers directly. It's also possible to expose a service type that acts like a factory or proxy. If, for example, `Analyzer` instances would be expensive to instantiate, or extra steps or arguments are required for initialization, the service type could be more akin to the `AnalyzerFactory`. This approach allows the consumer to be more in control of the instantiation.

Now let's refactor our first new analyzer implementation, the *Coleman-Liau* algorithm (provided by the `easytext.algorithm.coleman` module) to a service provider. This requires only a change to *module-info.java*, as shown in Example 4-2.

Example 4-2. Module descriptor providing an Analyzer service (➥ chapter4/easytext-services)

```
module easytext.analysis.coleman {

    requires easytext.analysis.api;

    provides javamodularity.easytext.analysis.api.Analyzer
        with javamodularity.easytext.analysis.coleman.ColemanAnalyzer;

}
```

The *provides with* syntax declares that this module provides an implementation of the `Analyzer` interface with the `ColemanAnalyzer` as an implementation class. Both the service type (after `provides`) and the implementation class (after `with`) must be fully qualified type names. Most important, the package containing the `ColemanAnalyzer` implementation class is not exported from this provider module.

This construct works only when the module declaring the `provides` has access to both the service type and the implementation class. Usually this means that an interface, `Analyzer` in this example, is either part of the module or is exported by another module that is required. The implementation class is typically part of the provider module, in an encapsulated (nonexported) package.

When you use nonexistent or inaccessible types in the `provides` clause, the module descriptor won't compile, and a compiler error is generated. The implementation class used in the `with` part of the declaration is normally not exported. After all, the whole point of services is to hide implementation details.

No code changes are necessary to the service type or implementation class to provide it as a service. Besides this *module-info.java* declaration, nothing needs to be done. Service implementations are plain Java classes. There are no special annotations to use, no APIs to implement.

Services allow a module to provide implementations to other modules without exporting the concrete implementation class. The module system has special privileges to reach into the provider module to instantiate the nonexported implementation class on behalf of the consumer. This means consumers of the service can use instances of this implementation class, without having access to it directly. Also, a service consumer doesn't know which module provided an implementation, nor does it need to. Because the only shared type between provider and consumer is the service type (most often an interface), there is true decoupling.

Now that we're done providing our first service, we can repeat this process for the other `Analyzer` implementations, and we're halfway done. Again, note that these service-providing modules don't export any packages. Having a module without exports may seem a bit counterintuitive at first. Nevertheless, these analysis implementation modules contribute useful functionality through the services mechanism at run-time, encapsulating their implementation details at compile-time.

The other half of the refactoring is consuming the services. Let's refactor the CLI module to use the `Analyzer` services.

Consuming Services

Providing services is useful if other modules can consume them. Consuming a service in the Java module system requires two steps. The first step is adding a `uses` clause to *module-info.java* in the CLI module:

```
module easytext.cli {
    requires easytext.analysis.api;

    uses javamodularity.easytext.analysis.api.Analyzer;
}
```

The uses clause instructs the ServiceLoader, which you will see in a moment, that this module wants to use implementations of Analyzer. The ServiceLoader then makes Analyzer instances available to the module.

The uses clause does not call for an Analyzer implementation to be available during compile-time. After all, a service implementation could be provided by a module that we don't have on the module path at compile-time. Services provide extensibility exactly because providers and consumers are bound only at run-time. Compilation will not fail when no service providers are found. The service type (Analyzer), on the other hand, must be accessible at compile-time—hence the requires easytext.anal ysis.api clause in the module descriptor.

A uses clause also doesn't guarantee there will be providers during run-time. The application will start successfully without any providers of services. This means there can be zero or more providers available at run-time, and our code has to deal with this.

Now that the module has declared that it wants to use Analyzer implementations, we can start writing code that uses the service. Consuming services happens through the ServiceLoader API. The ServiceLoader API itself has been around since Java 6 already. Although it is widely used in the JDK, few Java developers know or use Serv iceLoader. "ServiceLoader Before Java 9" on page 64 provides more historical background.

The ServiceLoader API is repurposed in the Java module system to work with modules, and is an important programming construct when working with the Java module system. Let's look at an example; see Example 4-3.

Example 4-3. Main.java

```
Iterable<Analyzer> analyzers = ServiceLoader.load(Analyzer.class); ❶

for (Analyzer analyzer: analyzers) { ❷
   System.out.println(analyzer.getName() + ": " + analyzer.analyze(sentences));
}
```

❶ Initialize a ServiceLoader for services of type Analyzer.

❷ Iterate over the instances and invoke the analyze method.

The ServiceLoader::load method returns a ServiceLoader instance that also conveniently implements Iterable. When you iterate over it as in the example, instances are created for all the provider types that have been discovered for the requested Analyzer interface. Note that we get only the actual instances here, with no additional information on which modules provided them.

After iterating over the services, we can use them like any other Java object. In fact, they *are* plain Java objects, except they are instantiated by ServiceLoader for us. Being just normal Java instances, there is zero overhead when invoking a service. Invoking a method on a service is just a direct method call; there are no proxies or other indirections that decrease performance.

With these changes, we have refactored our EasyText code from a partially decoupled factory structure to a fully modular and extensible setup as shown in Figure 4-2.

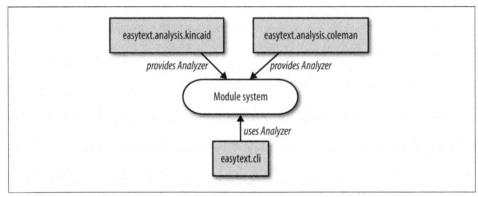

Figure 4-2. Structure of EasyText using ServiceLoader for extensibility

The code is fully decoupled because the CLI module doesn't need to know anything about modules providing Analyzer implementations. The application is easily extensible because we can add a new Analyzer implementation by simply adding a new provider module to the module path. Any services provided by these additional modules are picked up automatically through the ServiceLoader service discovery. No code changes or recompilation are necessary. Arguably the best part is that the code is clean. Programming with services is just as simple as writing plain Java code (that's because *it is* plain Java code), but the impact on architecture and design is quite positive.

ServiceLoader Before Java 9

ServiceLoader has been around since Java 6. It was designed to make Java more pluggable, and is used in the JDK in several places. It never received widespread use in application development, although several frameworks and libraries rely on the *old* ServiceLoader besides the JDK itself.

In principle, ServiceLoader had the same goal as services in the Java module system, but the mechanics were different, and there was no true strong encapsulation possible before modules. To register a provider, a file following a specific naming scheme must be created in the *META-INF* folder of a JAR file. For example, to provide an Analyzer implementation, a file named *META-INF/services/javamodularity.easytext.analy-sis.api.Analyzer* must be created. The contents of the file should be a single line representing the fully qualified name of the implementation class—for example, `javamodularity.easytext.analysis.coleman.ColemanAnalyzer`. Because these files are just text files, it is easy to make mistakes that the compiler won't catch.

With the Java module system, it's also possible to consume services provided the "old" way, as long as the service type is accessible to the consuming module.

You have seen that services provide an easy way to achieve decoupling. Think of services as the cornerstone of modular development. Although strong mechanisms for defining module boundaries are the first step toward modular design, services are required to create and use strictly decoupled modules.

Service Life Cycle

If the `ServiceLoader` is responsible for creating instances of provided services, it's important to know how this works exactly. In Example 4-3, the iteration caused the `Analyzer` implementation classes to be instantiated. `ServiceLoader` works lazily, meaning the `ServiceLoader::load` call doesn't immediately instantiate all known provider implementation classes.

A new `ServiceLoader` is instantiated every time you call `ServiceLoader::load`. Such a new `ServiceLoader` in turn reinstantiates provider classes when they are requested. Requesting services from an existing `ServiceLoader` instance returns cached instances of provider classes.

This is demonstrated by the following code:

```
ServiceLoader<Analyzer> first = ServiceLoader.load(Analyzer.class);
System.out.println("Using the first analyzers");
for (Analyzer analyzer: first) { ❶
  System.out.println(analyzer.hashCode());
}

Iterable<Analyzer> second = ServiceLoader.load(Analyzer.class);
System.out.println("Using the second analyzers");
for (Analyzer analyzer: second) { ❷
  System.out.println(analyzer.hashCode());
}

System.out.println("Using the first analyzers again, hashCode is the same");
for (Analyzer analyzer: first) { ❸
  System.out.println(analyzer.hashCode());
}

first.reload(); ❹
System.out.println("Reloading the first analyzers, hashCode is different");
```

```
for (Analyzer analyzer: first) {
  System.out.println(analyzer.hashCode());
}
```

❶ Iterating over `first`, `ServiceLoader` instantiates `Analyzer` implementations.

❷ A new `ServiceLoader`, `second`, will instantiate its own, fresh, `Analyzer` implementations. It returns different instances than `first`.

❸ The originally instantiated services are returned from `first` when iterating
again, as they are cached by the first `ServiceLoader` instance.

❹ After `reload`, the original `first` `ServiceLoader` provides fresh instances.

This code outputs something like the following (actual hashCodes will vary, of
course):

```
Using the first analyzers
1379435698
Using the second analyzers
876563773
Using the first analyzers again, hashCode is the same
1379435698
Reloading the first analyzers, hashCode is different
87765719
```

Because every invocation of `ServiceLoader::load` leads to new service instances,
different modules using the same service will all have their own instance. This is
something to remember when working with services that contain state. The state is,
without other provisions, not shared between usages across different `ServiceLoaders`
for the same service type. There is no *singleton* service instance, unlike what is typically the case in dependency injection frameworks.

Service Provider Methods

Service instances can be created in two ways. Either the service implementation class
must have a public no-arg constructor, or a static provider method can be used. It's
not always desirable for a service implementation class to have a public no-arg constructor. In cases where more information needs to be passed to the constructor, a
static provider method is the better option. Or, you may want to expose an existing
class without a no-arg constructor as a service.

A provider method is a `public static` no-arg method called `provider`, where the
return type is the service type. It must return a service instance of the correct type (or
a subtype). How the service is instantiated in this method is completely up to the `pro
vider` implementation. Possibly a singleton is cached and returned, or it just instanti-
ates a new service instance for each call.

When using the provider method approach, the `provides .. with` clause refers to the class containing the provider method after `with`. This can very well be the service implementation class itself, but it can also be another class. A class appearing after `with` must have either a provider method or a public no-arg constructor. If there is no static provider method, the class is assumed to be the service implementation itself and must have a public no-arg constructor. The compiler will complain when this is not the case.

Let's look at a provider method example (Example 4-4). We'll use another `Analyzer` implementation for this, just to highlight the use of a provider method.

Example 4-4. ExampleProviderMethod.java (➡ chapter4/providers/ provider.method.example)

```
package javamodularity.providers.method;

import java.util.List;
import javamodularity.easytext.analysis.api.Analyzer;

public class ExampleProviderMethod implements Analyzer {

  private String name;

  ExampleProviderMethod(String name) {
    this.name = name;
  }

  @Override
  public String getName() {
    return name;
  }

  @Override
  public double analyze(List<List<String>> sentences) {
      return 0;
  }

  public static ExampleProviderMethod provider() {
    return new ExampleProviderMethod("Analyzer created by static method");
  }
}
```

The `Analyzer` implementation is fairly useless, but it does show the usage of a provider method. The *module-info.java* for this example would be exactly the same as we have seen so far; the Java module system will figure out the right way to instantiate the class. In this example, the provider method is part of the implementation class. Alternatively, we can place the provider method in another class, which then serves as a factory for the service implementation. Example 4-5 shows this approach.

*Example 4-5. ExampleProviderFactory.java (➥ chapter4/providers/
provider.factory.example)*

```
package javamodularity.providers.factory;

public class ExampleProviderFactory {
  public static ExampleProvider provider() {
    return new ExampleProvider("Analyzer created by factory");
  }
}
```

Now we do have to change *module-info.java* to reflect this change. The provides ..
with must now point to the class containing the static provider method as shown in
Example 4-6.

Example 4-6. module-info.java (➥ chapter4/providers/provider.factory.example)

```
module provider.factory.example {
    requires easytext.analysis.api;

    provides javamodularity.easytext.analysis.api.Analyzer
        with javamodularity.providers.factory.ExampleProviderFactory;
}
```

 ServiceLoader can instantiate a service only if the provider class is
public. Only the provider class itself needs to be public; our second
example shows that the implementation can be package-private as
long as the provider class is public.

Note that in all cases the exposed service type Analyzer remains unchanged. From
the perspective of the consumer, it makes no difference how the service is instantiated. A static provider method offers more flexibility on the provider side. In many
cases, a public no-arg constructor on the service implementation class suffices.

Services in the module system don't offer a shutdown or service de-registration
mechanism. The death of a service is implicit, through garbage collection. Garbage
collection behaves the same for service instances as for any other objects in Java.
Once there are no hard references to the object anymore, it can be garbage collected.

Factory Pattern Revisited

Consumer modules can obtain services through the ServiceLoader API. You can
employ a useful pattern to avoid the use of this API in consumers, if desired. Instead,
you can offer an API to consumers similar to the factory example in the beginning of
this chapter. It's based on the ability to have static methods in interfaces as of Java 8.

The service type itself is extended with a static method (factory method) that does the
ServiceLoader lookup, as shown in Example 4-7.

*Example 4-7. Provide a factory method on the service interface (➡ chapter4/easytext-
services-factory)*

```
public interface Analyzer {

    String getName();

    double analyze(List<List<String>> text);

    static Iterable<Analyzer> getAnalyzers() {
      return ServiceLoader.load(Analyzer.class); ❶
    }

}
```

❶ Lookup is now done inside the service type itself.

Because the ServiceLoader lookup is done in Analyzer in the API module, its module descriptor must express the uses constraint:

```
module easytext.analysis.api {
    exports javamodularity.easytext.analysis.api;

    uses javamodularity.easytext.analysis.api.Analyzer;
}
```

Now, the API module both exports the interface and uses implementations of the
Analyzer interface. Consumer modules that want to obtain Analyzer implementations no longer need to use ServiceLoader (though they still can, of course). Instead,
all a consumer module needs to do is require the API module and call Ana
lyzer::getAnalyzers. No need for a uses constraint or the ServiceLoader API anymore from the perspective of the consumer.

Through this mechanism, you can use the power of services unobtrusively. Users of
an API are not forced to know about services or ServiceLoader but still get the benefits of decoupling and extensibility.

Default Service Implementations

So far, we've worked from the assumption that there is an API module, and there are
several distinct provider modules implementing this API. That's not unreasonable,
but it's far from the only way to set things up. It's perfectly possible to put an implementation into the same module exporting the service type. When a service type has

an obvious default implementation, why not provide it from the same module directly?

You see this pattern a lot in the way the JDK itself uses services. Even though it is possible to provide your own implementations for `javax.sound.sampled.spi.Audio FileWriter` or `javax.print.PrintServiceLookup`, most of the time the default implementations provided by the `java.desktop` module are adequate. These service types are exported from `java.desktop`, and at the same time default implementations are provided.

In fact, `java.desktop` itself even has `uses` constraints for those service types. This shows how a module can play the role of API owner, service provider, and consumer at the same time.

Bundling a default service implementation with the service type guarantees that at least one implementation is always available. In that case, no defensive coding is necessary on the consumer's part. Some service dependencies are intended to be optional. A default implementation in the same module as the service type precludes this scenario. Then, having a separate API module is necessary. In "Implementing Optional Dependencies with Services" on page 104, this pattern is explored in more detail.

Service Implementation Selection

When there are multiple providers, you don't necessarily want to use them all. Sometimes you want to filter and select an implementation based on certain characteristics.

 It's always the consumer deciding which service to use based on properties of the providers. Because providers should be completely unaware of each other, there is no way to favor a certain implementation from a provider's perspective. What would happen if, for example, two providers designate themselves as *default* or *best* implementation? The logic to select the right service(s) is application-dependent and belongs to the consumer.

You have seen that the `ServiceLoader` API itself is fairly limited. Until now, we have iterated only over all existing service implementations. What if we have multiple providers but are interested in only "the best" implementation? The Java module system can't possibly know what the best implementation is for your needs. Each domain has its own requirements in that regard. Therefore, it's up to you to equip your service type with methods to discover the capabilities of a service and make decisions based on these methods. This need not be complicated, and usually comes down to adding self-describing methods to a service interface.

For example, the `Analyzer` service interface offers a `getName` method. `ServiceLoader` doesn't know or care about this method, but we can use it in consumer modules to identify an implementation. Besides selecting an algorithm by name, you can also think of describing different characteristics, for example, with `getAccuracy` or `get Cost` methods. This way, a consumer of the `Analyzer` service can make a well-informed choice between implementations. There's no explicit support from the `ServiceLoader` API necessary: it all boils down to designing self-describing interfaces.

Service Type Inspection and Lazy Instantiation

In some scenarios, the mechanism described previously is still not sufficient. What if there's no method on the service interface to distinguish the right implementation? Or instantiation of the services is expensive? We would incur the cost of initialization for all service implementations just to find the right one, using a `ServiceLoader` iteration. In most scenarios, this is not an issue, but a solution exists for problematic cases.

With Java 9, `ServiceLoader` is enhanced to support service implementation type inspection before instantiation. Besides iterating over all provided instances as we've done so far, it's also possible to inspect a stream of `ServiceLoader.Provider` descriptions. The `ServiceLoader.Provider` class makes it possible to inspect a service provider before requesting an instance. The `stream` method on `ServiceLoader` returns a stream of `ServiceLoader.Provider` objects to inspect.

Let's look at an example based on EasyText again.

First we introduce our own annotation that can be used to select the right service implementation in Example 4-8. Such an annotation can be part of the API module that is shared between providers and consumers. The example annotation describes whether an `Analyzer` is fast.

Example 4-8. Define an annotation to annotate the service implementation class (➥ chapter4/easytext-filtering)

```
package javamodularity.easytext.analysis.api;

import java.lang.annotation.Retention;
import java.lang.annotation.RetentionPolicy;

@Retention(RetentionPolicy.RUNTIME)
public @interface Fast {

  public boolean value() default true;

}
```

We can now use this annotation to add metadata to a service implementation. Here, we add it to an example `Analyzer`:

```
@Fast
public class ReallyFastAnalyzer implements Analyzer {
  // Implementation of the analyzer
}
```

Now we just need some code to filter the `Analyzers`:

```
public class Main {
  public static void main(String args[]) {
    ServiceLoader<Analyzer> analyzers =
      ServiceLoader.load(Analyzer.class);

    analyzers.stream()
      .filter(provider -> isFast(provider.type()))
      .map(ServiceLoader.Provider::get)
      .forEach(analyzer -> System.out.println(analyzer.getName()));
  }

  private static boolean isFast(Class<?> clazz) {
    return clazz.isAnnotationPresent(Fast.class)
      && clazz.getAnnotation(Fast.class).value() == true;

  }
}
```

Through the `type` method on `Provider`, we get access to the `java.lang.Class` representation of the service implementation, which we pass to the `isFast` method for filtering.

Encapsulation Versus java.lang.Class

It might seem strange that we can get a `java.lang.Class` representation of the implementation class. Doesn't that violate strong encapsulation? The package the class comes from isn't even exported!

This is a clear case of "the map isn't the territory"—even though `Class` describes the implementation class, you can't actually do anything with it. When you try to get an instance through reflection (using `provider.type().newInstance()`), you will get an `IllegalAccessError` if the class is indeed not exported. So, having a `Class` object doesn't necessarily mean you can instantiate it in your module. All access checks of the module system still apply.

The `isFast` method checks for the presence of our `@Fast` annotation, and checks the value explicitly for `true` (which is the default value). `Analyzer` implementations that are not annotated as being fast are ignored, but services annotated `@Fast` or

`@Fast(true)` are instantiated and invoked. If you remove the `filter` from the stream pipeline, all `Analyzers` will be invoked indiscriminately.

The examples in this chapter demonstrate that although the `ServiceLoader` API is basic, the services mechanism is powerful. Services are an important construct in the Java module system when modularizing code.

 Using services as a means to improve decoupling is not new. For example, OSGi offers a services-based programming model as well. To be successful in creating truly modular code in OSGi, you *must* use services. So we're building on a proven concept.

Module Resolution with Service Binding

Remember learning in "Module Resolution and the Module Path" on page 28 that modules are resolved based on `requires` clauses in module descriptors? By recursively following all `requires` relations starting from a root module, the set of resolved modules is built from modules on the module path. During this process, missing modules are detected, giving the benefit of reliable configuration. The application won't start if a required module is missing.

Service `provides` and `uses` clauses add another dimension to the resolution process. Whereas `requires` clauses indicate strict compile-time relations between modules, service binding happens at run-time. Because service provider and consumer modules both declaratively state their intentions in module descriptors, this information can be used during the module resolution process as well.

In theory, an application can start without any of its services being bound at runtime. Calling `ServiceLoader::load` won't result in any instances. That's hardly useful, so the module system locates service provider modules on the module path at startup in addition to modules that are required.

When a module with a `uses` clause is resolved, the module system locates all provider modules for the given service type on the module path and adds them to the resolution process. These provider modules, and their dependencies, become part of the run-time module graph.

The implications of this extension to module resolution become clearer by looking at an example. In Figure 4-3 we look at our EasyText example again from the perspective of module resolution.

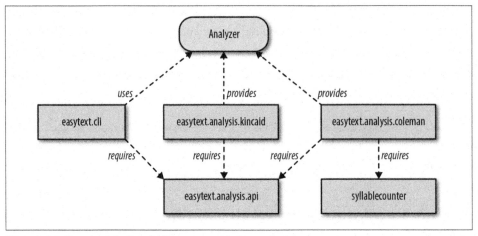

Figure 4-3. Service binding influences module resolution

We assume there are five modules on the module path: cli (the root module), api, kincaid, coleman, and an imaginary module syllablecounter. Module resolution starts with cli. It has a requires relation to api, so this module is added to the set of resolved modules. So far, nothing new.

However, cli also has a uses clause for Analyzer. There are two provider modules on the module path providing implementations of this interface. Hence the provider modules kincaid and coleman are added to the set of resolved modules. Module resolution stops for cli because it doesn't have any other requires or uses clauses.

For kincaid, there's nothing left to add to the resolved modules. The api module that it requires has already been resolved. With coleman, things are more interesting. Service binding caused coleman to be resolved. In this example, the coleman module requires another module: syllablecounter. Therefore, syllablecounter is resolved as well, and both modules are added to the run-time module graph.

If syllablecounter itself would have had requires (or even uses!) clauses, these would be subject to module resolution as well. Conversely, if syllablecounter is not found on the module path, resolution fails, and the application won't start. Even though cli, the consumer module, doesn't have any static knowledge of the coleman provider module, it is still resolved with all its dependencies through service binding.

There is no way for a consumer to specify that it needs at least one implementation. When no service provider modules are found, the application starts just as well. Code using ServiceLoader needs to account for this possibility. You've already seen that many JDK service types have default implementations. When there's a default implementation in the module exposing the service type, you're guaranteed to always have at least one service implementation available.

In the example, module resolution also succeeds when `coleman` isn't on the module path. At run-time, the `ServiceLoader::load` call finds the implementation only from `kincaid` in that case. However, as we've explained, if `coleman` is on the module path but `syllablecounter` isn't, the application won't start because of module-resolution failure. Silently ignoring this problem would be possible for the module system, but runs counter to the mantra of reliable configuration based on module descriptors.

Services and Linking

In "Linking Modules" on page 41, you learned how to use jlink to create *custom run-time images*. We can create an image for the EasyText implementation with services as well. Based on what you've learned in the previous chapter, we can come up with the following jlink command:

```
$ jlink --module-path mods/:$JAVA_HOME/jmods --add-modules easytext.cli \
        --output image
```

jlink creates a directory `image`, containing a `bin` directory. We can inspect the modules included in the image by using the following command:

```
$ image/bin/java --list-modules

java.base@9
easytext.analysis.api
easytext.cli
```

The `api` and `cli` modules are part of the image as expected, but what about the two analysis provider modules? If we run the application this way, it starts correctly because service providers are optional. But it is pretty useless without any analyzers.

jlink performs module resolution starting from the root module `easytext.cli`. All resolved modules are included in the resulting image. However, the resolution process differs from the resolution done by the module system at startup, which we discussed in the previous section. No service binding is done by jlink during module resolution. That means service providers are *not* automatically included in the image based on `uses` clauses.

Although this will certainly cause unexpected results for users who are not aware of this, it is a deliberate choice. Services are often used for extensibility. The EasyText application is a good example of this; new types of algorithms can be added by adding new service provider modules to the module path. Services used this way are not necessarily required to run the application. Which service providers you want to combine is an application-dependent concern. At build-time, there is no dependency to the service providers, and at link-time, it's really up to the creator of the desired image to choose which service providers should be available.

A more down-to-earth reason to not do automatic service binding in jlink is that `java.base` has an enormous number of uses clauses. The providers for all these service types are in various other platform modules. Binding all these services by default would result in a much larger minimum image size. Without automatic service binding in jlink, you can create an image containing just `java.base` and application modules, as in our example. In general, automatic service binding can lead to unexpectedly large module graphs.

Let's try to create a runtime image for the EasyText application, configured to run from the command line. To include analyzers, we use the `--add-modules` argument when executing jlink for each provider module we want to add:

```
$ jlink --module-path mods/:$JAVA_HOME/jmods \
        --add-modules easytext.cli              \
        --add-modules easytext.analysis.coleman \
        --add-modules easytext.analysis.kincaid \
        --output image

$ image/bin/java --list-modules

java.base@9
easytext.analysis.api
easytext.analysis.coleman
easytext.analysis.kincaid
easytext.cli
```

This looks better, but we will still find a problem when starting the application:

```
$ image/bin/java -m easytext.cli input.txt
```

The application exits with an exception: `java.lang.IllegalStateException: Sylla bleCounter not found`. The kincaid module uses another service of type `Syllable Counter`. This is a case where a service provider uses another service to implement its functionality. We already know that jlink doesn't automatically include service providers, so the module containing the `SyllableCounter` example wasn't included either. We use `--add-modules` once more to finally get a fully functional image:

```
$ jlink --module-path mods/:$JAVA_HOME/jmods \
        --add-modules easytext.cli              \
        --add-modules easytext.analysis.coleman \
        --add-modules easytext.analysis.kincaid \
        --add-modules easytext.analysis.naivesyllablecounter \
        --output image
```

The fact that jlink doesn't include service providers by default requires some extra work at link-time, especially when services use other services transitively. In return, it does give a lot of flexibility for fine-tuning the contents of a runtime image. Different images can serve different types of users, just by reconfiguring which service providers are included. In "Finding the Right Service Provider Modules" on page 256, we'll see that jlink offers additional options to discover and link relevant service provider modules.

The previous chapters covered the basics of the Java module system. Modularity is a lot about design and architecture, and this is where it really gets interesting. In the next chapter, we are going to look at patterns that improve the maintainability, flexibility, and reusability of systems built by using modules.

CHAPTER 5
Modularity Patterns

Mastering a new technology or language feature in some ways feels like acquiring a new superpower. You immediately see the potential, and you want to change the world by applying it everywhere. If anything, superheroes from comics have shown us the world isn't this black-and-white—even when you believe you have a super-power. Rarely is good and bad use of new powers immediately apparent; with great superpower comes great responsibility.

Learning the Java module system is no different. Knowing the module system does nothing for you if you do not also know about modular design principles to wield its power. Modularity is more than just an implementation concern, eased by the intro-duction of new language features. It's a matter of design and architecture as well. Applying modular design also is a long-term investment. With it, you can hedge against changes in requirements, environments, teams, and other unforeseen events.

In this chapter, we discuss common patterns to improve the maintainability, flexibil-ity, and reusability of systems built using modules. It's essential to remember that many of these patterns and design practices are technology agnostic. Although there is code in this chapter, it serves to illustrate these sometimes abstract patterns in the context of the Java module system. The focus is on effectively modularizing a system by applying established patterns of modularity.

If these patterns seem obvious to you, congratulations! You've been doing modular development all along. Still, the Java module system offers more support for writing modular code than ever before in the language. And not just for you, but across your whole team and even the Java ecosystem at large. If, on the other hand, these patterns are new to you, congratulations as well. By learning and applying these patterns and design practices, your applications become easier to maintain and extend.

This chapter discusses basic modularity patterns that you will encounter frequently in application development. We start with some general module design guidelines, followed by more concrete module patterns. In Chapter 6, we discuss more advanced patterns that may appeal only to developers of extremely flexible applications, such as generic application containers or plug-in-based systems.

Determining Module Boundaries

What makes a good module? It may surprise you that this question is in fact age-old. Dividing systems into small, manageable modules has been identified as a winning strategy since the inception of our profession. Take, for example, this quote from a 1972 paper (*http://bit.ly/parnas-on-the*):

> The effectiveness of a "modularization" is dependent upon the criteria used in dividing the system into modules.
>
> —D.L. Parnas, *"On the Criteria To Be Used in Decomposing Systems into Modules"*

One of the main points this paper makes is that modularization starts before any code is written. Module boundaries should be derived from the system's design and intent. In the following sidebar, you can read how Parnas approached this challenge. Like the quote says, the criteria used to draw boundaries determine the success of a modularization effort. So what are those criteria? As always, it depends.

Parnas Partitioning

Based on his 1972 paper, D.L. Parnas devised an approach to modularization called *Parnas partitioning*. It's always a good idea to take possible change into account when thinking about module boundaries. With Parnas partitioning, you construct a *hiding assumption list*. The list contains areas from the system that are expected to change or have contentious design decisions, along with their estimated probability of changing later. Functionality is divided into modules using this list to minimize the impact of change. High-probability items on the hiding assumption list are prime candidates to be encapsulated in a module. Creating such a list is not a hard science. It's something you can do together with technical and nontechnical stakeholders.

Read more about constructing a hiding assumption list in this primer on Parnas partitioning (*http://www.jodypaul.com/SWE/HAL/hal.html*).

There's a big difference between creating a modular library designed for reuse versus building a large enterprise application where understandability and maintainability are chief concerns. In general, we can distinguish several axes you can align with when designing modules:

Comprehension

Modules and their relations reflect the overall structure and intent of the system. Whenever someone looks at the codebase without prior knowledge, the high-level structure and functionality is immediately apparent. The module structure guides developers through the system when looking for specific functionality.

Changeability

Requirements change constantly. By using modules to encapsulate decisions that are likely to change, the impact of change decreases. Two systems with similar functionality but different anticipated areas of change may have different optimal module boundaries.

Reuse

Modules are an ideal unit of reuse. To increase reusability, modules should be narrowly focused and as independent as possible. Reusable modules can be composed in many ways across different applications.

Teamwork

Sometimes you want to use module boundaries to clearly divide work across multiple teams. Rather than using technical considerations, you align module boundaries with organizational boundaries.

Some tension exists between these axes. There's no one-size-fits-all answer here. By designing for change in a particular area, abstractions can be introduced that decrease comprehension at first sight. Say, for example, a step from a larger process is put in a separate module because it's expected to change more frequently than the surrounding parts. Logically, the step still belongs with the main process, but it's now in a separate module. This makes the whole a bit less comprehensible in a way, while changeability increases.

Another important trade-off comes from the tension between reuse and use. Generic components or reusable libraries may become complex because they need to be adaptable to different usage scenarios. Nonreusable application components, not directly burdened by the needs of many consumers, can be more straightforward and specific.

When designing for reuse, you have two main drivers:

- Adhering to the *Unix philosophy* of doing only one thing and doing it well.
- Minimizing the number of dependencies the module has itself. Otherwise, you're burdening all reusing consumers with those transitive dependencies.

These drivers do not necessarily work for application modules, where ease of use, comprehension, and speed of development are more important. If you can use a library module to speed up the development of your application module, and make the application module simpler in the process, you do so. On the other hand, if you want to create a reusable library module, your future consumers will thank you for not bringing in a multitude of transitive dependencies. There is no right or wrong here, only deliberate trade-offs. The module system makes these choices explicit.

Typically, reusable modules will be smaller and more focused than single-use application modules. On the other hand, orchestrating many small modules brings about its own complexity. When reuse is of no immediate concern, having larger modules can make sense.

In the next section, we'll explore the notion of module size.

Lean Modules

How big should a module be? Although it sounds like a natural question, it's like asking how big your application should be. Just big enough to serve its purpose, but no bigger—which isn't terribly useful advice.

There are more important concerns to address when thinking about module design than just size. When thinking about the measure of a module, take into account two metrics: the size of its public *surface area* and of its internal implementation.

Simplifying and minimizing the publicly exported part of your module is beneficial for two reasons. First, a simple and small API is easier to use than a large and convoluted one. Users of the module are not burdened with unnecessary details. The whole point of modularity is to break down concerns into manageable chunks.

Second, minimizing the public part of a module reduces the liability of the module's maintainer. You don't have to support what others can't access, leaving the module authors free to change internal details without grave consequences. The less is revealed, the less is relied upon by consumers, and the more stable an API can be. Whatever is put in the exported part of a module becomes a contract between the module producer and its consumers. This is not something to be taken lightly if you want to evolve the module in a backward-compatible manner (which should be the default position). Ergo, minimizing the public surface area of a module is recommended.

That leaves the other metric: the measure of the nonexported part of a module. Here it makes less sense to talk about raw size as with the public part of a module. Again, a module's private implementation should be as big as it needs to be to fulfill its API contract. More interesting is the question: how many other modules does it need to accomplish its goals? A lean module is as independent as possible, avoiding dependencies on other modules where possible. Nothing is more discouraging than to see a load of (transitive) dependencies being added to your system because you want to use a specific module. As discussed previously, when wide reuse is not a main concern for the module, this becomes less of an issue.

You may have noticed parallels between developing lean modules and the prevailing best practices around reusable microservices. Strive to be as small as possible. Have a well-defined contract to the outside world while at the same time being as independent as possible. Indeed, these are similar concerns at different levels in your system architecture. Modules with their public APIs and module descriptors facilitate intraprocess reuse and composition. Microservices function at a higher level in the architecture, through (networked) interprocess communication. Modules and microservices are therefore complementary concepts. A microservice may very well be implemented using Java modules on the inside. One important difference is that with modules and their descriptors, we can explicitly describe not only what they offer (export), but also what they require. Modules in the Java module system can therefore be resolved and linked reliably, something that cannot be said of most microservices environments.

API Modules

So far, you've seen that being deliberate about the API of a module is a must. API design becomes a first-class citizen when building proper modules. It may sound like this is a concern for only library authors, but that's not at all the case. When you modularize an application, crafting the public API of application modules is every bit as important. The API of a module is by definition the sum of its exported packages. Applications consisting of modules exporting everything they contain are typically a warning sign, leaving you no better off than before you used modules. A modular application hides implementation details from other parts of the application just as a good library hides its internals from applications. Whenever your module is used in different parts of your application, or by different teams in your organization, having a well-defined and stable API is paramount.

What Should Be in an API Module?

If you expect to have only a single implementation of an interface, you can combine the API and implementation in a single module. In that case, the exported part is visible to the consumers of the module, and your implementation packages are concealed. The implementation can be exposed as a service through the ServiceLoader. Even if you expect multiple implementations, in some cases it makes sense to bundle a default implementation into the API module. For the remainder of this discussion, we assume the API module does not contain such a default implementation, but stands on its own. In "API Module with a Default Implementation" on page 88, we discuss some caveats when a module contains both an exported API and an implementation of that API.

We already established that the public part of a module should be as lean as possible. But what do you export from an API module? Interfaces have been mentioned a lot, as they form the backbone of most APIs. Of course, there's more.

An interface contains methods with parameters and result types. In its most basic form, the interface stands on its own, using only types from java.base:

```
public interface SimpleTextRepository {
  String findText(String id);
}
```

Having such a simple interface is rare in practice. In an application such as EasyText, you'd expect a repository implementation to return a domain-specific type from get Text (see Example 5-1).

Example 5-1. An interface with nonprimitive types

```
public interface TextRepository {
  Text findText(String id);
}
```

In this case, the Text class is placed in the API module as well. It could be a typical JavaBean-style class, describing the data the caller can expect to get out of a service. As such, it's part of the public API. Exceptions declared in methods on an interface are part of the API, too. They should be colocated in the API module and exported alongside the methods that (declare to) throw them.

Interfaces are the primary means of achieving decoupling between the API provider and consumer. Of course, API modules can contain much more than interfaces—for example, (abstract) base classes you expect the API consumer to extend, enums, annotations, and so on. Whatever you put into an API module, remember: minimalism goes a long way.

When another module requires the API module, you want it to be usable as is. You don't want to require additional modules just to get readability of all the types used in the interface. Making the API module fully self-contained, as discussed so far, is one way to do this. Still, that's not always feasible. Often, an interface method returns or accepts a parameter of a type that resides in another module. To streamline this scenario, the module system offers *implied readability*.

Implied Readability

"Implied Readability" on page 23 provided an introduction to implied readability based on platform modules. Let's look at an example from the EasyText domain to see how implied readability helps create self-contained and fully self-describing API modules. You're going to look at an example consisting of three modules, shown in Figure 5-1.

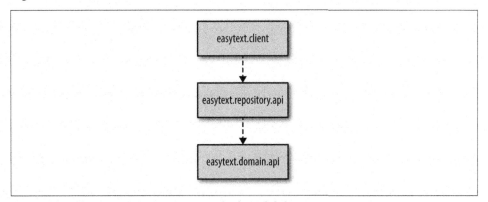

Figure 5-1. Three modules, without implied readability yet

In this example, the TextRepository interface in Example 5-1 lives in the module easytext.repository.api, and the Text class that its findText method returns lives in another module, easytext.domain.api. The *module-info.java* of easytext.client (which calls the TextRepository) starts out like Example 5-2.

Example 5-2. Module descriptor of a module using TextRepository (➥ chapter5/implied_readability)

```
module easytext.client {
  requires easytext.repository.api; ❶

  uses easytext.repository.api.TextRepository; ❷
}
```

❶ Requires the API module because we need to access TextRepository in it

❷ Indicates this client wants to use a service implementing TextRepository

The easytext.repository.api in turn depends on the easytext.domain.api, since it uses Text as the return type in the TextRepository interface:

```
module easytext.repository.api {
  exports easytext.repository.api; ❶
  requires easytext.domain.api; ❷
}
```

❶ Exposes the API package containing TextRepository

❷ Requires the domain API module because it contains Text, which is referenced in the TextRepository interface

Last, the easytext.domain.api module contains the Text class:

```
public class Text {

    private String theText;

    public String getTheText() {
        return this.theText;
    }

    public void setTheText(String theText) {
        this.theText = theText;
    }

    public int wordcount() {
        return 42; // Why not
    }

}
```

Note that Text has a wordcount method, which we'll be using later in the client code. The easytext.domain.api module exports the package containing this Text class:

```
module easytext.domain.api {
    exports easytext.domain.api;
}
```

The client module contains the following invocation of the repository:

```
TextRepository repository = ServiceLoader.load(TextRepository.class)
    .iterator().next();

repository.findText("HHGTTG").wordcount();
```

If we compile this, the following error is produced by the compiler:

```
./src/easytext.client/easytext/client/Client.java:13: error: wordcount() in
Text is defined in an inaccessible class or interface
        repository.findText("HHGTTG").wordcount();
                                     ^
```

Even though we're not mentioning the Text type directly in easytext.client, we're trying to call a method on this type as it is returned from the repository. Therefore, the client module needs to read the easytext.domain.api module, which exports Text. One way to solve this compilation error is to add a requires easy text.domain.api clause to the client's module descriptor. That's not a great solution, though; why should the client module have to handle the transitive dependencies of the repository module? A better solution is to improve the repository's module descriptor:

```
module easytext.repository.api {
  exports easytext.repository.api;
  requires transitive easytext.domain.api; ❶
}
```

❶ Sets up implied readability by adding the transitive keyword

Note the additional transitive keyword in the exports clause. It effectively says that
the repository module reads easytext.domain.api, *and* every module requiring
easytext.repository.api also automatically reads easytext.domain.api, as illustrated in Figure 5-2.

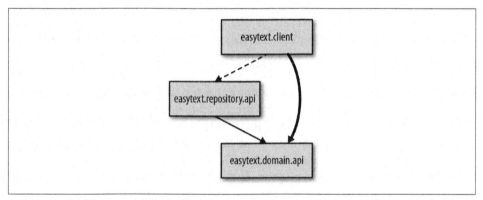

*Figure 5-2. Implied readability relation set up by requires transitive, shown as a bold
edge*

Now, the example compiles without problems. The client module can read the Text
class through the requires transitive clause in the repository's module descriptor.
Implied readability allows the repository module to express that its own exported
packages are not enough to use the module.

You've seen an example where the return type comes from a different module, neces-
sitating the use of requires transitive. Whenever a public, exported type refers to
types from another module, use implied readability. Besides return types, this applies
to argument types and thrown exceptions from different modules as well.

A compiler flag helps you spot dependencies in an API module that should be
marked as transitive. If you compile with -Xlint:exports, any types that are part
of exported types which are not transitively required (but should be) result in a warning. This way, you can find the problem while compiling the API module itself.
Otherwise, the error surfaces only when compiling a consuming module that is missing said dependency because no implied readability is set up. For example, when we
leave out the transitive modifier in the previous easytext.repository.api mod-

ule descriptor and compile it with `-Xlint:exports`, the following warning is produced:

```
$ javac -Xlint:exports --module-source-path src -d out -m easytext.repository.api
src/easytext.repository.api/easytext/repository/api/TextRepository.java:6:
warning: [exports] class Text in module easytext.domain.api is not indirectly
 exported using requires transitive
 Text findText(String id);
 ^
1 warning
```

When designing an API module, implied readability is a powerful technique to make modules easier to consume. There is a subtle danger to relying on implied readability in consuming modules. In our example, the client module can access the `Text` class by virtue of the transitive nature of implied readability. This works fine when the type is used through the interface, as in the example `repository.find Text("HHGTTG").wordcount()`. However, what if inside the client module we start using the `Text` class directly, without getting it as a return value through the interface's method—say, by instantiating `Text` directly and storing it in a field? That continues to compile and run correctly. But does the client's module descriptor now truly reflect our intentions? You can argue that the client module must take an explicit, direct dependency on the `easytext.domain.api` module in this case. That way, should the client module stop using the repository module (and thus lose the implied readability on the domain API), the client code continues to compile.

This may seem like an inconsequential issue. It compiles and works, so what's the big deal? However, as a module author, you are responsible for declaring the correct dependencies based on *your code*. Implied readability is meant only to prevent surprises such as the compiler error you saw previously. It is not a carte blanche to be lazy about real dependencies your module has.

API Module with a Default Implementation

Whether the implementation of the API should live in the same module or in a separate module is an interesting question. Separating the API and implementation is a useful pattern when you expect there to be multiple implementations of the API. On the other hand, when only a single implementation exists, bundling the API and implementation in the same module makes the most sense. It also makes sense when you want to offer a default implementation as a convenience.

A combined API/implementation module doesn't preclude alternative implementations in separate modules, at a later point in time. However, those alternative implementation modules then need a dependency on the combined module for the API. This combined module also contains an implementation. That may lead to superfluous transitive dependencies, because of the combined module's implementation dependencies that are of no use to the alternative implementation but still need to be resolved.

Figure 5-3 illustrates this problem. Modules easytext.analysis.coleman and easy text.analysis provide an implementation of the Analyzer interface as service. The latter module exports the API in addition to providing an implementation. However, the implementation inside easytext.analysis (but not the API) requires the sylla blecounter module. Now, the alternative implementation of the API in easy text.analysis.coleman cannot run without syllablecounter being present on the module path, even though the alternative implementation doesn't need it. Separating the API into its own module avoids such problems, as shown in Figure 5-4.

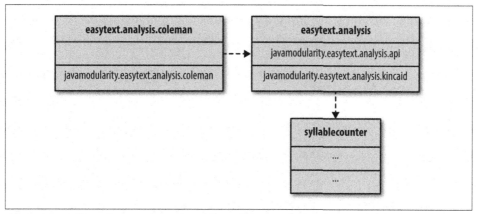

Figure 5-3. When the API is in a module with an implementation (as in the easy-text.analysis module here), the dependencies of the implementation (in this case syllable-counter) transitively burden alternative implementations as well

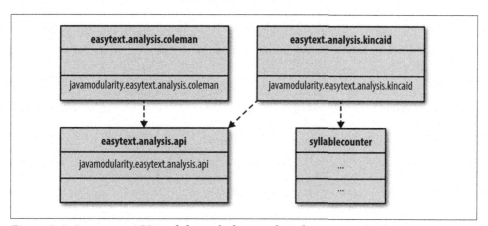

Figure 5-4. A separate API module works better when there are multiple implementations

Towards the end of Chapter 3 and in Chapter 4, we introduced a separate API module for the EasyText `Analyzer` interface. Whenever you have (or expect to have) multiple implementations of the API, it makes sense to extract the public API into its own module. This is certainly the case here: the whole idea was to make EasyText extensible with new analysis functionality. When the implementations are provided as a service, this leads to the pattern in Figure 5-4 when extracting an API module.

In this case, you end up with multiple implementation modules that do not export anything, which depend on the API module and publish their implementation as a service. The API module, in turn, only exports packages and does not contain any encapsulated implementation code. With this setup, the implementation dependency of the `easytext.analysis.kincaid` module on `syllablecounter` is not imposed on the alternative `easytext.analysis.coleman` module. You can use `easytext.analy sis.coleman` without having `easytext.analysis.kincaid` or `syllablecounter` on your module path.

Aggregator Modules

With implied readability fresh in your mind, you're ready for a new module pattern: the aggregator module. Imagine you have a library consisting of several loosely related modules. A user of your imaginary library can use either one or several modules, depending on their needs. So far, nothing new.

Building a Facade over Modules

Sometimes you don't want to burden the user of the library with the question of which exact modules to use. Maybe the modules of the library are split up in a way that benefits the library maintainer but might confuse the user. Or maybe you just want to have a way for people to quickly get started by having to depend on only a single module representing the whole library. One way to do this would be to build both the individual modules and a "super-module" combining all content from the individual modules. That works but is not a particularly nice solution.

Another way to achieve a similar result is to use implied readability to construct an aggregator module. Essentially, you are building a *facade* over the existing library modules. An aggregator module contains no code; it has only a module descriptor setting up implied readability to all other modules:

```
module library {
    requires transitive library.one;
    requires transitive library.two;
    requires transitive library.three;
}
```

Now, if the library user adds a dependency on `library`, all three library modules are transitively resolved, and their exported types are readable for the application.

Figure 5-5 shows the new situation. Of course, it's still possible to depend on a single specific module if so desired.

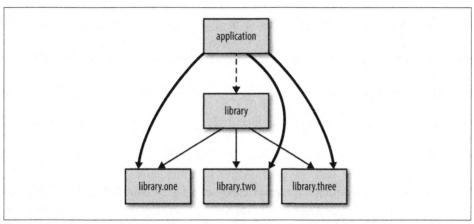

Figure 5-5. The application module can use all exported types from the three library modules through the aggregator module library. Implied readability edges are shown with bold edges.

Because aggregator modules are lightweight, it's perfectly possible to create several different aggregator modules. For example, you could provide several profiles or distributions of a library, targeted towards specific users.

The JDK contains a good example of this approach, as we saw before in Chapter 2. It has several aggregator modules, listed in Table 5-1.

Table 5-1. Aggregator modules in the JDK

Module	Aggregates
java.se	All modules officially belonging to the Java SE specification
java.se.ee	The java.se modules, plus all Java EE modules bundled with the Java SE platform

On the one hand, creating an aggregator module is convenient for consumers. Consumer modules can just require the aggregator module, without thinking too hard about the underlying structure. On the other hand, it poses a risk as well. The consuming module can now transitively access all exported types of the aggregated modules through the aggregator module. That may include types from modules you don't want to depend on as a consumer. Because of implied readability, you will not be warned by the module system anymore when you do use those types. Specifying precise dependencies on the exact underlying modules you need protects you from these pitfalls.

Having aggregator modules available is a convenience. From the point of view of the JDK developers, it's more than just a convenience. Aggregator modules are a great way to compose the platform into manageable chunks without having to repeat yourself. Let's take a look at one of the platform aggregator modules, `java.se.ee`, to see what this means. As you've seen before, you can use `java --describe-module <modulename>` to view the module descriptor content of a module:

```
$ java --describe-modules java.se.ee
java.se.ee@9
requires java.se transitive
requires java.xml.bind transitive
requires java.corba transitive
...
```

The aggregator module `java.se.ee` transitively requires relevant EE modules. It also transitively requires another aggregator module, `java.se`. Implied readability works transitively, so when a module reads `java.se.ee`, it also reads everything that is required transitively by `java.se`, and so on. This pattern of hierarchical aggregation is a clean way to organize a large number of modules.

Safely Splitting a Module

There is another useful application of the aggregator module pattern. It's when you have a single, monolithic module that you need to split up after it has been released. It may have grown too large to maintain, for example, or you might want to separate out unrelated functionality for improved reusability.

Suppose that a module `largelibrary` (shown in Figure 5-6) is in need of further modularization. However, there are already users of `largelibrary` in the wild, using its public API. The split needs to happen in a backward-compatible manner. That is, we can't rely on existing users of `largelibrary` to switch to the new, smaller modules right away.

The solution, shown in Figure 5-7, is to replace `largelibrary` with an aggregator module of the same name. In turn, this aggregator module arranges implied readability to the new, smaller modules.

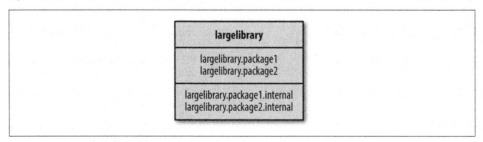

Figure 5-6. Module largelibrary before the split

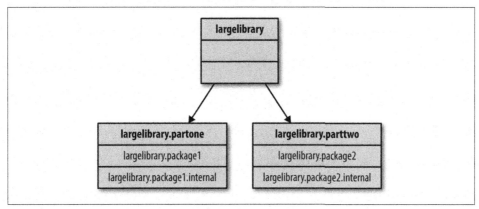

Figure 5-7. Module largelibrary after the split

The existing packages, both exported and encapsulated, are distributed over the newly introduced modules. New users of the library now have a choice of using either one of the individual modules, or `largelibrary` for readability on the whole API. Existing users of the library do not have to change their code or module descriptors when upgrading to this new version of `largelibrary`.

It's not necessary to always create a *pure* aggregator module, containing only a module descriptor and no code of its own. Often a library consists of core functionality that is independently useful. Going with the `largelibrary` example, package `largelibrary.part2` might build on top of `largelibrary.part1`.

In that case, it makes sense to create two modules, as shown in Figure 5-8.

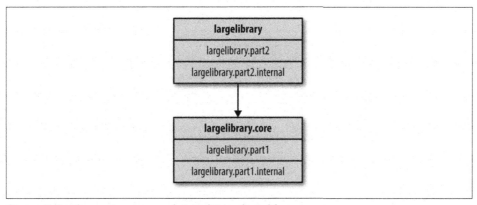

Figure 5-8. Alternative approach to splitting largelibrary

Consumers of `largelibrary` can keep using it as is, or require only the `largelibrary.core` module to use a subset of the functionality. This approach is implemented with the following module descriptor for `largelibrary`:

```
module largelibrary {
    exports largelibrary.part2;

    requires transitive largelibrary.core;
}
```

As you have seen, implied readability offers a safe way to split modules. Consumers of the new aggregator modules won't notice any difference to the situation where all code was in a single module.

Avoiding Cyclic Dependencies

In practice, safely splitting an existing module will be hard. The previous example assumed that the original package boundaries allow for cleanly splitting the module. What if different classes from the same package need to end up in different modules? You can't export the same package from two different modules for your users. Or, what if types across two packages have a mutual dependency? Putting each package into a separate module won't work in that case, because module dependencies cannot be circular.

We'll look at the problem of split packages first. Then we'll investigate how to refactor circular dependencies between modules.

Split Packages

One scenario you can run into when splitting modules is the introduction of split packages. A *split package* is a single package that spans multiple modules, as shown in Figure 5-9. It occurs when partitioning a module doesn't nicely align with existing package boundaries.

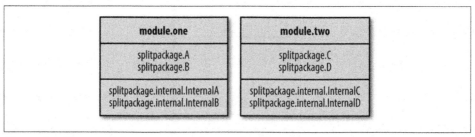

Figure 5-9. Two modules containing the same packages but different classes

In this example, module.one and module.two both contain classes from the same packages called splitpackage and splitpackage.internal.

Remember, packages in Java are nonhierarchical. Despite their appearance, `splitpackage` and `splitpackage.internal` are two unrelated packages that happen to share the same prefix.

Putting both `module.one` and `module.two` on the module path results in an error when starting the JVM. The Java module system doesn't allow split packages. Only one module may export a given package to another module. Because exports are declared in terms of package names, having two modules export the same package leads to inconsistencies. If this were allowed, a class with the exact same fully qualified name might be exported from both modules. When another module depends on both these modules and wants to use this class, conflicts arise as to which module the class should come from.

Even if the split package is not exported from the modules, the module system won't allow it. Theoretically, having a nonexported split package (such as `splitpack age.internal` in Figure 5-9) isn't a problem. It's all encapsulated, after all. In practice, the way the module system loads modules from the module path prohibits this arrangement. All modules from the module path are loaded within the same classloader. A classloader can have only a single definition of a package, and whether it's exported or encapsulated doesn't matter. In "Container Application Patterns" on page 128, you'll see how more advanced uses of the module system allow for multiple modules with the same encapsulated packages.

The obvious way to avoid split packages is to not create them in the first place. That works when you create modules from scratch, but is harder when you're transitioning existing JARs to modules.

The example in Figure 5-9 illustrates a *cleanly split* package, meaning no types with the same fully qualified name appear in the different modules. When converting existing JARs to modules, encountering unclean splits (where multiple JARs have the same types) is not uncommon. Of course, on the classpath these JARs might have worked together (but only accidentally). Not in the module system, though. In that case, merging the JARs and their overlapping packages into a single module is the solution.

Keep in mind that the module system checks for package overlap with all modules. That includes platform modules. Several JARs in the wild try to add classes to packages owned by modules in the JDK. Modularizing these JARs and putting them on the module path will not work, because they overlap with these platform modules.

When JARs containing packages that overlap with JDK packages are placed on the classpath, their types will be ignored and will not be loaded.

Breaking Cycles

Now that we've addressed the problem of split packages, we are still left with the issue of cyclic dependencies between packages. When splitting up a module with mutually dependent packages, this would give rise to cyclic module dependencies. You can create these modules, but they won't compile.

In "Module Resolution and the Module Path" on page 28, you learned that readability relations between modules must be acyclic at compile-time. Two modules cannot require each other from their module descriptors. Then, in "Creating a GUI Module" on page 49, you learned that cyclic readability relations can arise at run-time. Also note that services can use each other, forming a cyclic call-graph at run-time.

So, why this strict enforcement against cycles at compile-time? The JVM can load classes lazily at run-time, allowing for a multistage resolution strategy in the case of cycles. However, the compiler can compile a type only if all the other types it uses are either already compiled, or being compiled in the same compilation run.

The easiest way to achieve this would be to always compile mutually dependent modules together. Although not impossible, this leads to hard-to-manage builds and codebases. Indeed, that is a subjective statement. Disallowing cyclic module dependencies at compile-time is an opinionated choice made by the Java module system based on the premise that cyclic dependencies are generally bad news for modularity.

It's not controversial to say code containing cycles is harder to understand—especially because cycles can hide behind many levels of indirection. It is not always simply two classes in two different packages in two JARs that depend on each other. Cyclic dependencies significantly muddy the waters, and have no place in applications modularized with the Java module system.

What to do when you need to modularize an application that does have cyclic dependencies between existing JARs? Or, when splitting packages from a JAR would result in such cycles? You cannot just convert them to two modules that require each other, because the compiler disallows such a configuration.

One obvious solution is to merge these JARs into a single module. When there is such a tight (cyclic) relation between two components, it's not much of a stretch to conclude they're effectively one module. Of course, this solution assumes the cyclic relationship is benign to start with. It also breaks down when the cycle is indirect and involves several components, not just two, unless you want to merge all components participating in the cycle, which is unlikely.

Often, a cycle indicates questionable design. That means breaking the cycle involves a bit of redesign. As the saying goes, all problems in computer science can be solved by introducing another level of indirection (except the problem of too many indirections, of course). Let's see how adding an indirection can help break cycles.

We start out with two JAR files: *authors.jar* and *books.jar*. Each JAR contains a single class (respectively Author and Book), referencing each other. By naively turning the existing JARs into modular JARs, the cyclic dependency becomes apparent, as shown in Figure 5-10.

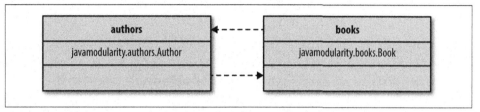

Figure 5-10. These modules won't compile or resolve because of their cyclic dependency

The first question we should answer is: what is the correct relation between those modules? There's no one-size-fits-all approach to be taken here. We need to zoom in on the code, and see what it's trying to accomplish. Only then can the question of what's appropriate be answered. We'll explore this question based on Example 5-3.

Example 5-3. Author.java (➥ chapter5/cyclic_dependencies/cycle)

```java
public class Author {
  private String name;
  private List<Book> books = new ArrayList<>();

  public Author(String name) {
    this.name = name;
  }

  public String getName() {
    return name;
  }

  public void writeBook(String title, String text) {
    this.books.add(new Book(this, title, text));
  }

}
```

An Author has a name and can write a book, which is added to the list of books:

```java
public class Book {
  private Author author;
```

```
  private String title;
  private String text;

  public Book(Author author, String title, String text) {
    this.author = author;
    this.text = text;
    this.title = title;
  }

  public void printBook() {
    System.out.printf("%s, by %s\n\n%s", title, author.getName(), text);
  }
}
```

A book can be created given an Author, a title, and some text. After creation, a Book can be printed using printBook. Looking at that method's code, we can see that its functionality is causing the dependency from Book to Author. In the end, the Author is just there to get a name for printing. This points to a new abstraction. The Book cares only about getting a name. Why should it be coupled to Author? Maybe there are even other ways of creating books than with authors (I heard deep learning is taking over our jobs any day now…).

All of these deliberations point to a new abstraction: the indirection we are looking for. Because the book's module is interested only in the name of things, let's introduce an interface Named, as shown in Example 5-4.

Example 5-4. Named.java (➥ chapter5/cyclic_dependencies/without_cycle)

```
public interface Named {
  String getName();
}
```

Now Author can implement this interface. It already has the required getName implementation. The Book implementation needs to switch out usages of Author for Named. In the end, this results in the module structure shown in Figure 5-11. As an added bonus, the javamodularity.authors package need not be exported anymore.

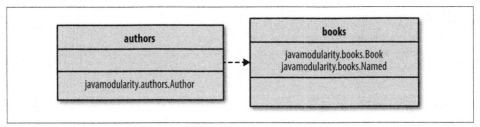

Figure 5-11. The Named interface breaks the cyclic dependency

---

This is far the from the only solution. In a larger system where multiple other components use `Author` similarly, the `Named` interface can also be lifted into its own module. For this example, that would lead to a triangular dependency graph with `Named` in the top module, and both the books and authors modules pointing to it.

In general, interfaces play a big role in breaking cyclic dependencies. An interface is one of the most powerful means of abstraction in Java. They enable the pattern of dependency inversion by which cycles can be broken.

Until now, we've assumed that the exact nature of the cyclic dependency is known. When cycles are indirect and arise through many steps, they can be hard to spot, though. Tools (for example SonarQube (*http://sonarqube.org*)) can help detect cyclic dependencies in existing code. Use them to your advantage.

Optional Dependencies

One of the hallmarks of a modular application is its explicit dependency graph. So far, you've seen how to construct such a graph through `requires` statements in module descriptors. But what if a module isn't strictly necessary at run-time, but nice to have?

Many frameworks currently work this way: by adding a JAR file (let's say *fastjsonlib.jar*) to the classpath, you get additional functionality. Whenever *fastjsonlib.jar* is not available, the framework uses a fallback mechanism or just doesn't offer the enhanced functionality. For the given example, parsing JSON might be a bit slower but it still works. The framework effectively has an optional dependency on `fastjson lib`. If your application already makes use of `fastjsonlib`, the framework also uses it; otherwise, it won't.

The Spring Framework is a famous example of a framework that has many optional dependencies. For instance, it has a `Base64Utils` helper class that delegates to either Java 8's `Base64` class or to an Apache Commons Codec `Base64` class if it's on the classpath. Regardless of the run-time environment, Spring itself must be compiled against both implementations.

Such optional dependencies cannot be expressed with our current knowledge of module descriptors. You can express a single module dependency graph for compile-time and run-time only through `requires` statements.

Services offer this flexibility and are a great way to address optional dependencies in your application, as you will see later in "Implementing Optional Dependencies with Services" on page 104. However, services are bound to the `ServiceLoader` API, which can be an intrusive change for existing code. Since optional dependencies are often used by frameworks and libraries, they might not want to force the use of the services

API on its users. When adopting services is not an option, another feature of the module system can be used to model optional dependencies: compile-time dependencies.

Compile-Time Dependencies

As the name already implies, compile-time dependencies are dependencies that are only required during compilation. You can express a compile-time dependency on a module by adding the `static` modifier to a `requires` clause, as shown in Example 5-5.

Example 5-5. Declaring a compile-time dependency (➡ chapter5/ optional_dependencies)

```
module framework {
  requires static fastjsonlib;
}
```

By adding `static`, the `fastjsonlib` module needs to be present when compiling, but not when running `framework`. This effectively makes `fastjsonlib` an optional dependency of `framework` from the perspective of the module consumer.

 Compile-time dependencies have other applications as well. For example, a module can export Java annotations that are used only during compilation. Requiring such a module should not lead to a run-time dependency, so `requires static` suits this scenario perfectly.

The question of course is, what happens when `framework` is run without `fastjson lib`? Let's explore the scenario where `framework` uses the class `FastJson` exported from `fastjsonlib` directly:

```
package javamodularity.framework;

import javamodularity.fastjsonlib.FastJson;

public class MainBad {

  public static void main(String... args) {
    FastJson fastJson = new FastJson();
  }

}
```

Running `framework` without `fastjsonlib` in this case leads to a `NoClassDefFound Error`. The resolver doesn't complain about the missing `fastjsonlib` module,

---

because it is a compile-time only dependency. Still, we get an error at run-time because FastJson clearly is necessary for framework in this case.

The onus is on the module expressing a compile-time dependency to guard against these problems at run-time. That means framework needs to code defensively around the usage of classes from compile-time dependencies. A direct reference to FastJson as in MainBad is problematic, because the VM will always try to load the class and instantiate it, leading to the NoClassDefFoundError.

Fortunately, Java has lazy loading semantics for classes: they are loaded at the last possible time. If we can somehow tentatively try to use the FastJson class and gracefully recover if it's not available, we achieve our goal. By using reflection with appropriate try-catch blocks, framework can prevent run-time errors:

```
package javamodularity.framework;

import javamodularity.fastjsonlib.FastJson;

public class Main {

  public static void main(String... args) {
    try {
      Class<?> clazz = Class.forName("javamodularity.fastjsonlib.FastJson");
      FastJson instance =
        (FastJson) clazz.getConstructor().newInstance();
      System.out.println("Using FastJson");
    } catch (ReflectiveOperationException e) {
      System.out.println("Oops, we need a fallback!");
    }
  }

}
```

When the FastJson class isn't found, the catch block can be used as a fallback. On the other hand, if fastjsonlib is there, we can use FastJson without any problems after the reflective instantiation.

 The requires static fastjsonlib clause does not cause fast jsonlib to be resolved at run-time, even if fastjsonlib is on the module path! There needs to be a direct requires clause on fast jsonlib, or you can add it as root module through --add-modules fastjsonlib for it to be resolved. In both cases, fastjsonlib is then resolved, and framework reads and uses it.

Guarding each and every use of classes from a compile-time dependency this way can be quite painful. Lazy loading also means that the moment a class is loaded can be surprising. A notorious example is the static initializer block in a class. That should already be a warning sign that `requires static` may not be the best way to create optional coupling between modules.

Whenever your module uses compile-time dependencies, try to concentrate the use of these optional types in one part of the module. Put the guard on the instantiation of a single top-level class, that in turn has all the (direct) references to types in the optional dependency. This way, the module won't get littered with defensive guard code.

There are other legitimate uses for `requires static`—for example, to reference compile-time-only annotations from another module. A `requires` clause (without `static`) would cause the dependency to be required at run-time as well.

Sometimes annotations on a class are used only at compile-time—for example, to perform static analysis (such as checking `@Nullable` or `@NonNull`), or to mark a type as input for code generation. When you retrieve annotations for an element at run-time and the annotation class is not present, the JVM gracefully degrades and won't throw any classloading exceptions. Still, you need access to the annotation types when compiling the code.

Let's look at a fictional `@GenerateSchema` annotation that can be put on entities. At build-time, these annotations are used to find classes to generate a database schema based on their signature. The annotation is not used at run-time. Therefore, we want code annotated with `@GenerateSchema` not to require the `schemagenerator` module (which exports the annotation) at run-time. Say we have the class in Example 5-6 in module `application`.

Example 5-6. An annotated class (➥ chapter5/optional_dependencies_annotations)

```
package javamodularity.application;

import javamodularity.schemagenerator.GenerateSchema;

@GenerateSchema
public class BookEntity {

  public String title;
  public String[] authors;

}
```

The module descriptor for `application` should have the right compile-time dependency:

```
module application {
  requires static schemagenerator;
}
```

In `application`, there's also a main class that instantiates the `BookEntity` and tries to obtain the annotations on that class:

```
package javamodularity.application;

public class Main {
  public static void main(String... args) {
    BookEntity b = new BookEntity();
    assert BookEntity.class.getAnnotations().length == 0;
    System.out.println("Running without annotation @GenerateSchema present.");
  }
}
```

When you run the application without the `schemagenerator` module, everything works out fine:

```
$ java -ea --module-path out/application \
       -m application/javamodularity.application.Main
Running without annotation @GenerateSchema present.
```

(The `-ea` flag enables run-time assertions in the JVM.)

There are no classloading or module resolution problems due to the missing `schema generator` module at run-time. Leaving out the module at run-time is possible because it's a compile-time dependency. Subsequently, the JVM gracefully handles the absence of annotation classes at run-time, as it always has. The call to `getAnnota tions` returns an empty array.

However, if we add the `schemagenerator` module explicitly, the `@GenerateSchema` annotation is found and returned:

```
$ java -ea --module-path out/application:out/schemagenerator \
       -m application/javamodularity.application.Main
Exception in thread "main" java.lang.AssertionError
        at application/javamodularity.application.Main.main(Main.java:6)
```

An `AssertionError` is thrown because now the `@GenerateSchema` annotation is returned. No longer is the annotations array empty.

There's no need for guard code to cope with missing annotation types at run-time, unlike the previous examples of compile-time dependencies we've seen. The JVM already takes care of this during classloading and reflective access to annotations.

It is also possible to combine the `static` modifier on `requires` with `transitive`:

```
module questionable {
  exports questionable.api;
  requires transitive static fastjsonlib;
}
```

You need to do this when a type from the optional dependency is referenced in an exported package. The fact that it's possible to combine `static` and `transitive` doesn't make it a good idea. It puts the responsibility of creating proper guards on the consumer of the API, which certainly doesn't adhere to the principle of the least surprise. In fact, the only reason this combination of modifiers is possible is to enable modularization of legacy code by using this pattern.

Optional dependencies can be approximated through `requires static`, but with services in the module system we can do better!

Implementing Optional Dependencies with Services

Using compile-time dependencies to model optional dependencies is possible but requires diligent use of reflection to safeguard classloading. Services are a better fit for this usage. You already saw in Chapter 4 that a service consumer can obtain zero or more implementations of a service type from service provider modules. Getting zero or one service implementation is just a special case of this general mechanism.

Let's apply this to the previous example with `framework` by using the optional `fast jsonlib`. Fair warning: we start with a naive refactoring, refining it into a real solution in several steps.

In Example 5-7, `framework` becomes a consumer of an optional service provided by `fastjsonlib`.

Example 5-7. Consuming a service, which may or may not be available at run-time (➡ chapter5/optional_dependencies_service)

```
module framework {
  requires static fastjsonlib;
  uses javamodularity.fastjsonlib.FastJson;
}
```

By virtue of the `uses` clause, we can now load `FastJson` with `ServiceLoader` in the framework code:

```
FastJson fastJson =
  ServiceLoader.load(FastJson.class)
          .findFirst()
          .orElse(getFallBack());
```

We no longer need reflection in the framework code to get `FastJson` when it's available. If there's no service found by `ServiceLoader` (meaning `findFirst` returns an empty `Optional`), we assume we can get a fallback implementation with `getFall Back`.

Of course, `fastjsonlib` must provide the class we're interested in as a service:

```
module fastjsonlib {
  exports javamodularity.fastjsonlib;
```

```
    provides javamodularity.fastjsonlib.FastJson
        with javamodularity.fastjsonlib.FastJson;
}
```

With this setup, the resolver even resolves `fastjsonlib` without having to add it explicitly, based on the `uses` and `provides` clauses.

There are several awkward problems with this refactoring from a pure compile-time dependency to a service, though. First of all, it's a bit strange to expose a class directly as a service, rather than exposing an interface and hiding the implementation. Splitting `FastJson` into an exported interface and encapsulated implementation solves this. This refactoring also enables the framework to implement a fallback class implementing the same interface.

A bigger problem surfaces when trying to run `framework` without `fastjsonlib`. After all, `fastjsonlib` is supposed to be optional so this should be possible. When `frame work` is started without `fastjsonlib` on the module path, the following error occurs:

```
Error occurred during initialization of VM
java.lang.module.ResolutionException: Module framework does not read a module
    that exports javamodularity.fastjsonlib
```

You cannot declare a service dependency with `uses` on a type that you can't read at run-time, regardless of whether there is a provider module. The obvious solution is to change the compile-time dependency on `fastjsonlib` into a normal dependency (`requires` without `static`). However, that's not what we want: the dependency on the library should be optional.

At this point, a more intrusive refactoring is warranted. It becomes clear that not everything can be optional in the relation between `framework` and `fastjsonlib` for this service setup to work. Why does the `FastJson` interface (assuming we refactored it into an interface) live in `fastjsonlib`? In the end, it's the framework which dictates that functionality it wants to use. The functionality is optionally provided by a library or by fallback code in the framework itself. Through this realization, it makes sense to put the interface in `framework` or in a separate API module that is shared between the framework and library.

This is an intrusive redesign. It almost inverts the relationship between the framework and the library. Instead of the framework optionally requiring the library, the library must require the framework (or its API module) to implement an interface and offer the implementation as a service. However, when such a redesign can be pulled off, it results in an elegant decoupled interaction between the framework and library.

Versioned Modules

Talking about modules for frameworks and libraries inevitably leads to questions around versioning. Modules are independently deployable and reusable units. Applications are built by combining the right deployment units (modules). Having just a module name is not sufficient to select the right modules that work together. You need versions as well.

Modules in the Java module system cannot declare a version in *module-info.java*. Still, it is possible to attach version information when creating a modular JAR. You can set a version by using the `--module-version=<V>` flag of the `jar` tool. The version `V` is set as an attribute on the compiled *module-info.class* and is available at run-time. Adding a version to your modular JARs is a good practice, especially the for API modules discussed earlier in this chapter.

Semantic Versioning

There are many different ways to version modules. The most important goal in versioning is to communicate the impact of changes to consumers of a module. Is a newer version a safe drop-in replacement for the previous version? Are there any changes to the API of the module? Semantic versioning (*http://semver.org*) formalizes a versioning scheme that is widely used and understood:

`MAJOR.MINOR.PATCH`

Breaking changes, such as changing a method signature in an interface, lead to a bump in the `MAJOR` version part. Changes to a public API that are backward compatible, such as adding a method on a public class, bump the `MINOR` part of the version string. Last, the `PATCH` part is incremented when implementation details change. This can be a bug fix, or optimizations to the code. In any case, a `PATCH` increment should always be a safe drop-in replacement for the previous version.

Note that it is not always straightforward to determine whether something is a major or minor change. For example, adding a method to an interface is a major change only if consumers of the interface are supposed to implement it. If, on the other hand, the interface is only called by consumers (but not implemented), consumers won't break when a method is added. To muddy the waters further, default methods on interfaces (introduced in Java 8) can turn the addition of a method on an interface into a minor change even in the first scenario. The important thing is to always reason from the perspective of the consumer of the module. The module's next version should reflect the impact of the upcoming changes for the consumers of a module.

Module Resolution and Versioning

Even though there's support for adding a version to modular JARs, it is not used in any way by the module system (yet). Modules are resolved purely by name. This may seem strange, because we already established that versions play an important role in deciding which modules play nice together. Ignoring versions during module resolution is not an oversight, but a deliberate design choice in the Java module system.

How you indicate which versions of deployment units work together is a rather controversial topic. What are the syntax and semantics of the version string? Do you specify a version range for dependencies? Or only exact versions? What happens if you end up requiring two versions at the same time, in the latter case? Such conflicts must be addressed.

Tools and frameworks (such as Maven and OSGi) have opinionated answers to each of those questions. It turns out these version-selection algorithms and associated conflict-resolution heuristics are both complex and (sometimes subtly) different. That's why the Java module system, for now, eschews the notion of version selection during the module-resolution process. Whatever strategy adopted would end up deeply ingrained in the module system and, hence, in the compiler, language specification, and JVM. The cost of not getting it right was simply too high. Therefore, the requires clause in module descriptors takes only a module name, not a module version (or range).

That still leaves us developers with a challenge. How do we select the right module versions to put on the module path? The answer is surprisingly straightforward, if a bit unsatisfactory: just as we did before with the classpath. Selection and retrieval of the right versions of dependencies are delegated to existing build tools. Maven and Gradle et al. handle this by externalizing the dependency version information into a POM file. Other tools may use other means, but the fact remains this information must be stored outside the module.

Figure 5-12 shows the steps involved with building a source module application that depends on two other modular JARs, lib and foo. At build-time, build tools download the right versions of the dependencies from a repository, using information from POM files. Any version conflicts arising during this process must be resolved by the build tool's conflict-resolution algorithm. The downloaded modular JARs are put on the module path for compilation. Then, the Java compiler resolves the module graph guided by information from module-info descriptors on the module path and application itself. More details on how existing build tools handle modules can be found in Chapter 11.

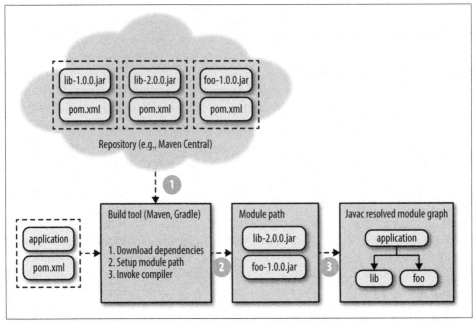

Figure 5-12. Build tools select the right version of a dependency to put on the module path

❶ A build tool such as Maven or Gradle downloads dependencies from a repository such as Maven Central. Version information in a build descriptor (for example, *pom.xml*) controls which versions are downloaded.

❷ The build tool sets up the module path with the downloaded versions.

❸ Then, the Java compiler or runtime resolves the module graph from the module path, which contains the correct versions without duplicates for the application to work. Duplicate versions of a module result in an error.

The Java module system ensures that all necessary modules are present when compiling and running `application` through the module-resolution process. However, the module system is oblivious to which version of a module is resolved. As long as there is a module with the correct name, it will be resolved. In addition, if multiple modules with the same name (but possibly a different version) are found in a directory on the module path, this leads to an error.

If two modules with the same name are in *different directories* on the module path, the resolver uses the first one it encounters and ignores the second. No errors are produced in this case.

There are genuine situations where having multiple versions of the same module at the same time is expedient. We've seen that by default, this scenario is not supported when launching an application from the module path. This is similar to the situation before the module system. On the classpath, two JARs of a different version can lead to undefined run-time behavior, which is arguably worse.

In application development, it is highly advisable to find a way to unify dependencies on a single module version. Often, the desire for running multiple concurrent versions of the same module stems from laziness rather than a pressing need. When developing generic, container-like applications, this may not always be possible. In Chapter 6, you will see that there is a way to resolve multiple versions of a module by using a more sophisticated module system API to construct module graphs at run-time. Another option in these cases is to adopt an existing module system such as OSGi, which offers the possibility to run multiple versions concurrently out of the box.

Resource Encapsulation

We've spent a considerable amount of time talking about strongly encapsulating code in modules. Although that's the most obvious use of strong encapsulation, applications typically have more resources than just code. Think of files containing translations (localized resource bundles), configuration files, images used in user interfaces, and so on. It's worthwhile to encapsulate such resources in a module as well, colocating them with the code using the resources. Having modules nose into another module's resources is just as bad as depending on private implementation classes.

Historically, resources on the classpath were even more free-for-all than code, because no access modifiers can be applied to resources. Any class can read any resource on the classpath. With modules, that changes. By default, resources within packages in a module are strongly encapsulated. Those resources can be used only from within the module, just as with classes in nonexported packages.

However, many tools and frameworks depend on finding resources regardless of where they come from. Frameworks might scan for certain configuration files (for example, *persistence.xml* or *beans.xml* in Java EE) or otherwise depend on resources from application code. This requires resources within a module to be accessible from other modules. To handle these cases gracefully and maintain backward compatibility, many exceptions have been added to the default of encapsulating resources in modules.

First, we are going to look at loading resources from within the same module. Second, we are going to look at how modules can share resources and which exceptions to the default of strong encapsulation are in place. Last, we turn our attention to a special case of resource loading: ResourceBundles. This mechanism is mainly used for localization and has been updated for the module system.

Loading Resources from a Module

Here's an example of a compiled module `firstresourcemodule` containing both code and resources:

```
firstresourcemodule
├── javamodularity
│   └── firstresourcemodule
│       ├── ResourcesInModule.class
│       ├── ResourcesOtherModule.class
│       └── resource_in_package.txt
├── module-info.class
└── top_level_resource.txt
```

There are two resources in this example alongside two classes and the module descriptor: `resource_in_package.txt` and `top_level_resource.txt`. We assume the resources are put into the module during the build process.

Resources are typically loaded through resource loading methods provided by the `Class` API. This still works within a module, as shown in Example 5-8.

Example 5-8. Various ways of loading resources in a module (➥ chapter5/ resource_encapsulation)

```
public static void main(String... args) throws Exception {
    Class clazz = ResourcesInModule.class;
    InputStream cz_pkg = clazz.getResourceAsStream("resource_in_package.txt"); ❶
    URL cz_tl = clazz.getResource("/top_level_resource.txt"); ❷

    Module m = clazz.getModule(); ❸
    InputStream m_pkg = m.getResourceAsStream(
        "javamodularity/firstresourcemodule/resource_in_package.txt"); ❹
    InputStream m_tl = m.getResourceAsStream("top_level_resource.txt"); ❺

    assert Stream.of(cz_pkg, cz_tl, m_pkg, m_tl)
                 .noneMatch(Objects::isNull);
}

}
```

❶ Reading a resource with `Class::getResource` resolves the name relative to the package the class is in (`javamodularity.firstresourcemodule` in this case).

❷ When reading a top-level resource, a slash must be prefixed to avoid relative resolution of the resource name.

❸ You can obtain a `java.lang.Module` instance from `Class`, representing the module the class is from.

❹ The `Module` API introduces new ways to obtain resources from a module.

❺ This `getResourceAsStream` method also works for top-level resources. The `Module` API always assumes absolute names, so no leading slash is necessary for a top-level resource.

All of these methods work for loading resources within the same module. Existing code does not have to be changed for loading resources. As long as the `Class` instance you're calling `getResource{AsStream}` on belongs to the current module containing the resource, you get back a proper `InputStream` or `URL`. On the other hand, when the `Class` instance comes from another module, `null` will be returned because of resource encapsulation.

 You can also load resources through `ClassLoader::getResource*` methods. In a module context, it is better to use the methods on `Class` and `Module` instead. The `ClassLoader` methods do not take into account the current module context like the methods `Class` and `Module` do, leading to potentially confusing results.

There's a new way to load resources as well. It's through the new `Module` API, which is discussed in more detail in "Reflection on Modules" on page 124. The `Module` API exposes `getResourceAsStream` to load a resource from that module. Resources in a package can be referred to in an absolute way by replacing the dots in the package name with slashes and appending the filename. For example, `javamodularity.first resourcemodule` becomes `javamodularity/firstresourcemodule`. After adding the filename, the argument to load a resource in a package becomes `javamodularity/firstresourcemodule/resource_in_package.txt`.

Any resource in the same module, whether it is in a package or at the top level, can be loaded by the methods discussed so far.

Loading Resources Across Modules

What happens if you obtain a `Module` instance representing a module other than the current module? It might seem you can call `getResourceAsStream` on this other `Module` instance and get access to all resources in that module. Thanks to strong encapsulation of resources, this is not (always) the case. Several exceptions to this rule exist, so let's add a module secondresourcemodule to our example to explore the different scenarios:

```
secondresourcemodule
├── META-INF
│   └── resource_in_metainf.txt
├── javamodularity
│   └── secondresourcemodule
│       ├── A.class
│       └── resource_in_package2.txt
├── module-info.class
└── top_level_resource2.txt
```

We assume that both module descriptors for firstresourcemodule and secondre sourcemodule have an empty body, meaning no package is exported. There's a package containing class A and a resource, there's a top-level resource, and a resource inside the *META-INF* directory. While looking at the following code, keep in mind resource encapsulation applies only to resources inside packages in a module.

We're going to try to access those resources in secondresourcemodule from a class in firstresourcemodule:

```
Optional<Module> otherModule =
    ModuleLayer.boot().findModule("secondresourcemodule"); ❶

otherModule.ifPresent(other -> {
    try {
        InputStream m_tl = other.getResourceAsStream("top_level_resource2.txt"); ❷
        InputStream m_pkg = other.getResourceAsStream(
            "javamodularity/secondresourcemodule/resource_in_package2.txt"); ❸
        InputStream m_class = other.getResourceAsStream(
            "javamodularity/secondresourcemodule/A.class"); ❹
        InputStream m_meta =
            other.getResourceAsStream("META-INF/resource_in_metainf.txt"); ❺
        InputStream cz_pkg =
          Class.forName("javamodularity.secondresourcemodule.A")
              .getResourceAsStream("resource_in_package2.txt"); ❻

        assert Stream.of(m_tl, m_class, m_meta)
                    .noneMatch(Objects::isNull);
        assert Stream.of(m_pkg, cz_pkg)
                    .allMatch(Objects::isNull);

    } catch (Exception e) {
        throw new RuntimeException(e);
```

❶ A Module can be obtained through the *boot layer*. The corresponding Module Layer API is introduced in the next chapter.

❷ Top-level resources from other modules can always be loaded.

❸ A resource from a package in another module is encapsulated by default, so this returns null.

❹ An exception is made for `.class` files; these can always be loaded from another module.

❺ Because *META-INF* is never a valid package name, resources from that directory can be accessed as well.

❻ While we can get a `Class<A>` instance by using `Class::forName`, loading the encapsulated resource through it will return null, just as in (3).

Resource encapsulation applies only to resources in packages. Class file resources (ending with `.class`) are the exception; they're not encapsulated even if they're inside a package. All other resources can be freely used by other modules. Even though you *can* doesn't mean you *should* do this. Relying on resources from another module is not quite modular. It's best to load resources only from within the same module. When you do need resources from another module, consider exposing the content of the resources through a method on an exported class or even as a service. This way, the dependency becomes explicit in the module descriptor.

Exposing Resources in Packages

You can expose encapsulated resources in packages to other modules by using *open modules* or *open packages*. These concepts are introduced in "Open Modules and Packages" on page 118. A resource that is in an open module or package can be loaded as if no resource encapsulation is applied.

Working with ResourceBundles

An example where the JDK itself heeds the advice of exporting resources through services is with ResourceBundles. ResourceBundles provide a mechanism for localization as part of the JDK. They're essentially lists of key-value pairs, specific to a locale. You can implement the ResourceBundle interface yourself, or use, for example, a properties file. The latter is convenient, because there is default support for loading properties files following a predefined format, as shown in Example 5-9.

Example 5-9. Properties files to be loaded by the ResourceBundle mechanism, where Translations is a user-defined basename

```
Translations_en.properties
Translations_en_US.properties
Translations_nl.properties
```

You then load a bundle for a specific locale, and get a translation for a key:

```
Locale locale = Locale.ENGLISH;
ResourceBundle translations =
   ResourceBundle.getBundle("javamodularity.resourcebundle.Translations",
                            locale);
String translation = translations.getString("modularity_key");
```

The translation properties files live in a package in a module. Traditionally, the `getBundle` implementation could scan the classpath for files to load. Then, the most appropriate properties file would be selected based on the locale, regardless of which JAR it comes from.

> Explaining how `ResourceBundle::getBundle` selects the right bundle given a basename and locale is beyond the scope of this book. If you're unfamiliar with this process, the `ResourceBundle` JavaDoc contains extensive information about how it loads the most specific file with fallback mechanisms. You will also find that an additional class-based format is supported besides properties files.

With modules, there is no classpath to scan. And you have already seen that resources in modules are encapsulated. Only files within the module calling `getBundle` are considered.

It's desirable to put translations for different locales into separate modules. At the same time, opening these modules or packages (see "Exposing Resources in Packages" on page 113) has more consequences than just exposing resources. This is why a services-based mechanism for ResourceBundles is introduced in Java 9. It's based on a new interface called `ResourceBundleProvider`, containing a single method with the signature `ResourceBundle getBundle(String basename, Locale locale)`. Whenever a module wants to offer additional translations, it can create an implementation of this interface and register it as a service. The implementation then locates the correct resource inside the module and returns it, or returns `null` if no suitable translation for the given locale is in the module.

Using this pattern, you can now extend the supported locales in an application by adding a module. As long as it registers a `ResourceBundleProvider` implementation, it's automatically picked up by the module requesting the translations through `ResourceBundle::getBundle`. A complete example can be found in the code accompanying this chapter (➥ *chapter5/resourcebundles*).

CHAPTER 6

Advanced Modularity Patterns

The previous chapter presented general design guidelines and patterns for modular application development. This chapter contains more advanced patterns and module system APIs that may not apply to everyday development. Still, it is an important part of the module system. Not only is the module system meant to be used directly by application developers, but it also serves as a basis for other frameworks to build upon. The advanced APIs primarily revolve around such usage.

The next section explores the need for reflection that many libraries and frameworks currently have. Open modules and packages are introduced as a feature to relax strong encapsulation at run-time. It's an important feature during migration too, so it will be revisited in Chapter 8.

After open modules and packages, the focus shifts to patterns for dynamically extensible applications. Think of plug-in-based systems or application containers. Central to these systems is the challenge of adding modules at run-time, instead of working only with a fixed configuration of modules from the module path.

 Feel free to skip this latter part of the chapter when first learning about the module system. Most applications get by fine without ever using the module system's more dynamic and advanced features. You can always come back later to gain a better understanding of these features after getting more experience with typical modular scenarios first.

Strong Encapsulation Revisited

We discussed the virtues of strong encapsulation at length in the previous chapters. In general, it is beneficial to be strict about what is and what is not a public, exported API. But in practice, the line isn't drawn quite as clearly. Many libraries and frameworks exist that rely on accessing implementation classes of your application to do their work. Think of serialization libraries, object-relational mappers, and dependency injection frameworks. All these libraries want to manipulate classes that you'd otherwise deem internal implementation details.

An object-relational mapper or serialization library needs to access entity classes so it can instantiate them and fill them with the right data. Even if an entity class never leaves the module, the ORM library module somehow needs access. Dependency injection frameworks, as another example, need to inject service instances into service implementation classes. Exporting just the interfaces is not enough. By strongly encapsulating implementation classes within modules, these frameworks are denied the usual access they previously enjoyed on the classpath.

Reflection is almost without exception the tool of choice for these frameworks. Reflection is an important part of the Java platform, allowing code to inspect code at run-time. If that sounds a bit esoteric, that's because it is. Using reflection in application code is not something to strive for. Still, without reflection, many generic frameworks (such as Hibernate or Spring) would not have been possible. But even reflection cannot break the walls of strong encapsulation around nonexported packages in modules, as you have learned in previous chapters.

The wrong reaction here is to export those packages indiscriminately. Exporting a package means its API can be compiled against and relied upon from different modules. That's not what we want to express in this case. We need a mechanism to indicate that it's OK for some libraries to get (reflective) *run-time* access to certain types.

Deep Reflection

Two orthogonal issues need to be addressed to make traditional reflection-based libraries play nice with strong encapsulation:

- Provide access to internal types without exporting packages.
- Allow reflective access to all parts of these types.

We'll zoom in on the second problem first. Let's assume we export a package so a library can get access. You already know that means we can compile against just the public types in those packages. But does it also mean we can use reflection to break into private parts of those types at run-time? This practice of *deep reflection* is used by many libraries. For example, Spring or Hibernate inject values into nonpublic fields of classes.

Back to our question: can you do deep reflection on public types from exported packages? The answer is no. It turns out that even if a type is exported, this does not mean you can unconditionally break into private parts of those types with reflection.

From a modularity perspective, this is the right thing to do. When arbitrary modules *can* break into private parts of exported types, they *will* do so. In effect, those private parts become part of the official API again. The same scenario played out already in the JDK itself, as discussed in "Using the Modular JDK Without Modules" on page 30.

Preventing access to nonpublic parts is not only a matter of API hygiene: private fields tend to be private for good reasons. For example, there is a `java.security.Key Store` class in the JDK that manages keys and credentials. The authors of this class specifically do not want anyone to access the private fields guarding those secrets!

Exporting a package does not allow a module using those exported types to reflect over nonpublic parts. Deep reflection is supported in Java by the `setAccessible` method that is available on reflective objects. It circumvents checks that otherwise block access to inaccessible parts. Before the module system and strong encapsulation, `setAccessible` would basically never fail. With the module system, the rules have changed. Figure 6-1 shows which scenarios won't work anymore.

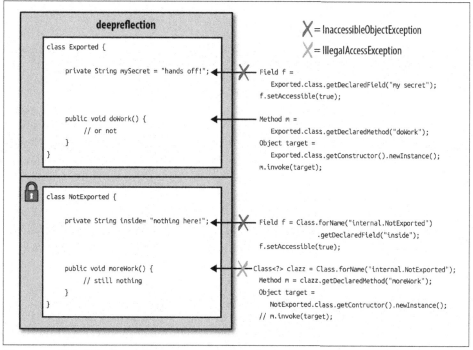

Figure 6-1. Module deepreflection exports a package containing class Exported and encapsulates the NotExported class. The snippets (assumed to be in another module) show reflection works only on public parts of exported types. Only Exported::doWork can be accessed reflectively; all others lead to exceptions.

So we're left in the situation where many popular libraries want to perform deep reflection, whether a type is exported or not. Because of strong encapsulation, they can't. And even if implementation classes were exported, deep reflection on nonpublic parts is prohibited.

Open Modules and Packages

What we need is a way to make types accessible for deep reflection at run-time without exporting them. With such a feature, the frameworks can do their work again, while strong encapsulation is still upheld at compile-time.

Open modules offer exactly this combination of features. When a module is open, all its types are available for deep reflection by other modules at run-time. This property holds regardless of whether any packages are exported.

Making a module open is done by putting the open keyword in the module descriptor:

```
open module deepreflection {
    exports api;
}
```

All previous failure modes from Figure 6-1 disappear when a module is open, as shown in Figure 6-2.

The open keyword opens all packages in a module for deep reflection. In addition to a package being open, it can also be exported, as is the case for the api package containing the class Exported in this example. Any module reflectively accessing nonpublic elements from Exported or NotExported can do so after calling setAccessible. Readability to the module deepreflection is assumed by the JVM when using reflection on its types, so no special code has to be written for this to work. At compile-time, NotExported still is inaccessible, while Exported is accessible because of the exports clause in the module descriptor. From the application developer's point of view, the NotExported class is still strongly encapsulated at compile-time. From the framework's perspective, the NotExported class is freely accessible at run-time.

 With Java 9, two new methods for reflection objects are added: canAccess and trySetAccessible (both are defined in java.lang.reflect.AccessibleObject). These methods take into account the new reality where deep reflection is not always allowed. You can use these methods instead of dealing with exceptions from setAccessible.

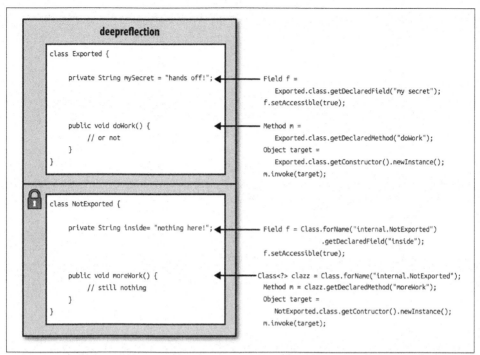

Figure 6-2. With an open module, all types in all packages are open for deep reflection at run-time. No exceptions are thrown when performing deep reflection from another module.

Opening a whole module is somewhat crude. It's convenient for when you can't be sure what types are used at run-time by a library or framework. As such, open modules can play a crucial role in migration scenarios when introducing modules into a codebase. More on this in Chapter 8.

However, when you know which packages need to be open (and in most cases, you should), you can selectively open them from a normal module:

```
module deepreflection {
    exports api;
    opens internal;
}
```

Notice the lack of open before the module keyword. This module definition is *not* equivalent to the previous open module definition. Here, only the types in package internal are open for deep reflection. Types in api are exported, but are not open for deep reflection. At run-time this module definition provides somewhat stronger encapsulation than the fully open module, since no deep reflection is possible on types in package api.

We can make this module definition equivalent to the open module by also opening the api package:

```
module deepreflection {
    exports api;
    opens api;
    opens internal;
}
```

A package can be both exported and open at the same time.

In practice, this combination is a bit awkward. Try to design exported packages in such a way that other modules don't need to perform deep reflection on them.

opens clauses can be qualified just like exports:

```
module deepreflection {
    exports api;
    opens internal to library;
}
```

The semantics are as you'd expect: only module library can perform deep reflection on types from package internal. A qualified opens reduces the scope to just one or more other explicitly mentioned modules. When you can qualify an opens statement, it's better to do so. It prevents arbitrary modules from snooping on internal details through deep reflection.

Sometimes you need to be able to perform deep reflection on a third-party module. In some cases, libraries even want to reflectively access private parts of JDK platform modules. It's not possible to just add the open keyword and recompile the module in these cases. For these scenarios, a command-line flag is introduced for the java command:

```
--add-opens <module>/<package>=<targetmodule>
```

This is equivalent to a qualified opens for package in module to targetmodule. If, for example, a framework module myframework wants to use nonpublic parts of java.lang.ClassLoader, you can do so by adding the following option to the java command:

```
--add-opens java.base/java.lang=myframework
```

This command-line option should be considered an escape hatch, especially useful during migration of code that's not written with the module system in mind yet. In Part II, this option and others like it will reappear for these purposes.

Dependency Injection

Open modules and packages are the gateway to supporting existing dependency injection frameworks in the Java module system. In a fully modularized application, a dependency injection framework relies on open packages to access nonexported types.

Replacing Reflection

Java 9 offers an alternative to reflection-based access of frameworks to nonpublic class members in applications: MethodHandles and VarHandles. The latter are introduced in Java 9 through JEP 193 (*http://openjdk.java.net/jeps/193*). Applications can pass a java.lang.invoke.Lookup instance with the right permissions to the framework, explicitly delegating private lookup capabilities. The framework module can then, using MethodHandles.privateLookupIn(Class, Lookup), access nonpublic members on classes from the application module. It is expected that frameworks, in time, move to this more principled and performance-friendly approach to access application internals. An example of this approach can be found in the code accompanying this chapter (➥ *chapter6/lookup*).

To illustrate the abstract concept of open modules and packages, we'll look at a concrete example. Instead of using services with the module system as described in Chapter 4, this example features a fictional third-party dependency injection framework in a module named spruce. Figure 6-3 shows the example. An open package is indicated by an "open" label in front of the types of a package.

Our example application covers two domains: orders and customers. These are clearly visible as separate modules, with the customers domain split into an API and implementation module. The main module uses both services but doesn't want to be coupled to the implementation details of either service. Both service implementation classes are encapsulated to that end. Only the interfaces are exported and accessible to the main module.

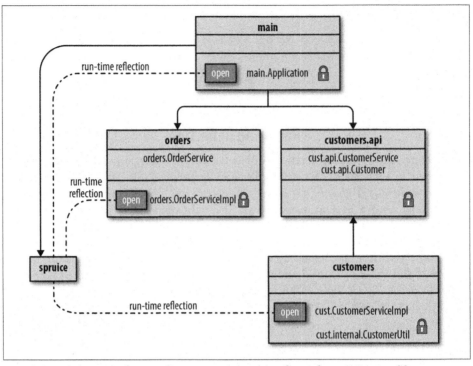

Figure 6-3. Overview of an application main using a dependency injection library spruice. Requires relations between modules are shown as solid edges, and run-time deep reflection on types in open packages is shown as dashed edges.

So far, the story is quite similar to the approach described in Chapter 4 on services. The `main` module is nicely decoupled from implementation specifics. However, this time we're not going to provide and consume the services through `ServiceLoader`. Rather, we are going to use the DI framework to inject `OrderService` and `Customer Service` implementations into `Application`. Either we configure `spruice` explicitly with the correct wiring of services, or we use annotations, or a combination of both approaches. Annotations such as `@Inject` are often used to identify injection points that are matched on type with injectable instances:

```
public class Application {

    @Inject
    private OrderService orderService;

    @Inject
    private CustomerService customerService;

    public void orderForCustomer(String customerId, String[] productIds) {
        Customer customer = customerService.find(customerId)
```

```
        orderService.order(customer, productIds);
    }

    public static void main(String... args) {
        // Bootstrap Spruice and set up wiring
    }
}
```

In the main method of the Application class, spruice APIs are used to bootstrap the DI framework, Therefore, the main module needs a dependency on spruice for its wiring API. Service implementation classes must be instantiated by spruice and injected into the annotated fields (constructor injection is another viable alternative). Then, Application is ready to receive calls on orderForCustomer.

Unlike the module system's services mechanism, spruice does not have special privileges to instantiate encapsulated classes. What we can do is add opens clauses for the packages that need to be instantiated or injected. This allows spruice to access those classes at run-time and perform deep reflection where necessary (e.g., to instantiate and inject the OrderServiceImpl class into the orderService private field of Applica tion). Packages that are used only internally in a module, such as cust.internal in the customers module, don't need to be opened. The opens clauses *could* be qualified to open to spruice only. Unfortunately, that also ties our orders and customers modules to this specific DI framework. An unqualified opens leaves room for changing DI implementations without recompiling those modules later.

Figure 6-3 exposes spruice for what it really is: a module reaching into almost every dark corner of the application we're building. Based on the wiring configuration, it finds encapsulated implementation classes, instantiates them, and injects them into private fields of Application. At the same time, this setup allows the application to be just as nicely modularized as with services and ServiceLoader—without having to use the ServiceLoader API to retrieve services. They are injected as if by (reflection) magic.

What we lose is the ability of the Java module system to know about and verify the service dependencies between modules. There are no provides/uses clauses in module descriptors to verify. Also, packages in the application modules need to be opened. It is possible to make all application modules open modules. Application developers then aren't burdened with making that choice for each package. Of course, this comes at the expense of allowing run-time access and deep reflection on all packages in every application module. With a little insight into what your libraries and frameworks are doing, this heavyweight approach isn't necessary.

In the next section, we'll look at reflection on modules themselves. Again, this is an advanced use of the module system APIs, which should not come up in normal application development all that often.

Reflection on Modules

Reflection allows you to reify all Java elements at run-time. Classes, packages, methods, and so on all have a reflective representation. We've seen how open modules allow deep reflection on those elements at run-time.

With the addition of a new structural element to Java, the module, reflection needs to be extended as well. In Java 9, `java.lang.Module` is added to provide a run-time view on a module from code. Methods on this class can be grouped into three distinct responsibilities:

Introspection
Query properties of a given module.

Modification
Change characteristics of a module on-the-fly.

Access
Read resources from inside a module.

The last case was discussed already in "Loading Resources from a Module" on page 110. In the remainder of this section, we'll look at introspecting and modifying modules.

Introspection

The `java.lang.Module` class is the entry point for reflection on modules. Figure 6-4 shows `Module` and its related classes. It has a `ModuleDescriptor` that provides a run-time view on the contents of `module-info`.

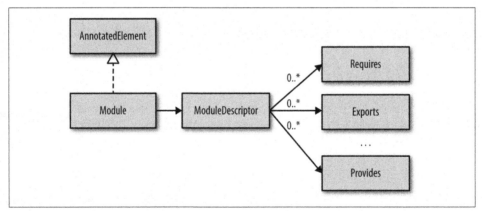

Figure 6-4. A simplified class diagram of Module and related classes

You can obtain a `Module` instance through a `Class` from within a module:

```
Module module = String.class.getModule();
```

The `getModule` method returns the module containing the class. For this example, the `String` class unsurprisingly comes from the `java.base` platform module. Later in this chapter, you will see another way to obtain `Module` instances by name through the new `ModuleLayer` API, without requiring knowledge of classes in a module.

There are several methods to query information on a `Module`, shown in Example 6-1.

Example 6-1. Inspecting a module at run-time (➥ chapter6/introspection)

```
String name1 = module.getName(); // Name as defined in module-info.java
Set<String> packages1 = module.getPackages(); // Lists all packages in the module

// The methods above are convenience methods that return
// information from the Module's ModuleDescriptor:
ModuleDescriptor descriptor = module.getDescriptor();
String name2 = descriptor.name(); // Same as module.getName();
Set<String> packages2 = descriptor.packages(); // Same as module.getPackages();

// Through ModuleDescriptor, all information from module-info.java is exposed:
Set<Exports> exports = descriptor.exports(); // All exports, possibly qualified
Set<String> uses = descriptor.uses(); // All services used by this module
```

The preceding examples are by no means exhaustive but illustrate that all information from *module-info.class* is available through the `ModuleDescriptor` class. Instances of `ModuleDescriptor` are read-only (immutable). It is not possible to, for example, change the name of a module at run-time.

Modifying Modules

You can perform several other operations on a `Module` that affect the module and its environment. Let's say you have a package that is not exported, but based on a run-time decision you want to export it:

```
Module target = ...; // Somehow obtain the module you want to export to
Module module = getClass().getModule(); // Get the module of the current class
module.addExports("javamodularity.export.atruntime", target);
```

You can add a *qualified export* only to a specific module through the `Module` API. Now, the target module can access code that was in the previously encapsulated `java modularity.export.atruntime` package.

You may wonder whether this is a security hole: can you just call `addExports` on an arbitrary module so it gives up its secrets? That's not the case. When you try to add an export to any module other than the current module where the call is executing from, an exception is thrown by the VM. You cannot escalate privileges of a module from the outside through the module reflection API.

Caller Sensitive

Methods that behave differently when called from different places are *caller sensitive* methods. You will find methods such as addExports to be annotated with @CallerSensitive in the JDK source code. Caller sensitive methods can find out which class (and module) is calling them, based on the current call-stack. The privilege of getting this information and basing decisions on it is reserved for code in java.base (although the new StackWalker API introduced through JEP 259 (*http://openjdk.java.net/jeps/259*) in JDK 9 opens this possibility for application code as well). Another example of this mechanism can be found in the implementation of setAccessible, as discussed in "Open Modules and Packages" on page 118. Calling this method from a module to which the package is not opened leads to an exception, whereas calling it from a module that is allowed to perform deep reflection succeeds.

Module has four methods that allow run-time modifications:

addExports(String packageName, Module target)
    Expose previously nonexported packages to another module.

addOpens(String packageName, Module target)
    Opens a package for deep reflection to another module.

addReads(Module other)
    Adds a reads relation from the current module to another module.

addUses(Class<?> serviceType)
    Indicates that the current module wants to use additional service types with ServiceLoader.

There's no addProvides method, because exposing new implementations that were not known at compile-time is deemed to be a rare use case.

It's good to know about the reflection API on modules. However, in practice this API is used only on rare occasions during regular application development. Always try to expose enough information between modules through normal means before reaching for reflection. Using reflection to change module behavior at run-time goes against the philosophy of the Java module system. Implicit dependencies arise that are not taken into account at compile-time or at startup, voiding a lot of guarantees the module system otherwise offers in those early phases.

Annotations

Modules can also be annotated. At run-time, those annotations can be read through the `java.lang.Module` API. Several default annotations that are part of the Java platform can be applied to modules, for example, the `@Deprecated` annotation:

```
@Deprecated
module m {

}
```

Adding this annotation indicates to users of the module that they should look for a replacement.

> As of Java 9, a deprecated element can also be marked for removal in a future release: `@Deprecated(forRemoval=true)`. Read JEP 277 (*http://openjdk.java.net/jeps/277*) for more details on the enhanced deprecation features. Several platform modules (such as `java.xml.ws` and `java.corba`) are marked for removal in JDK 9.

When you require a deprecated module, the compiler generates a warning. Another default annotation that can be applied to modules is `@SuppressWarnings`.

It's also possible to define your own annotations for modules. To this end, a new target element type `MODULE` is defined, as shown in Example 6-2.

Example 6-2. Annotating a module (➥ chapter6/annotated_module)

```
package javamodularity.annotatedmodule;

import java.lang.annotation.*;
import static java.lang.annotation.ElementType.*;

@Retention(RetentionPolicy.RUNTIME)
@Target(value={PACKAGE, MODULE})
public @interface CustomAnnotation {

}
```

This `CustomAnnotation` can now be applied to packages and modules. Using a custom-defined annotation on a module reveals another curious fact: module declarations can have `import` statements.

```
import javamodularity.annotatedmodule.CustomAnnotation;

@CustomAnnotation
module annotated { }
```

Without the `import` statement, the module descriptor doesn't compile. Alternatively, you can use the fully qualified name of the annotation directly, without an `import`.

> You can also use `import` in module descriptors to shorten `uses/pro vides` clauses.

Figure 6-4 shows how `Module` implements `AnnotatedElement`. In code, you can use `getAnnotations` on a `Module` instance to get an array of all annotations on a module. The `AnnotatedElement` interface offers various other methods to find the right annotation.

> This works only if the retention policy of the annotation is set to `RUNTIME`.

Besides platform-defined annotations such as `@Deprecated`, it will most probably be frameworks (or even build tools) that make use of annotations on modules.

Container Application Patterns

At this point, we're switching gears to even more advanced uses of the module system. This is a good moment to reiterate the advice from the beginning of this chapter: you can safely skip the remainder of this chapter when first learning about the module system.

With that out of the way, let's dive into the advanced APIs! Up to this point, we've looked at modular applications as a single entity. You gather modules, put them on the module path, and start the application. Although that's a valid view in most cases, another range of applications is structurally different.

You can think of applications acting as a container for other applications. Or, think of applications that define just their core functionality, with the expectation that this will be extended by third parties. In the former case, new applications can be deployed into a running container application. The latter case is often achieved through a plug-in-like architecture. In both cases, you don't start with a module path containing all modules up front. New modules can come (and go) during the life cycle of the container application. Many of these applications are currently built on module systems such as OSGi or JBoss Modules.

In this section, you'll look at architecting such a container or plug-in-based system by using the Java module system. Before looking at the realization of these container application patterns, you'll explore the new APIs that enable them. Keep in mind that these new APIs are introduced specifically for the use cases discussed so far. When you're not building an extensible, container-like application, you are unlikely to use those APIs.

Layers and Configurations

A module graph is resolved upon starting a module with the java command. The resolver uses modules from the platform itself and the module path to create a consistent set of resolved modules. It does so based on requires clauses and provides/uses clauses in the module descriptors. When the resolver is finished, the resulting module graph cannot be changed anymore.

That seems to run counter to the requirements of container applications. There, the ability to add new modules to a running container is crucial. A new concept must be introduced to allow for this functionality: layers. Layers are to modules as classloaders are to classes: a loading and instantiation mechanism.

A resolved module graph lives within a ModuleLayer. Layers set up coherent sets of modules. Layers themselves can refer to parent layers and form an acyclic graph. But before we get ahead of ourselves, let's look at the ModuleLayer you already had without knowing.

When plainly starting a module by using java, an initial layer called the *boot layer* is constructed by the Java runtime. It contains the resulting module graph after resolving the root modules provided to the java command (either as an initial module with -m or through --add-modules).

In Figure 6-5, a simplified example of the boot layer is shown after starting a module application that requires java.sql.

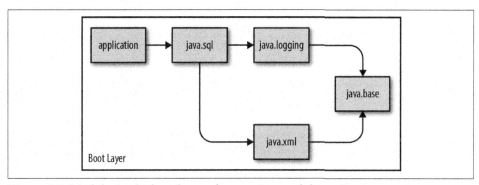

Figure 6-5. Modules in the boot layer after starting module application

(In reality, the boot layer contains many more modules because of service binding of platform modules.)

You can enumerate the modules in the boot layer with the code in Example 6-3.

Example 6-3. Printing all modules in the boot layer (➥ chapter6/bootlayer)

```
ModuleLayer.boot().modules()
          .forEach(System.out::println);
```

Because the boot layer is constructed for us, the question of how to create another layer remains. Before you can construct a `ModuleLayer`, a `Configuration` must be created describing the module graph inside that layer. Again, for the boot layer this is done implicitly at startup. When constructing a `Configuration`, a `ModuleFinder` needs to be provided to locate individual modules. Setting up this Russian doll of classes to create a new `ModuleLayer` looks as follows:

```
ModuleFinder finder = ModuleFinder.of(Paths.get("./modules")); ❶

ModuleLayer bootLayer = ModuleLayer.boot();

Configuration config = bootLayer.configuration()
    .resolve(finder, ModuleFinder.of(), Set.of("rootmodule")); ❷

ClassLoader scl = ClassLoader.getSystemClassLoader();
ModuleLayer newLayer = bootLayer.defineModulesWithOneLoader(config, scl); ❸
```

❶ A convenience method to create a `ModuleFinder` that locates modules in one or more paths on the filesystem.

❷ Configurations are resolved relative to parent configurations; in this case, to the configuration of the boot layer.

❸ With `Configuration`, a `ModuleLayer` can be constructed, materializing the resolved modules from the configuration.

In principle, modules could come from anywhere. Typically, they're somewhere on the filesystem, so the `ModuleFinder::of(Path...)` factory method is convenient to use. It returns a `ModuleFinder` implementation that can load modules from the filesystem. Every `ModuleLayer` and `Configuration` points to one or more parents, with the exception of instances returned by the `ModuleLayer::empty` and `Configuration::empty` methods. Those special instances serve as root for the `ModuleLayer` and `Configuration` hierarchy in the module system. The boot layer and corresponding configuration have their empty counterparts as a parent.

While constructing the new layer, we use the boot layer and configuration as a parent. In the `resolve` call, the `ModuleFinder` is passed as the first argument. The second argument to `resolve` is another `ModuleFinder`, in this case, an empty one. This second finder is consulted when a module could not be found in the first finder or through the parent configuration.

When resolving modules in the new configuration, modules from the parent configuration are taken into account as well. A module from the newly constructed configuration can read a module from the parent configuration. Root modules to kickstart the resolver are passed as a third argument to the configuration's `resolve` method. In this case, `rootmodule` serves as a initial module for the resolver to start from. Resolution in a new configuration is subject to the same constraints you've seen so far. It fails if a root module or one of its dependencies cannot be found. Cycles between modules are not allowed, nor can two modules exporting the same package be read by a single other module.

To expand on the example, let's say `rootmodule` requires the `javafx.controls` platform module and `library`, a helper module that also lives in the *./modules* directory. After resolving the configuration and constructing the new layer, the resulting situation looks like Figure 6-6.

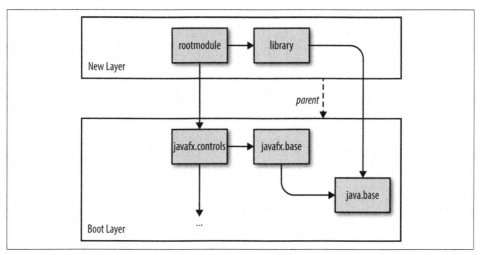

Figure 6-6. A new layer with the boot layer as its parent

Readability relations can cross layer boundaries. The `requires` clause of `rootmodule` to `javafx.controls` has been resolved to the platform module in the boot layer. On the other hand, the `requires` clause to `library` was resolved in the newly constructed layer, because that module is loaded along with `rootmodule` from the filesystem.

Besides the `resolve` method on `Configuration`, there's also `resolveAndBind`. This variation also does service binding, taking into account the `provides`/`uses` clauses of the modules in the new configuration. Services can cross layer boundaries as well. Modules in the new layer can use services from the parent layer, and vice versa.

Last, the `defineModulesWithOneLoader` method is called on the parent (boot) layer. This method materializes the module references resolved by the `Configuration` into real `Module` instances inside the new layer. The next section discusses the significance of the classloader passed to this method.

All examples of layers you've seen so far consisted of new layers pointing to the boot layer as the parent. However, layers can point to a parent layer other than the boot layer as well. It's even possible for a layer to have multiple parents. This is illustrated in Figure 6-7: Layer 3 points to Layer 1 and Layer 2 as its parents.

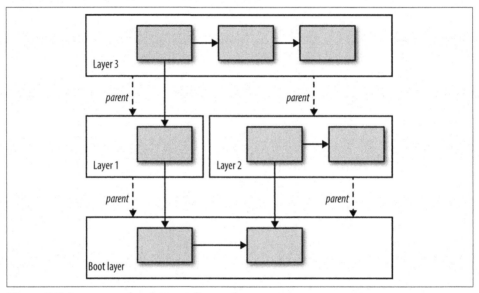

Figure 6-7. Layers can form an acyclic graph

Static `defineModules*` methods on `ModuleLayer` accept a list of parent layers when constructing new layers, instead of calling any of the nonstatic `defineModules*` methods on a parent layer instance directly. Later, in Figure 6-12, you'll see those static methods in action. The important thing to remember is that layers can form an acyclic graph, just like modules within a layer.

Classloading in Layers

You may still be wondering about the last two lines of the layer construction code in the previous section:

```
ClassLoader scl = ClassLoader.getSystemClassLoader();
ModuleLayer newLayer = bootLayer.defineModulesWithOneLoader(config, scl);
```

What's up with the classloader and the defineModulesWithOneLoader method? The answer to this question is nontrivial. Before we get to the method in question, it's good to brush up on what classloaders do and what that means for the module system.

Classloaders, no surprise, load classes at run-time. Classloaders dictate *visibility*: a class can be loaded if it is visible to a certain classloader, or any other classloaders it delegates to. In a way, it's peculiar to introduce classloaders this far into the book. Earlier module systems such as OSGi use classloaders as the primary means to enforce encapsulation. Every bundle (OSGi module) gets its own classloader, and the delegation between classloaders follows the wiring of bundles as expressed in the OSGi metadata.

Not so in the Java module system. There, a whole new mechanism encompassing readability and new accessibility rules is put in place, while leaving classloading mostly unchanged. That's a deliberate choice, because using classloaders for isolation is not a foolproof solution. After classes have been loaded, Class instances can be passed around freely, bypassing any schemes set up through classloader isolation and delegation. You can try to do that in the module system, but you've seen that creating instances from Class objects you're not allowed to access because of encapsulation leads to exceptions. The module system enforces encapsulation at a much deeper level. Furthermore, classloaders are only a run-time construct, whereas the Java module system enforces encapsulation at compile-time as well. Last, many existing codebases make assumptions about the way classes are loaded by default. Changing these defaults (for example, by giving each module its own classloader) would break existing code.

Still, it's good to be aware of the way classloaders interact with the module system. Let's revisit Figure 6-5, where a module application is loaded in the boot layer. This time, we're interested in what classloaders are involved, as shown in Figure 6-8.

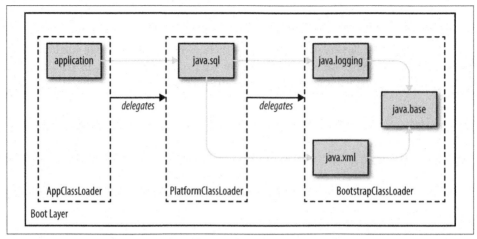

Figure 6-8. Classloaders in the boot layer when starting module application

Three classloaders are active in the boot layer when running an application from the module path. At the bottom of the delegation hierarchy is `BootstrapClassLoader`, also known as the *primordial classloader*. It's a special classloader loading all essential platform module classes. Care has been taken to load classes from as few modules as possible in this classloader, because classes are granted all security permissions when loaded in the bootstrap loader.

Then there's `PlatformClassLoader`, which loads less privileged platform module classes. Last in the chain is `AppClassLoader`, responsible for loading user-defined modules and some JDK-specific tooling modules (such as `jdk.compiler` or `jdk.java doc`). All classloaders delegate to the underlying classloader. Effectively, this gives `App ClassLoader` visibility to all classes. This three-way setup is quite similar to the way classloaders worked before the module system, mainly for backward compatibility.

We started this section with the question of why a classloader needs to be passed to the method creating a `ModuleLayer`:

```
ClassLoader scl = ClassLoader.getSystemClassLoader();
ModuleLayer newLayer = bootLayer.defineModulesWithOneLoader(config, scl);
```

Even though the mapping from modules to classloaders is predefined in the boot layer, the creator of a new layer must indicate which classloaders load classes for which modules. The `ModuleLayer::defineModulesWithOneLoader(Configuration, ClassLoader)` method is a convenience method. It sets up the new layer so that all modules in the layer are loaded by a single, freshly created classloader. This class-loader delegates to the parent classloader passed as an argument. In the example, we pass the result of `ClassLoader::getSystemClassLoader`, which returns `AppClass`

`Loader`, the classloader responsible for loading classes of user-defined modules in the boot layer (there's also a `getPlatformClassLoader` method).

So, the classloader view on the newly constructed layer from the example (as seen earlier in Figure 6-6) looks like Figure 6-9.

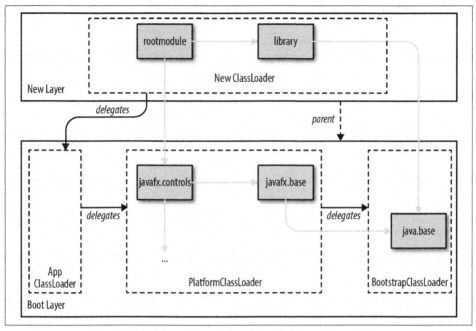

Figure 6-9. A single classloader is created for all modules in the new layer

The delegation between classloaders must respect the readability relations between modules, even across layers. It would be problematic if the new classloader didn't delegate to `AppClassLoader` in the boot layer, but, for example, to `BootstrapClass Loader`. Because `rootmodule` reads `javafx.controls`, it must be able to see and load those classes. Parent delegation of the new layer's classloader to `AppClassLoader` ensures this. In turn, `AppClassLoader` delegates to `PlatformClassLoader`, which loads the classes from `javafx.controls`.

There are other methods to create a new layer. Another convenience method called `defineModulesWithManyLoaders` creates a new classloader for each module in the layer, as shown in Figure 6-10.

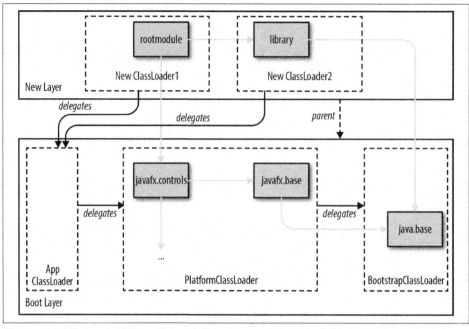

Figure 6-10. Every module within a layer constructed using defineModulesWithMany-Loaders gets its own classloader

Again, each of these new classloaders delegates to the parent that is passed as an argument to `defineModulesWithManyLoaders`. If you need even more control over classloading in a layer, there's the `defineModules` method. It takes a function mapping a string (module name) to a classloader. Providing such a mapping gives ultimate flexibility on when to create new classloaders for a new module or to assign existing classloaders to modules in the layer. An example of such a mapping can be found in the JDK itself. The boot layer is created using `defineModules` with a custom mapping to one of the three classloaders shown previously in Figure 6-8.

Why is it important to control classloading when using layers? Because it can make many limitations in the module system disappear. For example, we discussed how only a single module can contain (or export) a certain package. It turns out this is just a side effect of how the boot layer is created. A package can be defined to a classloader only once. All modules from the module path are loaded by `AppClassLoader`. Therefore, if any of these modules contain the same package (exported or not), they will be defined to the same `AppClassLoader` leading to run-time exceptions.

When you instantiate a new layer with a new classloader, the same package may appear in a different module in that layer. In that case, there is no inherent problem because the package gets defined twice to different classloaders. You'll see later that this also means multiple versions of the same module can live in distinct layers. That's quite an improvement on the situation we discussed in "Versioned Modules" on page 106, although it comes at the expense of the complexity of creating and managing layers.

Plug-in Architectures

Now that you have seen the basics of layers and classloading in layers, it's time to apply them in practice. First, you'll look at creating an application that can be extended with new plug-ins at run-time. In many ways, this is similar to what we did with EasyText and services in Chapter 4. With the services approach, when a new analysis provider is put on the module path, it is picked up when starting the application. This is already quite flexible, but what if those new provider modules come from third-party developers? And what if they aren't put on the module path at startup, but can be introduced at run-time?

Such requirements lead to a more flexible plug-in architecture. A well-known example of a plug-in-based application is the Eclipse IDE. Eclipse itself offers baseline IDE functionality but can be extended in many ways by adding plug-ins. Another example of an application that uses plug-ins is the new jlink tool in the JDK. It can be extended with new optimizations through a plug-in mechanism similar to the one we're going to look at now. Chapter 13 discusses more details on what plug-ins the jlink tool can use.

In general, we can identify a plug-in host application that gets extended by plug-ins, as shown in Figure 6-11.

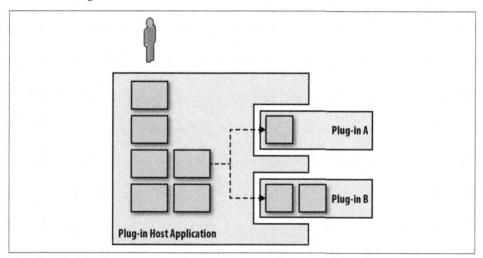

Figure 6-11. Plug-ins provide additional functionality on top of the host application's functionality

Users interact with the host application, but experience extended functionality by virtue of the plug-ins. In most cases, the host application can function fine without any plug-ins as well. Plug-ins are usually developed independently of the host application. A clear boundary exists between the host application and the plug-ins. At run-time, the host application calls into the plug-ins for additional functionality. For this to work, there must be an agreed-upon API that the plug-ins implement. Typically, this is an interface that plug-ins implement.

You may have already guessed that layers play a role in the implementation of a dynamic, plug-in-based application. We're going to create a pluginhost module that spins up a new ModuleLayer for each plug-in. These plug-in modules, plugin.a and plugin.b in this example, live in separate directories along with their dependencies (if any). Crucially, these directories are not on the module path when starting plugin host.

The example uses services with a pluginhost.api module exposing the interface pluginhost.api.Plugin, which has a single method, doWork. Both plug-in modules require this API module, but otherwise don't have a compile-time relation to the pluginhost application module. A plug-in module consists of an implementation of the Plugin interface, provided as service. Take the module descriptor of module plugin.a, shown in Example 6-4.

Example 6-4. module-info.java (➡ chapter6/plugins)

```
module plugin.a {
  requires pluginhost.api;

  provides pluginhost.api.Plugin
      with plugina.PluginA;
}
```

The plug-in implementation class PluginA is not exported.

In pluginhost, the main method loads plug-in modules from directories provided as arguments:

```
if (args.length < 1) {
  System.out.println("Please provide plugin directories");
  return;
}

System.out.println("Loading plugins from " + Arrays.toString(args));

Stream<ModuleLayer> pluginLayers = Stream
  .of(args)
  .map(dir -> createPluginLayer(dir)); ❶
```

```
pluginLayers
  .flatMap(layer -> toStream(ServiceLoader.load(layer, Plugin.class))) ❷
  .forEach(plugin -> {
    System.out.println("Invoking " + plugin.getName());
    plugin.doWork(); ❸
  });
}
```

❶ For each directory provided as an argument, a ModuleLayer is instantiated in createPluginLayer (implementation shown later).

❷ A ServiceLoader::load call is performed with each layer as an argument, giving back Plugin services from that layer.

❸ After the services have been flattened into a single stream, we call the doWork method on all plug-ins.

We are using a yet-to-be discussed overload of ServiceLoader::load. It takes a layer as an argument. By passing it the newly constructed layer for the plug-in, the call returns the freshly loaded Plugin service provider from the plug-in module that was loaded into the layer.

The application is started by running the pluginhost module from the module path. Again, none of the plug-in modules are on the module path. Plug-in modules live in separate directories, and will be loaded at run-time by the host application.

After starting pluginhost with the two plug-in directories as arguments, the run-time situation in Figure 6-12 emerges.

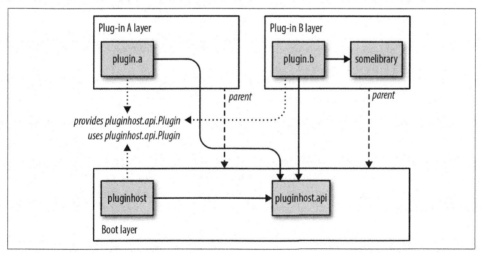

Figure 6-12. Every plug-in is instantiated in its own layer

The first plug-in consists of a single module. Plug-in B, on the other hand, has a dependency on somelibrary. This dependency is automatically resolved when creating the configuration and layer for this plug-in. As long as somelibrary is in the same directory as plugin.b, things just work. Both plug-ins require the plugin host.api module, which is part of the boot layer. All other interactions happen through services published by the plug-in modules and consumed by the host application.

Here's the createPluginLayer method:

```
static ModuleLayer createPluginLayer(String dir) {
  ModuleFinder finder = ModuleFinder.of(Paths.get(dir));

  Set<ModuleReference> pluginModuleRefs = finder.findAll();
  Set<String> pluginRoots = pluginModuleRefs.stream()
        .map(ref -> ref.descriptor().name())
        .filter(name -> name.startsWith("plugin"))  ❶
        .collect(Collectors.toSet());

  ModuleLayer parent = ModuleLayer.boot();
  Configuration cf = parent.configuration()
    .resolve(finder, ModuleFinder.of(), pluginRoots);  ❷

  ClassLoader scl = ClassLoader.getSystemClassLoader();
  ModuleLayer layer = parent.defineModulesWithOneLoader(cf, scl);  ❸

  return layer;
}
```

❶   In order to identify the root modules when resolving the Configuration, we retain all modules with a name that starts with plugin.

❷   The Configuration is resolved with respect to the boot layer, so that plug-in modules can read pluginhost.api.

❸   All modules in the plug-in layer will be defined with the same (fresh) classloader.

Because the createPluginLayer method is called for each plug-in directory, multiple layers are created. Each layer has a single root module (respectively, plugin.a and plugin.b) that gets resolved independently. Because plugin.b requires somelibrary, a ResolutionException will be thrown if that module cannot be found. A configuration and layer will be created only if all constraints expressed in the module descriptors can be satisfied.

We can also call `resolveAndBind(finder, ModuleFinder.of(),`
`Set.of())` (providing no root modules to resolve) instead of
`resolve(..., pluginRoots)`. Because the `plugin` modules expose
a service, service binding causes the resolution of the `plugin` modules and their dependencies anyway.

There's another advantage to loading each plug-in module into its own layer with a
new classloader. By isolating plug-ins this way, it becomes possible for the plug-ins to
depend on different versions of the same module. In "Versioned Modules" on page
106, we discussed how only a single module of the same name exporting the same
packages can be loaded by the module system. That's still true, but we now know this
depends on the way classloaders are set up. Only when talking about the boot layer
constructed from the module path will this be problematic.

Different versions of modules can be loaded simultaneously when constructing multiple layers. If, for example, Plug-in A and B would depend on different versions of
`somelibrary`, that's perfectly possible, as shown in Figure 6-13.

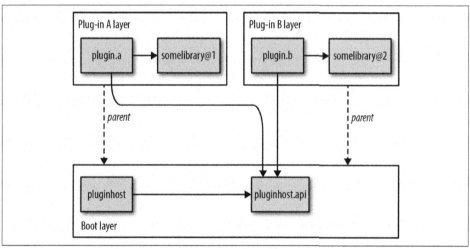

Figure 6-13. Different versions of the same module can be loaded in multiple layers

No code changes are necessary for this to work. Because in our layers modules are
loaded in a new classloader, no clashes in package definitions can occur.

This setup with a new layer for each plug-in brings many advantages. Plug-in authors
are free to choose their own dependencies. At run-time, they're guaranteed not to
clash with dependencies from other plug-ins.

One question to ponder is what happens when we create another layer *on top* of the
two plug-in layers. Layers can have multiple parents, so we can create a new layer
with both plug-in layers as parents:

```
List<Configuration> parentConfigs = pluginLayers
  .map(ModuleLayer::configuration)
  .collect(Collectors.toList());
Configuration newconfig = Configuration.resolve(finder, parentConfigs, ❶
  ModuleFinder.of(), Set.of("topmodule"));
ModuleLayer.Controller newlayer = ModuleLayer.defineModulesWithOneLoader(
  newconfig, pluginLayers, ClassLoader.getSystemClassLoader()); ❷
```

❶ This static method can take multiple configurations as parents.

❷ The same holds for the layer construction with multiple parents.

Let's say this new layer contains a single (root) module named topmodule, which requires somelibrary. Which version of somelibrary will topmodule be resolved against? The fact that the static resolve and defineModulesWithOneLoader methods take a List as a parameter for the parents should serve as a warning sign. Order matters. When the configuration is resolved, the list of parent configurations is consulted in order of the provided list. So depending on which plug-in configuration is put into the parentConfigs list first, the topmodule uses either version 1 or 2 of somelibrary.

Container Architectures

Another architecture that hinges on being able to load new code at run-time is the application container architecture. Isolation between applications in a container is another big theme. Throughout the years, Java has known many application containers, or application servers, most implementing the Java EE standard.

 Even though application servers offer some level of isolation between applications, in the end all deployed applications still run in the same JVM. True isolation (i.e., restricted memory and CPU utilization) requires a more pervasive approach.

Java EE served as one of the inspirations while designing the requirements around layers. That's not to say Java EE is aligned with the Java module system already. At the time of writing, it is unclear which version of Java EE will first make use of modules. However, it's not unthinkable (one might say, quite reasonable to expect) that Java EE will support modular versions of Web Archives (WARs) and Enterprise Application Archives (EARs).

To appreciate how layers enable application container architectures, we're going to create a small application container. Before looking at the implementation, let's review how an application container architecture differs from a plug-in-based one (see Figure 6-14).

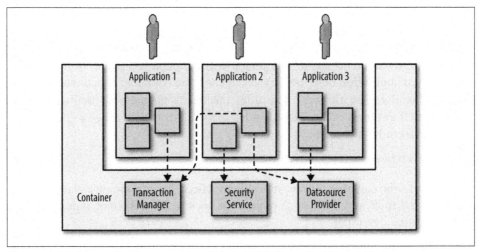

Figure 6-14. An application container hosts multiple applications, offering common functionality for use in those applications

As Figure 6-14 shows, many applications can be loaded into a single container. Applications have their own internal module structure, but crucially, they use common services offered by the container. Functionality such as transaction management or security infrastructure is often provided by containers. Application developers don't have to reinvent the wheel for every application.

In a way, the call-graph is reversed compared to Figure 6-11: applications use the implementations offered by the container, instead of the host application (container) calling into the newly loaded code. Of course, a shared API between the container and applications must exist for this to work. Java EE is an example of such an API. Another big difference with plug-in-based applications is that individual users of the system interact with the dynamically loaded applications themselves, not the container. Think of deployed applications directly exposing HTTP endpoints, web interfaces, or queues to users. Last, applications in a container can be deployed and undeployed, or replaced by a new version.

Functionally, a container architecture is quite different from a plug-in-based architecture. Implementation-wise, there's not that much difference. Application modules can be loaded at run-time into a new layer, just like plug-ins. An API module is offered by the container with interfaces for all the services it offers, which applications can compile against. Those services can be consumed in applications through `ServiceLoader` at run-time.

To make things interesting, we're going to create a container that can deploy and undeploy applications. In the plug-in example, we relied on the plug-in module to expose a service implementing a common interface. For the container, we're going to do things differently. After deployment, we're going to look for a class that implements `ContainerApplication`, which is part of the API offered by the container. The container will reflectively load the class from the application. By doing so, we cannot rely on the services mechanism to interact with the deployed application (although the deployed application does use services to consume container functionality). After instantiating the class through reflection, the `startApp` method (defined in `ContainerApplication`) is called. Before undeployment, `stopApp` is called so the application can gracefully shut down.

There are two new concepts to focus on:

- How can the container ensure it is able to reflectively instantiate a class from the deployed application? We don't require the package to be open or exported by the application developer.
- How can modules be properly disposed of after undeploying an application?

During layer creation, it's possible to manipulate the modules that are loaded into the layer and their relations. That's exactly what a container needs to do to get access to classes in the deployed application. Somehow the container needs to ensure that the package containing the class implementing `ContainerApplication` is open for deep reflection.

Cleaning up modules is done at the layer level and is surprisingly straightforward. Layers can be garbage collected just like any other Java object. If the container makes sure there are no strong references anymore to the layer, or any of its modules and classes, the layer and everything associated eventually get garbage collected.

It's time to look at some code. The container provided as an example in this chapter is a simple command-line launcher that lists applications you can deploy and undeploy. Its main class is shown in Example 6-5. If you deploy an application, it keeps running until it is undeployed (or the container is stopped). We pass information about where the deployable apps live as command-line arguments in the format `out-appa/app.a/app.a.AppA`: first the directory that contains the application modules, then the root module name, and last the name of the class that implements `ContainerApplication`, all separated by slashes.

Usually, application containers have a deployment descriptor format that would convey such information as part of the application package. There are other ways to achieve similar results, for example, by putting annotations on modules (as shown in "Annotations" on page 127) to specify some metadata. For simplicity, we derive `AppDescriptor` instances containing this information from the command-line arguments.

Example 6-5. Launching the application container (➥ chapter6/container)

```
public class Launcher {

  private static AppDescriptor[] apps;
  private static ContainerApplication[] deployedApps;

  public static void main(String... args) {
    System.out.println("Starting container");

    deployedApps = new ContainerApplication[args.length];
    apps = new AppDescriptor[args.length];
    for (int i = 0; i < args.length; i++)
      apps[i] = new AppDescriptor(args[i]);

    // handling keyboard input and calling deploy/undeploy omitted
  }

  // methods for deploy/undeploy discussed later
}
```

The main data structures for the container are an array of application descriptors and an array keeping track of started `ContainerApplication` instances. After the container starts, you can type commands such as `deploy 1` or `undeploy 2` or `exit`. The numbers refer to the index in the `apps` and `deployedApps` arrays. A layer is created for each application that is deployed. In Figure 6-15, we see two applications deployed (after `deploy 1` and `deploy 2`) in their own layers.

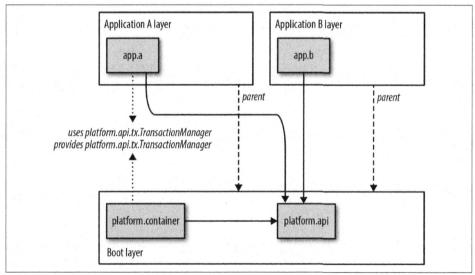

Figure 6-15. Two applications deployed in the container

The image is quite similar to Figure 6-12, save for the fact that the provides and uses relations are inverted. In platform.api, we find the service interfaces to the container functionality, such as platform.api.tx.TransactionManager. The platform.container module contains service providers for these interfaces, and contains the Launcher class we saw earlier. Of course, the container and applications in the real world probably consist of many more modules.

Creating a layer for an application looks similar to what we saw when loading plug-ins, with a small twist:

```
private static ModuleLayer.Controller createAppLayer(AppDescriptor appDescr) {
    ModuleFinder finder = ModuleFinder.of(Paths.get(appDescr.appDir));
    ModuleLayer parent = ModuleLayer.boot();

    Configuration cf = parent.configuration()
        .resolve(finder, ModuleFinder.of(), Set.of(appDescr.rootmodule)); ❶

    ClassLoader scl = ClassLoader.getSystemClassLoader();
    ModuleLayer.Controller layer =
      ModuleLayer.defineModulesWithOneLoader(cf, List.of(parent), scl); ❷

    return layer;
}
```

❶ A ModuleFinder and Configuration are created based on the AppDescriptor metadata.

❷ The layer is created with the static ModuleLayer.defineModulesWithOneLoader method, which returns a ModuleLayer.Controller.

Each application is loaded into its own isolated layer, with a single fresh classloader. Even if applications contain modules with the same packages, they won't conflict. By using the static ModuleLayer::defineModulesWithOneLoader, we get back a ModuleLayer.Controller object.

This controller is used by the calling method to open the package in the root module that contains the class implementing ContainerApplication in the deployed application:

```
private static void deployApp(int appNo) {
    AppDescriptor appDescr = apps[appNo];
    System.out.println("Deploying " + appDescr);

    ModuleLayer.Controller appLayerCtrl = createAppLayer(appDescr); ❶
    Module appModule = appLayerCtrl.layer() ❷
      .findModule(appDescr.rootmodule)
      .orElseThrow(() -> new IllegalStateException("No " + appDescr.rootmodule));

    appLayerCtrl.addOpens(appModule, appDescr.appClassPkg,
```

```
    Launcher.class.getModule()); ❸

    ContainerApplication app = instantiateApp(appModule, appDescr.appClass); ❹
    deployedApps[appNo] = app;
    app.startApp(); ❺
}
```

❶ Calling the previously defined createAppLayer method to obtain the Module Layer.Controller.

❷ From the controller, we can get the actual layer and locate the root module that has been loaded.

❸ Before using reflection to instantiate the application class in the root module, we ensure that the given package is open.

❹ Now, the instantiateApp implementation can use reflection to instantiate the application class without restrictions.

❺ Finally, the deployed application is started by calling startApp.

The most interesting line in the deployApp is where ModuleLayer.Control ler::addOpens is invoked. It opens the package mentioned in the AppDescriptor from the application's root module to the container module, as shown in Figure 6-16.

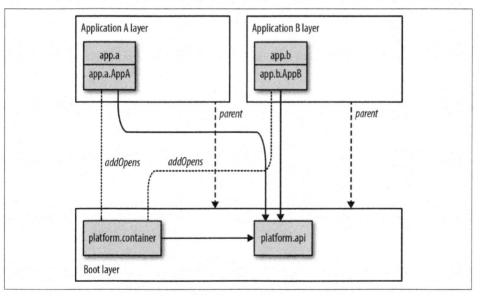

Figure 6-16. At layer creation, the packages app.a and app.b are opened to the platform.container module

This qualified `opens` enables the container to reflect over the packages `app.a` and `app.b`. In addition to `addOpens(Module source, String pkg, Module target)`, you can call `addExports(Module source, String pkg, Module target)` or `add Reads(Module source, Module target)` on a layer controller. With `addExports`, a previously encapsulated package can be exported (without being opened). And, by establishing readability with `addReads`, the target module can access the exported packages of the source module. In all cases, source modules must come from the layer that has been constructed. Layers can, in effect, reshape the dependencies and encapsulation boundaries of modules. As always, with great power comes great responsibility.

Resolving Platform Modules in Containers

Isolation in the container architectures described so far is achieved by resolving a new application or plug-in within its own `ModuleLayer`. Each application or plug-in can require its own libraries, possibly even different versions. As long as `ModuleFinder` can locate the necessary modules for `ModuleLayer`, everything is fine.

But what about dependencies to platform modules from these freshly loaded applications or plug-ins? At first sight, it might seem there is no problem. `ModuleLayer` can resolve modules in parent layers, eventually reaching the boot layer. The boot layer contains platform modules, so all is well. Or is it? That depends on which modules were resolved into the boot layer while starting the *container*.

Normal module resolution rules apply: the root module that is started determines which platform modules are resolved. When the root module is the container launcher, only the dependencies of the container launcher module are taken into account. Only the (transitive) dependencies of this root module end up in the boot layer at run-time.

When a new application or plug-in is loaded after startup, these might require platform modules that were not required by the container itself. In that case, module resolution fails for the new layer. This can be prevented by using `--add-modules ALL-SYSTEM` when starting the container module. All platform modules are in that case resolved, even if the module that is started doesn't depend on them. The boot layer has all possible platform modules because of the `ALL-SYSTEM` option. This ensures that applications or plug-ins loaded at run-time can require arbitrary platform modules.

You have seen how layers enable dynamic architectures. They allow constructing and loading new module graphs at run-time, possibly changing the openness of packages and readability relations to suit the container. Modules in different layers do not interfere, allowing for multiple versions of the same module to coexist in different layers. Services are a natural fit when interacting with newly loaded modules in layers.

However, it's also still possible to take a more traditional, reflection-based approach, as you have seen.

The ModuleLayer API is not expected to be widely used in normal application development. In some ways, the API is similar in nature to classloaders: a powerful feature, mostly wielded by frameworks to make the lives of developers easier. Existing Java module frameworks are expected to use layers as a means of interoperability. It's up to frameworks to put the new ModuleLayer API to good use, just as they did with classloaders over the past 20 years.

PART II

Migration

CHAPTER 7

Migration Without Modules

Backward compatibility has always been a major goal for Java. Usually, migration to a new Java version is mostly trivial from the developer perspective. The module system and the modularized JDK arguably represent the biggest change to the whole Java platform since its inception. Even so, backward compatibility is a top priority.

Migrating an existing application to Java 9 is best approached as a two-step process. This chapter focuses on migrating existing code to build and run on Java 9, without migrating code to modules. The next chapter dives into migrating code to modules, providing strategies to accomplish this.

 Why migrate to Java 9 when you don't anticipate using its flagship feature, the module system? An upgrade to Java 9 also gives access to the other features that are part of Java 9. Think of new APIs, tools, and performance improvements.

Whether you go all the way to modules or leave it at the first step depends. Is the application likely to see lots of extensions and new features? In that case, reaping the benefits of modularity may justify the cost of taking the second step. When an application is in maintenance mode and only has to run on Java 9, it makes sense to only take the first step, as described in this chapter.

For library maintainers, the question isn't *if* Java 9 support is necessary, but *when*. Migrating a library to Java 9 and modules raises different concerns than migrating applications. In Chapter 10, we address those concerns.

But first, what does it take to bring an application to Java 9, without adopting modules for the application yet? It should be clear that an application that has been developed for Java 8 or earlier, while following best practices such that only public JDK

APIs are used, will just work. JDK 9 is still backward compatible, but many internal changes have been made. Migration problems you might run into are often caused by improper use of the JDK, either by the application's code itself, or, more likely, by its libraries.

Libraries can be a source of frustration when it comes to migration. Many frameworks and libraries have made assumptions on (nonpublic, and therefore unsupported) implementation details of the JDK. Technically, the JDK can't be blamed for breaking this code. In reality, things are more nuanced. "Libraries, Strong Encapsulation, and the JDK 9 Classpath" on page 155 explains the compromise that was reached to work toward stronger encapsulation while not breaking existing libraries.

In an ideal world, libraries and frameworks update their implementations to be Java 9 compatible before Java 9 is released. That's not the world we live in, unfortunately. As a user of libraries and frameworks, you should know how to work around potential problems. The remainder of this chapter focuses on strategies to get your applications running on Java 9, even in a nonideal world. Hopefully, with time, this chapter becomes obsolete.

The Classpath Is Dead, Long Live the Classpath

Previous chapters introduced the module path. In many ways, you can view the module path as the successor of the classpath. Does this mean the classpath is gone in Java 9? Or that it's going away, at all? Absolutely not! History will tell whether the classpath is ever removed from Java. Meanwhile, the classpath is still available in Java 9, and works largely the same as in previous releases. The classpath can even be combined with the new module path, as you will see in the next chapter.

When we ignore the module path, and use the classpath to build and run applications, we're simply not using the new module features *in our application*. This requires minimal (if any) changes to existing code. Roughly speaking, when your application and its dependencies use only officially sanctioned APIs from the JDK, it should compile and run without issues on JDK 9.

If changes are necessary, they arise from the fact that the JDK itself has been modularized. Whether or not your application uses modules, the JDK it runs on always consists of modules as of Java 9. Although the module system is mostly ignored from an application perspective in this scenario, the changes to the JDK structure are still there. In many cases, the modular JDK doesn't pose any problems for classpath-based applications, but there are definitely some caveats. Those caveats are in most cases related to libraries. The remainder of the chapter covers the possible problems, and more important, their workarounds.

Libraries, Strong Encapsulation, and the JDK 9 Classpath

One of the problems you can run into when migrating a classpath-based application to Java 9 is caused by the strong encapsulation of code in platform modules. Many libraries use classes from the platform that are now encapsulated with Java 9. Or, they use deep reflection to pry their way into nonpublic parts of platform classes.

Deep reflection is using the reflection API to get access to nonpublic elements of a class. In "Deep Reflection" on page 116, you learned that exporting a package from a module does not make its nonpublic elements accessible for reflection. Unfortunately, many libraries call setAccessible on private elements found through reflection.

You have seen that when using modules, JDK 9 by default disallows access to encapsulated packages and deep reflection on code in other modules, which includes platform modules. There is a good reason for this: abuse of platform internals has been the source of many security issues, and allowing it hampers evolution of APIs. However, in this chapter, we're still dealing with classpath-based applications on top of a modular JDK. On the classpath, strong encapsulation of platform internals is not enforced as strictly, although it still plays a role.

Using deep reflection on JDK types is an obscure use case. Why would you want to make private parts of JDK classes accessible? It turns out some commonly used libraries do this. An example of this is the javassist runtime code-generation library, which is used by many other frameworks.

To ease migration of classpath-based applications to Java 9, the JVM by default shows a warning when deep reflection is applied on classes in platform modules. Or, when reflection is used to access types in nonexported packages. For example, when running code that uses the javassist library, we see the following warning:

```
WARNING: An illegal reflective access operation has occurred
WARNING: Illegal reflective access by javassist.util.proxy.SecurityActions
  (...javassist-3.20.0-GA.jar) to method
  java.lang.ClassLoader.defineClass(...)
WARNING: Please consider reporting this to the maintainers of
  javassist.util.proxy.SecurityActions
WARNING: Use --illegal-access=warn to enable warnings of further illegal
  reflective access operations
WARNING: All illegal access operations will be denied in a future release
```

Let that sink in for a bit. Code that ran without any issues on JDK 8 and earlier now prints a prominent warning to the console—even in production. It shows how seriously the breach of strong encapsulation is taken.

Besides this warning, the application will still run as usual. As indicated by the warning message, the behavior will change in a next version of Java. In the future, the JDK will enforce strong encapsulation of platform modules even for code on the classpath. The same application will not run on default settings in a future Java release. Therefore, it is important to investigate the warnings and to fix the underlying problems. When the warnings are caused by libraries, that usually means reporting the issue to the maintainers.

By default, only a single warning is generated on the first illegal access attempt. Following attempts will not generate extra errors or warnings. If we want to further investigate the cause of the problem, we can use different settings for the `--illegal-access` command-line flag to tweak the behavior:

`--illegal-access=permit`
> The default behavior. Illegal access to encapsulated types is allowed. Generates a warning on the first illegal access attempt through reflection.

`--illegal-access=warn`
> Like `permit`, but generates an error on *every* illegal access attempt.

`--illegal-access=debug`
> Also shows stack traces for illegal access attempts.

`--illegal-access=deny`
> Does not allow illegal access attempts. This will be the default in the future.

Notice that none of the settings allow you to suppress the printed warnings. This is by design. In this chapter, you'll learn how to address the underlying issues, in order to resolve the illegal access warnings. Because `--illegal-access=deny` will be the future default, your goal is to run your application with this setting.

If we run code that uses `javassist` with `--illegal-access=deny`, the application fails to run and we see the following error:

```
java.lang.reflect.InaccessibleObjectException: Unable to make protected final
    java.lang.Class java.lang.ClassLoader.defineClass(java.lang.String,byte[],
                                int,int,java.security.ProtectionDomain)
    throws java.lang.ClassFormatError accessible: module java.base does not
    "opens java.lang" to unnamed module @0x7b3300e5
```

This error explains that `javassist` tries to make the `defineClass` method on `java.lang.Class` public. We can use the `--add-opens` flag to grant the classpath deep reflection access to a specific package in a module. Open modules and open packages are discussed in detail in "Deep Reflection" on page 116. As a refresher, a package needs to be *open* to allow deep reflection. This is even true when the package is exported as is the case here with `java.lang`. A package is usually opened in a module descriptor, similar to the way packages are exported. We can do the same from the command line for modules that we don't control (for example, platform modules):

```
java --add-opens java.base/java.lang=ALL-UNNAMED
```

In this example, `java.base/java.lang` is the module/package we grant access to. The last argument is the module that gets the access. Because the code is still on the classpath, we use `ALL-UNNAMED`, which represents the classpath. The package is now open, so the deep reflection is no longer illegal. This will remove the warning (or error, when running with `--illegal-access=deny`). Similarly, when code on the classpath tries to access a type in a nonexported package, you can use `--add-exports` to force the package to be exported. We'll see an example of this scenario in the next section. Remember that this is still just a workaround. Ask the maintainers of a library that causes illegal access problems for an updated version of the library with a proper fix.

Illegal access is allowed by the default setting `--illegal-access=permit` only on packages that already existed before JDK 9, but are now encapsulated. Any new encapsulated packages in JDK 9 are not exempt from strong encapsulation, even when code is on the classpath.

Security Impact

How does the existence of `--add-opens` and `--add-exports` impact security? One of the reasons to not allow deep reflection by default for platform modules in a future Java version is to prevent malicious code from reaching dangerous JDK internals. Doesn't a flag to simply disable these checks void this important security benefit? One the one hand, yes, it selectively opens up a bigger attack surface when you choose to do so.

But consider this: there's no way to gain the privileges afforded by `--add-opens` or `--add-exports` at run-time by merely executing Java code. An attacker needs to have access to the startup scripts (the command line) of an application to add these flags. When that level of access is established, the breach already allows the attacker to make arbitrary modifications reaching much further than just adding JVM options.

Compilation and Encapsulated APIs

The JDK contains many private, internal APIs. They are not supposed to be used by anyone other than the JDK itself. This has been clearly documented since the early beginnings. Examples are the `sun.*` and `jdk.internal.*` packages. As an application developer, you likely are not using these types directly. Most of these internal classes serve obscure corner cases, which typical applications don't need. For this book, we even found it difficult to come up with a good example from the application development perspective.

Of course, some applications and (especially older) libraries *do* still use those internal classes. JDK internals were not strongly encapsulated previously, because there was no mechanism to do so. Pre-Java 9 compilers do emit warnings when using internal classes, but those are easily overlooked or ignored. We have seen that for the time being, code compiled with older versions of Java that uses encapsulated JDK types will still run on Java 9, because of the `--illegal-access=permit` default setting.

The same code will not compile on Java 9, however! Let's say we have code (see Example 7-1) compiled with the JDK 8 compiler that uses types from the `sun.security.x509` package.

Example 7-1. EncapsulatedTypes.java (➡ chapter7/encapsulation)

```
package encapsulated;

import sun.security.x509.X500Name;

public class EncapsulatedTypes {
    public static void main(String... args) throws Exception {
        System.out.println(new X500Name("test.com", "test",
                    "test", "US"));

    }
}
```

Compiling this code with JDK 9 results in the following compiler error:

```
./src/encapsulated/EncapsulatedTypes.java:3: error: package sun.security.x509
is not visible
import sun.security.x509.X500Name;
                  ^
    (package sun.security.x509 is declared in module java.base, which does not
      export it to the unnamed module)
```

By default, this code will still run successfully on Java 9, although the code is using an encapsulated package. You might wonder why there's a difference between javac and java when it comes to accessing encapsulated types. What's the point of being able to run code that accesses encapsulated types when you can't compile the same code?

The reason that such code is still able run is to provide backward compatibility for existing libraries. The reason compiling with those same encapsulated types is prohibited is to prevent future compatibility nightmares. For code that you control, you should take immediate action when it comes to encapsulated types and replace them with nonencapsulated alternatives. When using a library (compiled with an older Java version) that's using encapsulated types or deep reflection on JDK internals, you're in a more difficult spot. You can't fix the problem yourself, which would block you in your attempt to move to Java 9. Because of the lenient runtime, the library can still be used for the time being.

Allowing the usage of encapsulated JDK types at run-time is only a temporary situation. In a future Java release, this will be disabled. We can already prepare for this today by setting the `--illegal-access=deny` flag that we have seen in the previous section. Running the same code with java `--illegal-access=deny` generates an error:

```
Exception in thread "main" java.lang.IllegalAccessError:
class encapsulated.EncapsulatedTypes (in unnamed module @0x2e5c649) cannot
access class sun.security.x509.X500Name (in module java.base) because module
java.base does not export sun.security.x509 to unnamed module @0x2e5c649
        at encapsulated.EncapsulatedTypes.main(EncapsulatedTypes.java:7)
```

 Notice that no warnings are shown for this scenario if we configure `--illegal-access` with anything other than deny. Only reflective illegal access triggers the warnings we have seen, not static references to encapsulated types as in this case. This restriction is a pragmatic one: changing the VM to also generate warnings for static references to encapsulated types would be too invasive.

The right course of action is to report the issue to the maintainers of the library. But what if this is our own code, and we need to recompile with JDK 9 but can't make code changes right away? Changing code is always risky, so we have to find the right moment to do so.

We can use command-line flags to break encapsulation at compile-time as well. In the previous section, you saw how to use `--add-opens` to open a package from the command line. Both java and javac also support `--add-exports`. As the name suggests, we can use this to export an otherwise encapsulated package from a module. The syntax is `--add-exports <module>/<package>=<targetmodule>`. Because our code is still running on the classpath, we can use `ALL-UNNAMED` as the target module. Note that exporting an encapsulated package still does not allow deep reflection on its types. The package needs to be open for that. In this case, exporting the package is sufficient. In Example 7-1, we're referencing the encapsulated type directly, without any reflection involved. For our (admittedly contrived) `sun.security.x509.X500Name` example, we can compile and run with the following commands:

```
javac --add-exports java.base/sun.security.x509=ALL-UNNAMED \
    encapsulated/EncapsulatedTypes.java
```

```
java --add-exports java.base/sun.security.x509=ALL-UNNAMED \
    encapsulated.EncapsulatedTypes
```

The `--add-exports` and `--add-opens` flags can be used for any module and package, not only for JDK internals. During compilation, warnings are still emitted for the use of internal APIs. Ideally, the `--add-exports` flag is a temporary migration step. Use it until you adapt your code to the public APIs, or (if a library is in violation) until there is new release of the third-party library using the replacement API.

Too Many Command-Line Flags!

Some operating systems limit the length of the command line that can be executed. When you need to add many flags during migration, you can hit these limits. You can use a file to provide all the command-line arguments to java/javac instead:

```
$ java @arguments.txt
```

The argument files must contain all necessary command-line flags. Each line in the file contains a single option. For instance, *arguments.txt* could contain the following:

```
-cp application.jar:javassist.jar
--add-opens java.base/java.lang=ALL-UNNAMED
--add-exports java.base/sun.security.x509=ALL-UNNAMED
-jar application.jar
```

Even if you're not running into command-line limits, argument files can be clearer than a very long line somewhere in a script.

Removed Types

Code also could use internal types, which are now removed entirely. This is not directly related to the module system, but is still worth mentioning. One of the removed internal classes in Java 9 is sun.misc.BASE64Encoder, which was popular before Java 8 introduced the java.util.Base64 class. Example 7-2 shows code using BASE64Decoder.

Example 7-2. RemovedTypes.java (➡ chapter7/removedtypes)

```
package removed;

import sun.misc.BASE64Decoder;

// Compile with Java 8, run on Java 9: NoClassDefFoundError.
public class RemovedTypes {
    public static void main(String... args) throws Exception {
        new BASE64Decoder();
    }
}
```

This code will no longer compile or run on Java 9. When we try to compile, we see the following error:

```
removed/RemovedTypes.java:3: error: cannot find symbol
import sun.misc.BASE64Decoder;
               ^
  symbol:   class BASE64Decoder
  location: package sun.misc
removed/RemovedTypes.java:8: error: cannot find symbol
        new BASE64Decoder();
            ^
  symbol:   class BASE64Decoder
  location: class RemovedTypes
2 errors
```

If we compile the code with an older Java version, but try to run it with Java 9, it also fails:

```
Exception in thread "main" java.lang.NoClassDefFoundError: sun/misc/BASE64Decoder
    at removed.RemovedTypes.main(RemovedTypes.java:8)
Caused by: java.lang.ClassNotFoundException: sun.misc.BASE64Decoder
    ...
```

For an encapsulated type, we can work around the problem by forcing access to it with command-line flags. We can't do this for this BASE64Decoder example, because the class doesn't exist anymore. It's important to understand this difference.

Using jdeps to Find Removed or Encapsulated Types and Their Alternatives

jdeps is a tool shipped with the JDK. One of the things jdeps can do is find usages of removed or encapsulated JDK types, and suggest replacements. jdeps always works on class files, not on source code. If we compile Example 7-2 with Java 8, we can run jdeps on the resulting class:

```
jdeps -jdkinternals removed/RemovedTypes.class

RemovedTypes.class -> JDK removed internal API
    removed.RemovedTypes -> sun.misc.BASE64Decoder
    JDK internal API (JDK removed internal API)

Warning: JDK internal APIs are unsupported and private to JDK implementation
that are subject to be removed or changed incompatibly and could
break your application.
Please modify your code to eliminate dependence on any JDK internal APIs.
For the most recent update on JDK internal API replacements, please check:
https://wiki.openjdk.java.net/display/JDK8/Java+Dependency+Analysis+Tool

JDK Internal API                        Suggested Replacement
----------------                        ----------------------
sun.misc.BASE64Decoder                  Use java.util.Base64 @since 1.8
```

Similarly, encapsulated types such as X500Name in Example 7-1 are reported by jdeps with suggested replacements. More details on how to work with jdeps are discussed in "Using jdeps" on page 184.

Since Java 8, the JDK includes `java.util.Base64`, which is a much better alternative to use. The solution in this case is simple: we must migrate to the public API in order to run on JDK 9. In general, moving to Java 9 will expose a lot of technical debt in the areas discussed in this chapter.

technicalDebts.xls

Using JAXB and Other Java EE APIs

Certain Java EE technologies, such as JAXB, shipped with the JDK alongside Java SE APIs in the past. These technologies are still present in Java 9, but require special attention. They are shipped in the following list of modules:

- `java.activation`
- `java.corba`
- `java.transaction`
- `java.xml.bind`
- `java.xml.ws`
- `java.xml.ws.annotation`

In Java 9, these modules are *deprecated for removal*. The `@Deprecated` annotation has a new argument `forRemoval` in Java 9. When set to `true`, this means the API element will be removed in a future release. For API elements that are part of the JDK, this means removal may happen in a next *major* release. More details about deprecation can be found in JEP 277 (*http://openjdk.java.net/jeps/277*).

There is good reason for removing Java EE technologies from the JDK. The overlap between Java SE and Java EE in the JDK has always been confusing. Java EE application servers usually provide custom implementations of the APIs. Slightly simplified, this is done by putting the alternative implementation on the classpath, overriding the default JDK version. In Java 9, this becomes a problem. The module system does not allow the same package to be provided by multiple modules. If a duplicate package is found on the classpath (hence in the unnamed module), it is ignored. In any case, a situation where both Java SE and an application server provide `java.xml.bind` would not result in the expected behavior.

This is a serious practical problem, which would break many existing application servers and related tools. To avoid this problem, these modules are not resolved by default in classpath-based scenarios. Let's take a look at the module graph of the platform in Figure 7-1.

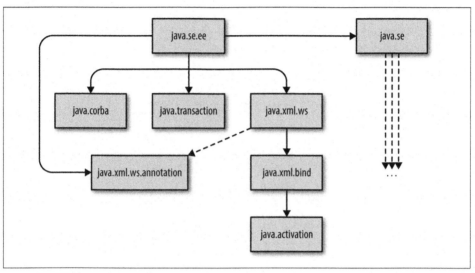

Figure 7-1. Subset of the JDK module graph showing modules reachable only through java.se.ee, not java.se

At the very top are the `java.se` and `java.se.ee` modules. Both are aggregator modules, modules that don't contain code but group a set of more fine-grained modules. Aggregator modules are discussed in detail in "Aggregator Modules" on page 90. Most platform modules reside under `java.se` and are not shown here (but you can see the whole graph in Figure 2-1). The `java.se.ee` module aggregates the modules we are discussing, which are not part of the `java.se` aggregator module. This includes the `java.xml.bind` module, containing JAXB types.

By default, both javac and java use `java.se` as the root when compiling and running classes in the unnamed module. Code can access any package exported by the transitive dependencies of `java.se`. Modules under `java.se.ee` but not under `java.se` are therefore not resolved, so they are not read by the unnamed module. Even though package `javax.xml.bind` is exported from module `java.xml.bind`, it doesn't matter because it is not resolved during compilation and run-time.

If modules under java.se.ee are necessary, we need to add them explicitly to the set of resolved platform modules. We can do so by adding them as root modules with the --add-modules flag of both javac and java.

Let's try this with Example 7-3, based on JAXB. This example serializes a Book to XML.

Example 7-3. JaxbExample.java (➥ chapter7/jaxb)

```
package example;

import javax.xml.bind.JAXBContext;
import javax.xml.bind.JAXBException;
import javax.xml.bind.Marshaller;

public class JaxbExample {
    public static void main(String... args) throws Exception {
      Book book = new Book();
      book.setTitle("Java 9 Modularity");

      JAXBContext jaxbContext = JAXBContext.newInstance(Book.class);
      Marshaller jaxbMarshaller = jaxbContext.createMarshaller();

      jaxbMarshaller.setProperty(Marshaller.JAXB_FORMATTED_OUTPUT, true);

      jaxbMarshaller.marshal(book, System.out);
    }
}
```

On Java 8, this example compiles and runs without problems. On Java 9, we get several errors at compile-time:

```
example/JaxbExample.java:3: error: package javax.xml.bind is not visible
import javax.xml.bind.JAXBContext;
                ^
  (package javax.xml.bind is declared in module java.xml.bind, which is not
    in the module graph)
example/JaxbExample.java:4: error: package javax.xml.bind is not visible
import javax.xml.bind.JAXBException;
                ^
  (package javax.xml.bind is declared in module java.xml.bind, which is not
    in the module graph)
example/JaxbExample.java:5: error: package javax.xml.bind is not visible
import javax.xml.bind.Marshaller;
                ^
  (package javax.xml.bind is declared in module java.xml.bind, which is not
    in the module graph)
3 errors
```

When you compile with Java 8 and run the code with Java 9, an exception reporting the same problem is generated at run-time. We already know how to fix this issue: add --add-modules java.xml.bind to both the javac and java invocation.

 Instead of adding the platform module that contains JAXB, you can add a JAR that provides JAXB to the classpath. Several popular (open source) libraries provide JAXB implementations. Since the Java EE modules in the JDK are marked for removal, this is a more future-proof solution.

Note that we wouldn't encounter this problem with the module path. If our code lives in a module, it must explicitly define a requirement on any modules other than java.base. That includes a dependency on java.xml.bind for the example code. Based on this, the module system resolves these modules without the need for a command-line flag.

Summing up, beware when using Java EE code from the JDK. When you're getting errors that the packages are not visible, add the relevant modules by using --add-modules. Be aware that they will be removed in a next major Java release, however. Adding your own versions of these technologies to the classpath instead avoids future problems.

The jdk.unsupported Module

Some internal classes from the JDK have proven to be harder to encapsulate. Chances are that you have never used sun.misc.Unsafe and the like. These have always been unsupported classes, meant to be used only in the JDK internally.

Some of these classes are widely used by libraries for performance reasons. Although it's easy to argue that this should never be done, in some cases it's the only option. A well-known example is the sun.misc.Unsafe class, which can perform low-level operations bypassing Java's memory model and other safety nets. The same functionality cannot be implemented by libraries outside the JDK.

If such classes would simply be encapsulated, libraries depending on them would no longer work with JDK 9, at least, not without warnings. Theoretically, this is not a backward-compatibility issue. Those libraries abuse nonsupported implementation classes, after all. For some of these highly used internal APIs, the real-world implications would be too severe to ignore, however—especially because there are no supported alternatives to the functionality they provide.

With that in mind, a compromise was reached. The JDK team researched which JDK platform internals are used by libraries the most, and which of those can be implemented only inside the JDK. Those classes are *not* encapsulated in Java 9.

Here's the resulting list of specific classes and methods that are kept accessible:

- `sun.misc.{Signal,SignalHandler}`
- `sun.misc.Unsafe`
- `sun.reflect.Reflection::getCallerClass(int)`
- `sun.reflect.ReflectionFactory::newConstructorForSerialization`

Remember, if these names don't mean anything to you, *that's a good thing*. Popular libraries such as Netty, Mockito, and Akka use these classes, though. Not breaking these libraries is a good thing as well.

Because these methods and classes were not primarily designed to be used outside the JDK, they are moved to a platform module called `jdk.unsupported`. This indicates that it is expected the classes in this module will be replaced by other APIs in a future Java version. The `jdk.unsupported` module exports and/or opens the internal packages containing the classes discussed. Many existing uses involve deep reflection. Using these classes through reflection *does not lead to warnings at run-time*, unlike the scenarios discussed in "Libraries, Strong Encapsulation, and the JDK 9 Classpath" on page 155. That's because `jdk.unsupported` opens the necessary packages in its module descriptor, so there is no illegal access from that point of view.

 Although these types can be used without breaking encapsulation, they are still unsupported; their use is still discouraged. The plan is to provide supported alternatives in the future. For example, some of the functionality in Unsafe is superseded by *variable handles* as proposed in JEP 193 (*http://openjdk.java.net/jeps/193*). Until then, the status quo is maintained.

When code still lives on the classpath, nothing changes. Libraries can use these classes from the classpath as before, running without any warnings or errors. The compiler generates warnings when compiling against classes from `jdk.unsupported`, rather than errors as with encapsulated types:

```
warning: Unsafe is internal proprietary API and may be
         removed in a future release
```

If you want to use these types from a module, you must require `jdk.unsupported`. Having such a `requires` statement in your module descriptor serves as a warning sign. In a future Java release, changes may be necessary to adapt to publicly supported APIs instead of the unsupported APIs.

Other Changes

Many other changes in JDK 9 can potentially break code. These changes affect, for example, tool authors, and applications that use the JDK extension mechanisms. Some of the changes include the following:

JDK layout

> Because of the platform modularization, the big *rt.jar* containing all platform classes doesn't exist anymore. The layout of the JDK itself has changed considerably as well, as is documented in JEP 220 (*http://openjdk.java.net/jeps/220*). Tools or code relying on the JDK layout must adapt to this new reality.

Version string

> Gone are the days that all Java platform versions start with the 1.x prefix. Java 9 is shipped with version 9.0.0. The syntax and semantics of the version string have changed considerably. If an application does any kind of parsing on the Java version, read JEP 223 (*http://openjdk.java.net/jeps/223*) for all the details.

Extension mechanisms

> Features such as the *Endorsed Standard Override Mechanism* and the extension mechanism through the `java.ext.dirs` property are removed. They are replaced by *upgradeable modules*. More information can be found in JEP 220 (*http://openjdk.java.net/jeps/220*).

These are all highly specialized features of the JDK. If your application does rely on them, it will not work with JDK 9. Because these changes are not really related to the Java module system, we won't go into further detail. The linked JDK Enhancement Proposals (JEPs) contain guidance on how to proceed in these cases.

Congratulations! You now know how to run your existing application on JDK 9. Even though several things *could* go wrong, in many cases things will just work. Remember to run your application with `--illegal-access=deny` as well, to be prepared for the future. After fixing all issues when running existing applications from the classpath, it's time to look at how to make them more modular.

CHAPTER 8

Migration to Modules

With all the module goodness from the previous chapters, you are hopefully excited to start using the Java module system. Writing new code based on modules is pretty straightforward now that you understand the basic concepts.

Back in the real world, there's also a lot of existing code that we may want to migrate to modules. The previous chapter showed how to migrate existing code to Java 9, without transforming the codebase to modules. This is the first step in any migration scenario. With that taken care of, we can focus on migrating toward the Java module system in this chapter.

 We're not suggesting that every existing application should be migrated to use the Java module system. If an application is not actively developed anymore, it might not be worth the work. Similarly, small applications may not really benefit from structuring in modules. Migrate to improve maintainability, changeability, and reusability when it makes sense—not just for the sake of it.

The amount of work required for a migration largely depends on how well-structured a codebase is. But even for a well-structured codebase, migration to a modular runtime can be a challenging task. Most applications use third-party libraries, which are an important factor when migrating. These libraries aren't necessarily modularized yet, nor do you want to take on that responsibility.

Luckily, the Java module system is designed with backward compatibility and migration as a primary concern. Several constructs were introduced in the Java module system to make gradual migration of existing code possible. In this chapter, you will learn about these constructs to migrate your own code to modules. Migration from the perspective of a library maintainer is, of course, related but requires a slightly different process. Chapter 10 focuses on that perspective.

Migration Strategies

A typical application has application code (your code) and library code. The application code uses code from third-party libraries. Ideally, all the libraries used are already modules, and we can focus on modularizing our own code. For the first years after the release of Java 9, this is probably not a realistic scenario. Some libraries may not be available as modules yet, and perhaps never will be, because they are no longer maintained.

If we were to wait until the whole ecosystem moved toward modules, we might have to wait very long. Also, this would require updating to new versions of those libraries, potentially causing its own set of issues. We could also manually patch the libraries, adding a module descriptor and transforming them to a module. This is clearly a lot of work, and requires forking the library, which makes future updates more painful. It would be much better if we can focus on migrating our own code, while leaving libraries the way they are for the moment.

A Simple Example

You will look at several migration examples in this chapter to understand the various cases you can run into in practice. To start, we take a simple application that uses the Jackson library to convert a Java object to JSON. For this application, we need three JAR files from the Jackson project:

- `com.fasterxml.jackson.core`
- `com.fasterxml.jackson.databind`
- `com.fasterxml.jackson.annotations`

The Jackson JAR files in the version used for this example (2.8.8) are not modules yet. They are plain JAR files without module descriptors.

The application consists of two classes, with the main class listed in Example 8-1. Not listed here is the `Book` class, a simple class with getters and setters representing a book. The `Main` class contains a main method using `ObjectMapper` from `com.fasterxml.jackson.databind` to convert a `Book` instance to JSON.

Example 8-1. Main.java (➡ chapter8/jackson-classpath)

```
package demo;

import com.fasterxml.jackson.databind.ObjectMapper;

public class Main {

  public static void main(String... args) throws Exception {
    Book modularityBook =
      new Book("Java 9 Modularity", "Modularize all the things!");

    ObjectMapper mapper = new ObjectMapper();
    String json = mapper.writeValueAsString(modularityBook);
    System.out.println(json);

  }
}
```

The `com.fasterxml.jackson.databind.ObjectMapper` class in the example is part of *jackson-databind-2.8.8.jar*. This JAR file has a dependency on both *jackson-core-2.8.8.jar* and *jackson-annotations-2.8.8.jar*. However, this dependency information is implicit because the JAR files are not modules. The example project has the following file structure to start with:

```
├── lib
│   ├── jackson-annotations-2.8.8.jar
│   ├── jackson-core-2.8.8.jar
│   └── jackson-databind-2.8.8.jar
└── src
    └── demo
        ├── Book.java
        └── Main.java
```

As you saw in the previous chapter, the classpath is still available in Java 9. Let's start with building and running on the classpath, before we start migration to modules. We can build and run the application with the commands in Example 8-2.

Example 8-2. run.sh (➡ chapter8/jackson-classpath)

```
CP=lib/jackson-annotations-2.8.8.jar:
CP+=lib/jackson-core-2.8.8.jar:
CP+=lib/jackson-databind-2.8.8.jar

javac -cp $CP -d out -sourcepath src $(find src -name '*.java')

java -cp $CP:out demo.Main
```

This application compiles and runs with Java 9 without any changes.

The Jackson libraries are not directly under our control, but the `Main` and `Book` code is, so that's what we focus on for migration. This is a common migration scenario. We want to move our own code toward modules, without worrying about libraries. The Java module system has some tricks up its sleeve to make gradual migration possible.

Mixing Classpath and Module Path

To make gradual migration possible, we can mix the usage of classpath and module path. This is not an ideal situation, since we only partially benefit from the advantages of the Java module system. However, it is extremely helpful for migrating in small steps.

Because the Jackson libraries are not our own source code, ideally we would not change them at all. Instead we start the migration top-down, by migrating our own code first. Let's put this code in a module named books. You will see in a moment that this isn't sufficient, but let's start by creating a simple *module-info.java* for our module:

```
module books {

}
```

Note that the module doesn't have any `requires` statements yet. This is suspicious because we clearly do have a dependency on classes from the *jackson-databind-2.8.8.jar* JAR file. Because we now have a real module, we can compile our code by using the `--module-source-path` flag. The Jackson libraries are not modules, so they stay on the classpath for now:

```
CP=lib/jackson-annotations-2.8.8.jar:
CP+=lib/jackson-core-2.8.8.jar:
CP+=lib/jackson-databind-2.8.8.jar

javac -cp $CP -d out --module-source-path src -m books

src/books/demo/Main.java:3: error:
package com.fasterxml.jackson.databind does not exist

import com.fasterxml.jackson.databind.ObjectMapper;
                                     ^
src/books/demo/Main.java:11: error: cannot find symbol
    ObjectMapper mapper = new ObjectMapper();
    ^
  symbol:   class ObjectMapper
  location: class Main
src/books/demo/Main.java:11: error: cannot find symbol
    ObjectMapper mapper = new ObjectMapper();
                              ^
  symbol:   class ObjectMapper
```

```
    location: class Main
  3 errors
```

The compiler is clearly not happy! Although *jackson-databind-2.8.8.jar* is still on the classpath, the compiler tells us that it is not usable in our module. Modules cannot *read* the classpath, so our module can't access types on the classpath, as illustrated in Figure 8-1.

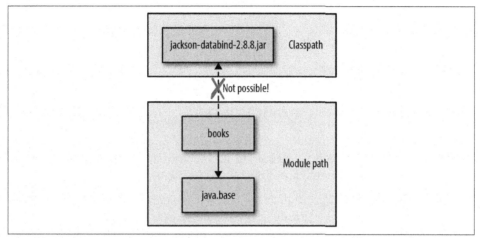

Figure 8-1. Modules don't read the classpath

Not being able to read from the classpath is a good thing, even when it requires some work during migration, because we want to be explicit about our dependencies. When modules can read the classpath, besides their explicit dependencies, all bets are off.

Even so, our application is not compiling now, so let's try to fix that first. If we can't rely on the classpath, the only way forward is to make the code that our module relies on available as a module as well. This requires us to turn *jackson-databind-2.8.8.jar* into a module.

Automatic Modules

The source code of the Jackson libraries is open source, so we could patch the code to turn it into a module ourselves. In a large application that uses a long list of (transitive) dependencies, patching all of them isn't appealing. Moreover, we probably don't have enough knowledge of the libraries to properly modularize them.

The Java module system has a useful feature to deal with code that isn't a module yet: *automatic modules*. An automatic module can be created by moving an existing JAR file from the classpath to the module path, without changing its contents. This turns the JAR into a module, with a module descriptor generated on the fly by the module system. In contrast, *explicit modules* always have a user-defined module descriptor. All modules we've seen so far, including platform modules, are explicit modules. Automatic modules behave differently than explicit modules. An automatic module has the following characteristics:

- It does not contain *module-info.class*.
- It has a module name specified in *META-INF/MANIFEST.MF* or derived from its filename.
- It `requires transitive` all other resolved modules.
- It exports all its packages.
- It reads the classpath (or more precisely, the *unnamed module* as discussed later).
- It cannot have split packages with other modules.

This makes the automatic module immediately usable for other modules. Mind you, it's not a well-designed module. Requiring all modules and exporting all packages doesn't sound like proper modularization, but at least it's usable.

What does it mean to *require all other resolved modules*? An automatic module requires every module in the already resolved module graph. Remember, there still is no explicit information in an automatic module telling the module system which other modules it really needs. This means the JVM can't warn at startup when dependencies of automatic modules are missing. We, as developers, are responsible for making sure the module path (or classpath) contains all required dependencies. This is not very different from working with the classpath.

All modules in the module graph are `required transitive` by automatic modules. This effectively means that if you require one automatic module, you get implied readability to all other modules "for free." This is a trade-off, which we will discuss in more detail soon.

Let's take the *jackson-databind-2.8.8.jar* JAR file and turn it into an automatic module, by moving it to the module path. First we move the JAR file to a new directory that we name *mods* in this example:

```
├── lib
│   ├── jackson-annotations-2.8.8.jar
│   └── jackson-core-2.8.8.jar
├── mods
│   └── jackson-databind-2.8.8.jar
└── src
    └── books
        ├── demo
        │   ├── Book.java
        │   └── Main.java
        └── module-info.java
```

Next we have to modify the *module-info.java* in our books module to require jackson.databind:

```
module books {
    requires jackson.databind;
}
```

The books module requires jackson.databind as if it were a normal module. But where did the module name come from? The name of an automatic module can be specified in the newly introduced Automatic-Module-Name field of a *META-INF/ MANIFEST.MF* file. This provides a way for library maintainers to choose a module name even before they fully migrate the library to be a module. See "Choosing a Library Module Name" on page 209 for more details about naming modules this way.

If no name is specified, the module name is derived from the JAR's filename. The naming algorithm is roughly the following:

- Dashes (-) are replaced by dots (.).
- Version numbers are omitted.

In the Jackson example, the module name is based on the filename.

We can now successfully compile the program by using the following command:

```
CP=lib/jackson-annotations-2.8.8.jar:
CP+=lib/jackson-core-2.8.8.jar

javac -cp $CP --module-path mods -d out --module-source-path src -m books
```

The *jackson-databind-2.8.8.jar* JAR file is removed from the classpath, and a module path is now configured, pointing to the *mods* directory. Figure 8-2 provides an overview of where all the code lives.

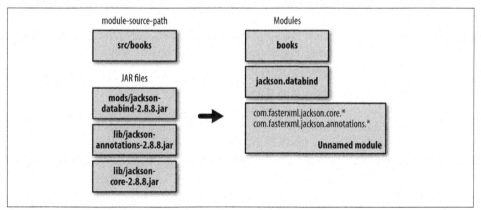

Figure 8-2. Nonmodular JARs on the module path become automatic modules. The classpath becomes the unnamed module.

To run the program, we also have to update the java invocation:

```
java -cp $CP --module-path mods:out -m books/demo.Main
```

We made the following change to the java command:

- Move the *out* directory to the module path.
- Move *jackson-databind-2.8.8.jar* from the classpath (*lib*) to the module path (*mods*).
- Start the application by using the `-m` flag to specify our module.

 Instead of moving just *jackson-databind* to the module path, we could have moved all the JARs to the module path. This makes the process a little easier, but makes it harder to see what happens. Feel free to move all JARs to the module path when migrating your own applications.

We're close to our first migrated application, but unfortunately we still get an exception when starting the application:

```
Exception in thread "main" java.lang.reflect.InaccessibleObjectException:
    Unable to make public java.lang.String demo.Book.getTitle() accessible:
    module books does not "exports demo" to module jackson.databind
    ...
```

This is a problem specific to Jackson Databind, but not an uncommon scenario. We use Jackson Databind to marshal the `Book` class, which is part of the `books` module. Jackson Databind uses reflection to look at the fields of a class to be able to serialize it. Therefore, Jackson Databind needs to access the `Book` class; otherwise, it can't use reflection to look at its fields. For this to be possible, the package containing the class must be *exported* or *opened* by its containing module (`books`, in this example). Exporting the package restricts Jackson Databind to reflect only over public elements, whereas opening the package allows for deep reflection as well. In our example, reflecting over public elements is enough.

This puts us in a difficult position. We don't necessarily want to export the package containing `Book` to other modules, just because Jackson needs it. If we did, we would give up on encapsulation, and that was one of the primary reasons to move to modules! There are multiple ways to work around this problem, each with its own trade-offs. The first way is to use a *qualified export*. Using a qualified export, we can export the package to *just* `jackson.databind`, so we don't lose encapsulation with respect to other modules:

```
module books {
  requires jackson.databind;
```

```
    exports demo to jackson.databind;
}
```

After recompiling, we can now successfully run the application! We have another option besides exporting that may better fit our needs when it comes to reflection, and we will explore this in the next section.

Warnings When Using Automatic Modules

Although automatic modules are essential to migration, they should be used with some caution. Whenever you write a `requires` on an automatic module, make a mental note to come back to this later. If the library is released as an explicit module, you want to use that instead.

Two warnings were added to the compiler to help with this as well. Note that it is only a recommendation that Java compilers support these warnings, so different compiler implementations may have different results. The first warning is opt out (enabled by default), and will give a warning for every `requires transitive` on an automatic module. The warning can be disabled with the `-Xlint:-requires-transitive-automatic` flag. Notice the dash (`-`) after the colon. The second warning is opt in (disabled by default), and will give a warning for every `requires` on an automatic module. This warning can be enabled with the `-Xlint:requires-automatic` (no dash after the colon) flag. The reason that the first warning is enabled by default is that it is a more dangerous scenario. You expose a (possibly volatile) automatic module to consumers of your module through implied readability.

Replace automatic modules with explicit modules when available, and ask the library maintainer for one if not available yet. Also remember that such a module may have a more restricted API, because the default of having all packages exported is likely not what the library maintainer intended. This can lead to extra work when switching from an automatic module to an explicit module, where the library maintainer has created a module descriptor.

Open Packages

Using `exports` in the context of reflection has some caveats. First of all, it's arguably strange that we need to give compile-time readability to a package, while we only expect run-time (reflection) usage. Frameworks often use reflection to work on application code, but they don't need compile-time readability. Also, we might not always know which module requires readability up front, so a qualified export isn't possible.

Using the Java Persistence API (JPA) is an example of such a scenario. When using JPA, you typically program to the standardized API. At run-time, you would use an implementation of this API such as Hibernate or EclipseLink. The API and the implementation live in separate modules. In the end, the implementation needs accessibility to your classes. If we put an `exports com.mypackage to hibernate.core` or something like that in our module, we'd be suddenly coupled to the implementation. Changing JPA implementations would require us to change the module descriptor of our code, which would be a clear sign of leaking implementation details.

As discussed in detail in "Open Modules and Packages" on page 118, another problem arises when it comes to reflection. Exporting a package exports only the public types in the package. Protected or package-private classes, and nonpublic methods and fields in exported classes, are not accessible. Deep reflection, using the `setAcces` `sible` method, will not work even when a package is exported. To allow deep reflection (which many frameworks need), a package must be *open*.

Going back to our Jackson example, we can use the `opens` keyword instead of the qualified export to `jackson.databind`:

```
module books {
    requires jackson.databind;

    opens demo;
}
```

An open package gives run-time access (including deep reflection) to its types to any module, but no compile-time access. This avoids others using your implementation code accidentally *at compile-time*, while frameworks can do their magic without problems *at run-time*. When only run-time access is required, `opens` is a good choice in most cases. Remember that an open package is not truly encapsulated. Another module can always access the package by using reflection. But at least we're protected against accidental usage during development, and it clearly documents that the package isn't meant to be used directly by other modules.

Like the `exports` keyword, the `opens` keyword can be qualified. This way, a package can be opened just to a limited set of modules:

```
module books {
    requires jackson.databind;

    opens demo to jackson.databind;
}
```

Now that you have seen two ways to work around the run-time accessibility problem, one question remains: why did we find out about this problem only when running the application, and not during compilation? Let's revisit the rules of readability again to understand this scenario better. For a class to able to read another class from another module, the following needs be true:

- The class needs to be public (ignoring the case of deep reflection).

- The package in the other module must be exported, or opened in the case of deep reflection.

- The consuming module must have a readability relation to the other module (requires).

Usually, this can all be checked at compile-time. Jackson Databind doesn't have a compile-time dependency on our code, however. It learns about our Book class only because we pass it in as an argument to ObjectMapper. This means the compiler can't help us. When doing reflection, the runtime takes care of automatically setting up a readability relation (requires), so this step is taken care of. Next it will find out that the class is not exported nor opened (and therefore not accessible) at run-time, and this is not automatically "fixed" by the runtime.

If the runtime is smart enough to add a readability relation automatically, why doesn't it also take care of opening the package? This is about intentions and module ownership. When code uses reflection to access code in another module, the intention from that module's perspective is clearly to read the other module. It would be unnecessary extra boilerplate to be (even more) explicit about this. The same is not true for exports/opens. The module owner should decide which packages are exported or opened. Only the module itself should define this intention, so it can't be automatically inferred by the behavior of some other module.

Many frameworks use reflection in a similar way, so it's always important to test well after migration.

 In "Libraries, Strong Encapsulation, and the JDK 9 Classpath" on page 155, you learned that by default Java 9 runs with --illegal-acces=permit. Why did we still have to explicitly open our package for reflection? Remember that the --illegal-access flag affects only code on the classpath. In this example, jackson.databind is a module itself, reflecting on code in our module (not a platform module). There's no code on the classpath involved.

Open Modules

In the previous section, you saw the use of open packages to give run-time-only access to a package. This is great to satisfy the reflection needs that many frameworks and libraries have. If we're in the middle of a large migration, in a codebase that is not completely modularized yet, it may not be immediately obvious which packages need to be open. Ideally, we know exactly how the frameworks and libraries that we use access our code, but maybe we're not intimately familiar with the codebase we're working with. This could result in a tedious trial-and-error process, trying to figure out which packages need to be open. For these situations, we can use *open modules*, which is a less precise but more powerful tool:

```
open module books {
  requires jackson.databind;
}
```

An open module is a module that gives run-time access to all its packages. This does not grant compile-time access to packages, which is exactly what we want for our migrated code. If a package needs to be used at compile-time, it must be exported. Create an open module first to avoid reflection-related problems. This helps you focus on `requires` and compile-time usage (`exports`) first. Once the application is working again, we can fine-tune run-time access to the packages as well by removing the `open` keyword from the module, and be more specific about which packages should be open.

VM Arguments to Break Encapsulation

In some scenarios, adding `export` or `opens` to a module is not an option. Maybe we don't have access to the code, or maybe access is required only during testing. In these scenarios, we can set up additional exports by using a VM argument. You have already seen this in action in "Compilation and Encapsulated APIs" on page 157 for platform modules, and we can do the same for other modules, including our own.

Instead of adding an `exports` or `opens` clause to the books module descriptor, we can use a command-line flag to achieve the same:

```
--add-exports books/demo=jackson.databind
```

The complete command to run the application then is as follows:

```
java -cp lib/jackson-annotations-2.8.8.jar:lib/jackson-core-2.8.8.jar \
  --module-path out:mods \
  --add-exports books/demo=jackson.databind \
  -m books/demo.Main
```

This sets up a qualified export when starting the JVM. A similar flag exists to open packages: `--add-opens`. Although these flags are useful in special cases, they should be treated as a last resort. The same mechanism can also be used to gain access to internal, nonexported packages, as you saw in the previous chapter. Although this can be a temporary workaround until code is properly migrated, it should be used with great care. Breaking encapsulation should not be done lightly.

Automatic Modules and the Classpath

In the previous chapter, you saw the *unnamed module*. All code on the classpath is part of the unnamed module. In the Jackson example, you learned that code in a module you're compiling can't access code on the classpath. How is it then possible for the `jackson.databind` automatic module to work correctly while the Jackson Core and Jackson Annotations JARs, which it depends on, are still on the classpath? This works because these libraries are in the unnamed module. The unnamed module exports all code on the classpath and reads all other modules. There is a big restriction, however: the unnamed module itself is readable only from automatic modules!

Figure 8-3 illustrates the difference between automatic modules and explicit modules when it comes to reading the unnamed module. An explicit module can read only other explicit modules, and automatic modules. An automatic module reads all modules including the unnamed module.

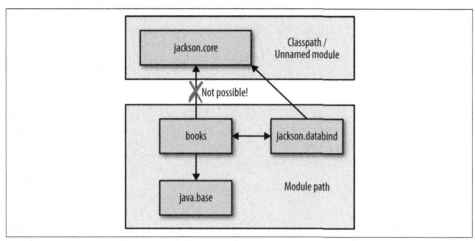

Figure 8-3. Only automatic modules can read the classpath

The readability to the unnamed module is only a mechanism to facilitate automatic modules in a mixed classpath/module path migration scenario. If we were to use a type from Jackson Core directly in our code (as opposed to from an automatic module), we would have to move Jackson Core to the module path as well. Let's try this in Example 8-3.

Example 8-3. Main.java (➡ chapter8/readability_rules)

```
package demo;

import com.fasterxml.jackson.databind.ObjectMapper;
import com.fasterxml.jackson.core.Versioned; ❶

public class Demo {

  public static void main(String... args) throws Exception {
```

```
Book modularityBook =
  new Book("Java 9 Modularity", "Modularize all the things!");

ObjectMapper mapper = new ObjectMapper();
String json = mapper.writeValueAsString(modularityBook);
System.out.println(json);

Versioned versioned = (Versioned) mapper;  ❷
System.out.println(versioned.version());

  }
}
```

❶ Importing the `Versioned` type from Jackson Core

❷ Using the `Versioned` type to print the library version

The Jackson Databind `ObjectMapper` type implements the interface `Versioned` from Jackson Core. Note that this wasn't a problem until we started to use this type explicitly in our module. Any time we use an external type in a module, we should immediately think `requires`. Let's demonstrate this by trying to compile the code, which will result in an error:

```
src/books/demo/Main.java:4: error:
package com.fasterxml.jackson.core does not exist

import com.fasterxml.jackson.core.Versioned;
                                  ^
src/books/demo/Main.java:16: error:
cannot find symbol
    Versioned versioned = (Versioned)mapper;
    ^
  symbol:   class Versioned
  location: class Main
src/books/demo/Main.java:16: error:
cannot find symbol
    Versioned versioned = (Versioned)mapper;
                           ^
  symbol:   class Versioned
  location: class Main
3 errors
```

Although the type exists in the unnamed module (the classpath), and the `jack son.databind` automatic module can access it, we can't access it from our module. To fix this problem, we need to move Jackson Core to the module path as well, making it an automatic module. Let's start with moving the JAR file to the *mods* directory, and removing it from the classpath, as we did for Jackson Databind:

```
javac -cp lib/jackson-annotations-2.8.8.jar \
  --module-path mods \
```

```
-d out \
--module-source-path src \
-m books
```

This works! Taking a step back, however, why does it work? We're clearly using a type from jackson.core, but we don't have a requires for jackson.core in our *module-info.java*. Why didn't the compilation fail? Remember that an automatic module requires transitive all other modules. This means that by requiring jackson.data bind, we also read jackson.core transitively. Although this is convenient, it's a big trade-off. We have an explicit code dependency on a module that we don't explicitly require. If jackson.databind moves to become an explicit module, and the Jackson maintainers choose to not requires transitive jackson.core, our code would suddenly break.

Be aware that although automatic modules look like modules, they miss the metadata to provide reliable configuration. In this specific example, it is better to explicitly add a requires to jackson.core as well:

```
module books {
    requires jackson.databind;
    requires jackson.core;

    opens demo;
}
```

Now that we're compiling happily again, we can also adapt the run command. We have to remove only the Jackson Core JAR file from the classpath, because the module path was already configured correctly:

```
java \
    -cp lib/jackson-annotations-2.8.8.jar \
    --module-path out:mods \
    -m books/demo.Main
```

If you are wondering why jackson.core was *resolved* in the first place (it's not explicitly added to the module graph as a root module, and no explicit module depends on it directly), you have been paying attention! "Module Resolution and the Module Path" on page 28 discussed in detail that the set of *resolved* modules is calculated based on a given set of *root modules*. In the case of automatic modules this would be confusing. Automatic modules don't have explicit dependencies, so they would not cause their transitive dependencies that are also automatic modules to be resolved. Because it would be time-consuming to add dependencies manually with --add-modules, all automatic modules on the module path are automatically resolved when the application requires any one of them. This behavior can cause unused automatic modules to be resolved (taking unnecessary resources), so keep the module path clean.

The behavior is similar to what we're used to with the classpath, however. Again, this illustrates how automatic modules are a feature squarely aimed at migrating from the classpath to modules.

Why isn't the JVM smarter about this? It has access to all the code in an automatic module, after all, so why not analyze dependencies? To analyze whether any of this code calls into other modules, the JVM needs to perform bytecode analysis of all the code. Although this isn't difficult to implement, it is an expensive operation potentially adding a lot of startup time in a large application. Moreover, such an analysis won't find dependencies arising through reflection. Because of these limitations, the JVM doesn't and probably never will do this. Instead, the JDK ships with another tool, jdeps, that does perform such bytecode analysis.

Using jdeps

In the preceding Jackson example, we've used kind of a trial-and-error approach to migrating the code. This gave you a good understanding of what happens, but is not efficient. jdeps is a tool shipped with the JDK that analyzes code and gives insights about module dependencies. We can use jdeps to optimize the process we've gone through to migrate the Jackson example.

We will start by using jdeps to analyze the classpath version of the demo, before we migrated to (automatic) modules. jdeps analyzes bytecode, not source files, so we're interested only in the application's output folder and JAR files. For reference, here's the compiled version of the books example when using just the classpath, as in the beginning of this chapter:

```
├── lib
│   ├── jackson-annotations-2.8.8.jar
│   ├── jackson-core-2.8.8.jar
│   └── jackson-databind-2.8.8.jar
└── out
    └── demo
        ├── Book.class
        └── Main.class
```

We can analyze this application by using the following command:

```
$ jdeps -recursive -summary -cp lib/*.jar out

jackson-annotations-2.8.8.jar -> java.base
jackson-core-2.8.8.jar -> java.base
jackson-databind-2.8.8.jar -> lib/jackson-annotations-2.8.8.jar
jackson-databind-2.8.8.jar -> lib/jackson-core-2.8.8.jar
jackson-databind-2.8.8.jar -> java.base
jackson-databind-2.8.8.jar -> java.desktop
jackson-databind-2.8.8.jar -> java.logging
jackson-databind-2.8.8.jar -> java.sql
```

```
jackson-databind-2.8.8.jar -> java.xml
out -> lib/jackson-databind-2.8.8.jar
out -> java.base
```

The -recursive flag makes sure that transitive run-time dependencies are also analyzed. Without it, *jackson-annotations-2.8.8.jar* would not be analyzed, for example. The -summary flag, as the name suggests, summarizes the output. By default, jdeps outputs the complete list of dependencies for each package, which can be a long list. The summary shows module dependencies only, and hides the package details. The -cp argument is the classpath we want to use during the analysis, which should correspond to the run-time classpath. The *out* directory contains the application's class files that must be analyzed.

We learn several things from the jdeps output:

- Our own code (in directory *out*) has only a direct, compile-time dependency on *jackson-databind-2.8.8.jar* (and java.base, of course).

- Jackson Databind has a dependency on Jackson Core and Jackson Annotations.

- Jackson Databind has dependencies on several platform modules.

Based on this output, we can already conclude that to migrate our code to a module, we need to make jackson-databind an automatic module as well. We also see that jackson-databind depends on jackson-core and jackson-annotations, so they need to be provided either on the classpath or as automatic modules. If we want to know *why* a dependency exists, we can print more details by using jdeps. Omitting the -summary argument in the preceding command prints the full dependency graph, showing exactly which packages require which other packages:

```
$ jdeps -cp lib/*.jar out

com.fasterxml.jackson.databind.util (jackson-databind-2.8.8.jar)
      -> com.fasterxml.jackson.annotation jackson-annotations-2.8.8.jar
      -> com.fasterxml.jackson.core jackson-core-2.8.8.jar
      -> com.fasterxml.jackson.core.base jackson-core-2.8.8.jar

... Results truncated for readability
```

If this is still not enough detail, we can also instruct jdeps to print dependencies at the class level:

```
$ jdeps -verbose:class -cp lib/*.jar out

out -> java.base
   demo.Main (out)
      -> java.lang.Object
      -> java.lang.String
   demo.Main (out)
      -> com.fasterxml.jackson.databind.ObjectMapper jackson-databind-2.8.8.jar
```

```
... Results truncated for readability
```

So far, we have used jdeps on a classpath-based application. We can also use jdeps with modules. Let's in this case try jdeps on the Jackson demo, where all Jackson JARs are available as automatic modules:

```
├── mods
│   ├── jackson-annotations-2.8.8.jar
│   ├── jackson-core-2.8.8.jar
│   └── jackson-databind-2.8.8.jar
├── out
│   └── books
│       ├── demo
│       │   ├── Book.class
│       │   └── Main.class
│       └── module-info.class
```

To invoke jdeps, we now have to pass in the module path that contains the application module and the automatic Jackson modules:

```
$ jdeps --module-path out:mods -m books
```

This prints the dependency graph as before. Looking at the (long) output, we can see the following:

```
module jackson.databind (automatic)
  requires java.base
    com.fasterxml.jackson.databind
      -> com.fasterxml.jackson.annotation jackson.annotations
    com.fasterxml.jackson.databind
      -> com.fasterxml.jackson.core jackson.core
    com.fasterxml.jackson.databind
      -> com.fasterxml.jackson.core.filter jackson.core

...

module books
  requires jackson.databind
  requires java.base
   demo -> com.fasterxml.jackson.databind jackson.databind
   demo -> java.io java.base
   demo -> java.lang java.base
```

We can see that `jackson.databind` has a dependency on both `jackson.annotations` and `jackson.core`. We also see that `books` has only a dependency on `jackson.data bind`. The `books` code is not using `jackson.core` classes at compile-time, and transitive dependencies are not defined for automatic modules. Remember that the JVM won't do this analysis at application startup, which means we have to take care of adding `jackson.annotations` and `jackson.core` to either the classpath or the module path ourselves. jdeps provides the information to set this up correctly.

jdeps can output *dot* files for module graphs using the `-dotoutput` flag. This is a useful format to represent graphs, and it's easy to generate images from this format. Wikipedia has a nice introduction (*https://en.wikipedia.org/wiki/DOT_(graph_description_language)*) to the format.

Loading Code Dynamically

A situation that might require some special care when migrating to modules is the use of reflection to load code. A well-known example is loading JDBC drivers. You will see that in most cases loading a JDBC driver "just works," but some corner cases give us better insights into the module system. Let's start with an example that loads a JDBC driver that sits in the *mods* directory of the project as shown in Example 8-4. The HSQLDB driver JAR is not a module yet, so we can use it only as an automatic module.

Because the name of the class is just a string, the compiler will not know about the dependency, so compilation succeeds.

Example 8-4. Main.java (➥ chapter8/runtime_loading)

```
package demo;

public class Main {

  public static void main(String... args) throws Exception {
    Class<?> clazz = Class.forName("org.hsqldb.jdbcDriver");
    System.out.println(clazz.getName());
  }
}
```

The module descriptor (shown in Example 8-5) is empty; it does not require *hsqldb*, which is the driver we're trying to load. Although this would normally be a reason to be suspicious, it could still work in theory, because the runtime will automatically create a readability relation when using reflection on code in another module.

Example 8-5. module-info.java (➥ chapter8/runtime_loading)

```
module runtime.loading.example {
}
```

Still, if we run the code, it fails with a `ClassNotFoundException`:

```
java --module-path mods:out -m runtime.loading.example/demo.Main

Exception in thread "main" java.lang.ClassNotFoundException:
  org.hsqldb.jdbcDriver
```

All observable automatic modules are resolved *when the application uses at least one of them*. Resolving happens at startup, so effectively our module is not causing the automatic module to load. If we had other automatic modules that are required directly, this would cause the hsqldb module to resolve as well as a side effect. In this case, we can add the automatic module ourselves with --add-modules hsqldb.

Now the driver loads but gives another error, because the driver depends on java.sql, which wasn't resolved yet. Remember, automatic modules lack the metadata to specifically require other modules. When using JDBC in practice, we would need to require java.sql in our module to be able to use the JDBC API after loading the driver. This means adding it to the module descriptor as shown in Example 8-6.

Example 8-6. module-info.java (➥ chapter8/runtime_loading)

```
module runtime.loading.example {
    requires java.sql;
}
```

The code now runs successfully. With java.sql required by our module, we can see another interesting case of automatic module resolving. If we remove --add-modules hsqldb again, the application still runs! Why does requiring java.sql cause an automatic module to be loaded? It turns out that java.sql defines a java.sql.Driver service interface, and has a uses constraint for this service type as well. Our *hsqldb* JAR provides a service, which is registered via the "old" way of using a file in *META-INF/services*. Because of service binding, the JAR is automatically resolved from the module path. This goes into the subtleties of the module system but is good to understand.

Why didn't we just put requires hsqldb in our module descriptor? Although typically we like to be as explicit as possible about dependencies by putting them in the module descriptor, this is a good example of where this rule of thumb does not apply. The JDBC driver to use often depends on the deployment environment of the application, where the exact driver name is configured in a configuration file. Application code should not be coupled to a specific database driver in that case (although in our example, it is). Instead we simply make sure that the driver is resolved by adding --add-modules. The module containing the driver will be in the resolved module graph, and the reflective instantiation establishes the readability relation to this module.

If the JDBC driver supports it (as HSQLDB does), it is even better to avoid reflective instantiation from application code altogether and use services instead. Services are discussed in detail in Chapter 4.

Split Packages

"Split Packages" on page 94 explained the problem of *split packages*. Just as a refresher, a split package means two modules contain the same package. The Java module system doesn't allow split packages.

When using automatic modules, we can run into split packages as well. In large applications, it is common to find split packages due to dependency mismanagement. Split packages are always a mistake, because they don't work reliably on the classpath either. Unfortunately, when using build tools that resolve transitive dependencies, it's easy to end up with multiple versions of the same library. The first class found on the classpath is loaded. When classes from two versions of a library mix, this often leads to hard-to-debug exceptions at run-time.

> Modern build tools often have a setting to fail on duplicate dependencies. This makes dependency management issues clearer and forces you to deal with them early. It is highly recommended to use this.

The Java module system is much stricter about this issue than the classpath. When it detects that a package is exported from two modules on the module path, it will refuse to start. This fail-fast mechanism is much better than the unreliable situation we used to have with the classpath. Better to fail during development than in production, when some unlucky user hits a code path that is broken by an obscure classpath problem. But it also means we have to deal with these issues. Blindly moving all JARs from the classpath to the module path may result in split packages between the resulting automatic modules. These will then be rejected by the module system.

To make migration a little easier, an exception to this rule exists when it comes to automatic modules and the unnamed module. It acknowledges that a lot of classpaths are simply incorrect and contain split packages. When both a (automatic) module and the unnamed module contain the same package, the package from the module will be used. The package in the unnamed module will be ignored. This is also the case for packages that are part of the platform modules. It's common to override platform packages by putting them on the classpath. This approach is no longer working in Java 9. You already saw this in the previous chapter, and learned that `java.se.ee` modules are not included in the `java.se` module for this reason.

If you run into split package issues while migrating to Java 9, there's is no way around them. You must deal with them, even when your classpath-based application works correctly from a user's perspective.

This chapter presented many techniques to make gradual migration to the Java module system possible. These techniques are extremely valuable, because it will take time before the Java ecosystem moves to the Java module system in its entirety. Automatic modules play an important role in migration scenarios; therefore, it's important to fully understand how they work.

Migration Case Study: Spring and Hibernate

Chapter 8 presented all the available tools for migrating applications to modules. This chapter brings everything together in a case study. We'll migrate a fully functional application that uses Spring and Hibernate to modules. Note that we're deliberately using an example of "traditional" Spring/Hibernate development, instead of using the most modern way of doing things. We're using pre-Java 9 versions, to create an interesting case study. Many applications have been written this way, which makes it extra interesting to see how these applications can be migrated toward the future. Newer versions of frameworks will support Java 9 better out of the box, and migrations based on these versions will probably be even easier. If you are not familiar with these frameworks, don't worry. You don't have to understand all the code and configuration to learn about common problems you may face during a migration toward modules.

You will get a lot more value out of this chapter if you check out the code repository and try to migrate the code while you're reading the chapter. In the code repository, we have provided three versions:

chapter9/spring-hibernate-starter
    The classpath version of the application before migration.

chapter9/spring-hibernate
    The migrated application.

chapter9/spring-hibernate-refactored
    The migrated application after additional modularization.

We recommend opening the *spring-hibernate-starter* project in an editor, and applying each step described in this chapter on the code. You should end up with roughly the same result as the finished *spring-hibernate* example.

Getting Familiar with the Application

The application represents a bookstore. Books are stored in a database by using Hibernate. Spring is used to bootstrap Hibernate, including transaction management and dependency injection. The Spring configuration uses a mix of XML and annotation-based configuration.

Before migration, the application code, direct dependencies, and transitive dependencies are on the classpath, as shown in Figure 9-1.

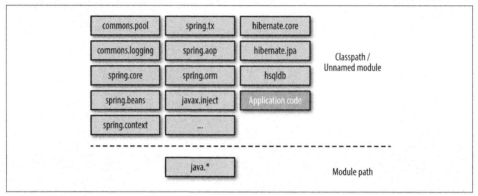

Figure 9-1. Migration starting point (➥ chapter9/spring-hibernate-starter)

The end result of the migration is a codebase with a single module, using automatic modules for dependencies where necessary. Figure 9-2 shows the end result.

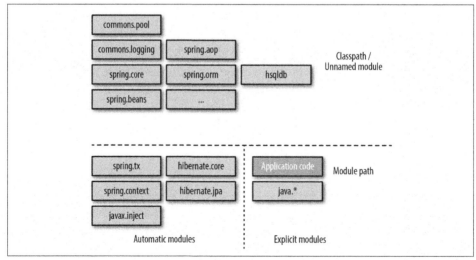

Figure 9-2. Application migrated (➥ chapter9/spring-hibernate)

At the end of the chapter, we will also look at refactoring the application code itself to be more modular.

Before we even start thinking about splitting our code in modules, we should get over some technical issues coming from our dependencies. Remember that we're dealing with pre-Java 9 libraries, which were not designed to work with the Java module system. Specifically, we are using the following framework versions:

- Spring 4.3.2
- Hibernate 5.0.1

Also note that great progress has been made within these frameworks when it comes to module support. At the time of writing, the first Release Candidate of Spring 5 was released, with explicit support for usage as automatic modules. We do not use these updated versions because that wouldn't make a realistic migration example. Even without special support from frameworks and libraries, migration to modules is possible.

The focus of this section is to create a single module for our code. This means defining `requires` for dependencies, and moving libraries to automatic modules. We will also have to deal with `exports` and `opens` to make our code accessible to the frameworks. Once this migration is complete, we can take a good look at the design of our code, and potentially split the code into smaller modules. Because we already solved all the technical issues, this becomes a design exercise.

Let's start by looking at the most important parts of the code to get an idea of the application. For optimal readability of the code, we strongly advise opening the code in your favorite editor.

The `Book` class (shown in Example 9-1) is a JPA entity that can be stored in a database by using Hibernate (or another JPA implementation). It has annotations such as `@Entity` and `@Id` to configure the mapping to the database.

Example 9-1. Book.java (➦ chapter9/spring-hibernate)

```
package books.impl.entities;

import books.api.entities.Book;
import javax.persistence.*;

@Entity
public class BookEntity implements Book {
  @Id @GeneratedValue
  private int id;
  private String title;
  private double price;
```

```
//Getters and setters omitted for brevity
```

}

The `HibernateBooksService` is a Spring `Repository`. This is a service that automatically takes care of transaction management, which is required to successfully store something in the database. It implements our service interface `BooksService`, and uses the Hibernate API (such as `SessionFactory`) to store and retrieve books from the database.

The `BookstoreService` is a simple interface, whose implementation in `BookStoreSer viceImpl`, shown in Example 9-2, can calculate the total price of a given list of books. It is annotated with Spring's `@Component` annotation so that it becomes available for dependency injection.

Example 9-2. BookstoreServiceImpl.java (➡ chapter9/spring-hibernate)

```java
package bookstore.impl.service;

import java.util.Arrays;
import books.api.entities.Book;
import books.api.service.BooksService;
import bookstore.api.service.BookstoreService;
import org.springframework.stereotype.Component;

@Component
public class BookstoreServiceImpl implements BookstoreService {

  private static double TAX = 1.21d;

  private BooksService booksService;

  public BookstoreServiceImpl(BooksService booksService) {
    this.booksService = booksService;
  }

  public double calculatePrice(int... bookIds) {
    double total = Arrays
      .stream(bookIds)
      .mapToDouble(id -> booksService.getBook(id).getPrice())
      .sum();

    return total * TAX;
  }

}
```

Finally, we have a main class that bootstraps Spring, and stores and retrieves some books, as shown in Example 9-3.

Example 9-3. Main.java (➡ chapter9/spring-hibernate)

```java
package main;

import org.springframework.context.ApplicationContext;
import org.springframework.context.support.ClassPathXmlApplicationContext;
import books.api.service.BooksService;
import books.api.entities.Book;
import bookstore.api.service.BookstoreService;

public class Main {

  public void start() {
    System.out.println("Starting...");

    ApplicationContext context =
        new ClassPathXmlApplicationContext(new String[] {"classpath:/main.xml"});

    BooksService booksService = context.getBean(BooksService.class);
    BookstoreService store = context.getBean(BookstoreService.class);

      // Create some books
      int id1 = booksService.createBook("Java 9 Modularity", 45.0d);
      int id2 = booksService.createBook("Modular Cloud Apps with OSGi", 40.0d);
      printf("Created books with id [%d, %d]", id1, id2);

      // Retrieve them again
      Book book1 = booksService.getBook(id1);
      Book book2 = booksService.getBook(id2);
      printf("Retrieved books:\n  %d: %s [%.2f]\n  %d: %s [%.2f]",
        id1, book1.getTitle(), book1.getPrice(),
        id2, book2.getTitle(), book2.getPrice());

      // Use the other service to calculate a total
      double total = store.calculatePrice(id1, id2);
      printf("Total price (with tax): %.2f", total);

  }

  public static void main(String[] args) {
    new Main().start();
  }

  private void printf(String msg, Object... args) {
      System.out.println(String.format(msg + "\n", args));
  }
}
```

Spring is bootstrapped by using `ClassPathXmlApplicationContext`, which requires an XML configuration. In this configuration, shown in Example 9-4, we set up component scanning, which automatically registers `@Component` and `@Repository` annotated classes as Spring beans. We also set up transaction management and Hibernate.

Example 9-4. main.xml (➥ chapter9/spring-hibernate)

```xml
<context:component-scan base-package="books.impl.service"/>
<context:component-scan base-package="bookstore.impl.service"/>

<bean id="myDataSource"
class="org.apache.commons.dbcp.BasicDataSource" destroy-method="close">
    <property name="driverClassName" value="org.hsqldb.jdbcDriver"/>
    <property name="url" value="jdbc:hsqldb:mem:testdb"/>
    <property name="username" value="sa"/>
    <property name="password" value=""/>
</bean>

<bean id="mySessionFactory"
  class="org.springframework.orm.hibernate5.LocalSessionFactoryBean">
    <property name="dataSource" ref="myDataSource"/>
    <property name="annotatedClasses">
  <list>
    <value>books.impl.entities.BookEntity</value>
  </list>
</property>

<property name="hibernateProperties">
  <props>
    <prop key="hibernate.hbm2ddl.auto">create</prop>
  </props>
</property>
</bean>

 <bean id="transactionManager"
    class="org.springframework.orm.hibernate5.HibernateTransactionManager">
    <property name="sessionFactory" ref="mySessionFactory"/>
</bean>

<tx:annotation-driven/>
```

The directory structure of the project is currently as follows:

```
├── lib
├── run.sh
└── src
    ├── books
    │   ├── api
    │   │   ├── entities
    │   │   │   └── Book.java
    │   │   └── service
```

```
|   |        └─ BooksService.java
|   └─ impl
|       ├─ entities
|       |   └─ BookEntity.java
|       └─ service
|           └─ HibernateBooksService.java
├─ bookstore
|   ├─ api
|   |   └─ service
|   |       └─ BookstoreService.java
|   └─ impl
|       └─ service
|           └─ BookstoreServiceImpl.java
├─ log4j2.xml
├─ main
|   └─ Main.java
└─ main.xml
```

The *src* directory contains the configuration files and the source code packages. The *lib* directory contains the JAR files of Spring, Hibernate, and transitive dependencies of both, which is a long list of 31 JAR files in total. To build and run the application, we can use the following commands:

```
javac -cp [list of JARs in lib] -d out -sourcepath src $(find src -name '*.java')

cp $(find src -name '*.xml') out

java -cp [list of JARs in lib]:out main.Main
```

Running on the Classpath with Java 9

The first step toward any migration to modules should start with compiling and running the code with Java 9, while still using the classpath. This also shows the first problem to solve. Hibernate relies on some JAXB classes. In "Using JAXB and Other Java EE APIs" on page 162, you learned that JAXB is part of the `java.se.ee` subgraph, but not of the default `java.se` module subgraph. Without modification, running `Main` results in `java.lang.ClassNotFoundException: javax.xml.bind.JAXBException`. We need to add JAXB to our application by using the `--add-modules` flag:

```
java -cp [list of JARs in lib]:out --add-modules java.xml.bind main.Main
```

We're now seeing another, rather obscure, warning:

```
WARNING: An illegal reflective access operation has occurred
WARNING: Illegal reflective access by javassist.util.proxy.SecurityActions
(file:.../lib/javassist-3.20.0-GA.jar)
to method java.lang.ClassLoader.defineClass(...)
WARNING: Please consider reporting this to the maintainers
  of javassist.util.proxy.SecurityActions
```

```
WARNING: Use --illegal-access=warn to enable warnings of further illegal
    reflective access operations
WARNING: All illegal access operations will be denied in a future release
```

We discussed exactly this issue in "Libraries, Strong Encapsulation, and the JDK 9 Classpath" on page 155. The `javassist` library tries to use deep reflection on JDK types, which is by default allowed, but generates a warning. If we were to run the application with `--illegal-access=deny`, this would even turn into an error. Remember, in a future Java release, this will be the default. We don't want to fix this issue right now by updating to a possibly fixed version of `javassist`. Still, we can get rid of the warning by using `--add-opens`:

```
java -cp [list of JARs in lib]:out \
--add-modules java.xml.bind \
--add-opens java.base/java.lang=ALL-UNNAMED main.Main
```

It's up to you whether you want to silence the warning by adding `--add-opens`. Doing so prepares you for the next Java releases, where illegal access from the classpath isn't treated as friendly as in Java 9. The problematic behavior of `javassist` is still there. Raising such issues with library maintainers is the right course of action.

Setting Up for Modules

With these problems out of the way, we can start migrating toward modules. First, we migrate the code to a single module. Keeping the code's internal structure unchanged first is a good strategy when migrating to modules. Although this structure might not be the final structure you want, it can be easier to first focus on the technical problems.

The first step is to change `-sourcepath` to `--module-source-path`. To do this, we need to slightly change the structure of the project. The *src* directory should not contain packages directly, but a module directory first. The module directory should also contain *module-info.java*:

```
├── lib
├── mods
├── run.sh
└── src
    └── bookapp
        ├── books
        │   ├── api
        │   │   ├── entities
        │   │   │   └── Book.java
        │   │   └── service
        │   │       └── BooksService.java
        │   └── impl
        │       ├── entities
        │       │   └── BookEntity.java
        │       └── service
```

```
|              └─ HibernateBooksService.java
├─ bookstore
│   ├─ api
│   │   └─ service
│   │       └─ BookstoreService.java
│   └─ impl
│       └─ service
│           └─ BookstoreServiceImpl.java
├─ log4j2.xml
├─ main
│   └─ Main.java
├─ main.xml
└─ module-info.java
```

We modify the compile/run script to use `--module-source-path` and to start the main class from our module:

```
javac -cp [list of JARs in lib] \
  --module-path mods \
  -d out \
  --module-source-path src \
  -m bookapp

cp $(find src -name '*.xml') out/bookapp

java -cp out:[list of JARs in lib] \
  --module-path mods:out \
  --add-modules java.xml.bind \
  -m bookapp/main.Main
```

We didn't move any libraries to the module path yet, nor did we put anything in *module-info.java*, so the preceding commands are obviously going to fail.

Using Automatic Modules

To be able to compile our module, we need to add `requires` statements to *module-info.java* for any compile-time dependencies. This also implies that we need to move some of the JAR files from the classpath to the module path to make them automatic modules. To figure out which compile-time dependencies we have exactly, we can look at `import` statements in our code or use jdeps. For our example application, we can come up with the following list of `requires` statements, based on direct compile-time dependencies:

```
requires spring.context;
requires spring.tx;

requires javax.inject;

requires hibernate.core;
requires hibernate.jpa;
```

All are pretty self-explanatory; packages from these modules are used directly from the sample code. To be able to require these libraries, we move their corresponding JAR files to the module path to make them automatic modules. Transitive dependencies can stay on the classpath, as shown in Figure 9-3.

 Remember "Using jdeps" on page 184? jdeps is useful when you have to figure out what modules to require during migration. For example, we could have found our requires by running the following on our classpath version of the application:

```
jdeps -summary -cp lib/*.jar out

out -> lib/hibernate-core-5.2.2.Final.jar
out -> lib/hibernate-jpa-2.1-api-1.0.0.Final.jar
out -> java.base
out -> lib/javax.inject-1.jar
out -> lib/spring-context-4.3.2.RELEASE.jar
out -> lib/spring-tx-4.3.2.RELEASE.jar
```

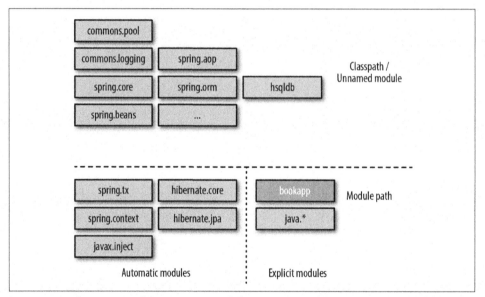

Figure 9-3. Migration with automatic modules

Besides these compile-time dependencies, we have both an additional compile-time and run-time requirement that we can add by using --add-modules. Types from the java.naming platform module are used in the Hibernate API, requiring it to be available at compile-time, even when we don't use this type explicitly in our code. Without adding the module explicitly, we would see this error:

```
src/bookapp/books/impl/service/HibernateBooksService.java:19:
    error: cannot access Referenceable
    return sessionFactory.getCurrentSession().get(BookEntity.class, id);
                                              ^
  class file for javax.naming.Referenceable not found
1 error
```

Because Hibernate is used as an automatic module, it does not cause extra platform modules to resolve. Our code does have an indirect compile-time dependency on it, though, because Hibernate uses a type from `java.naming` in its API (the `SessionFac` `tory` interface extends `Referenceable`). This means we have a compile-time dependency, without having a `requires`, which doesn't work. If Hibernate were an explicit module, it should have `requires transitive java.naming` in its *module-info.java* to set up implied readability and prevent this problem.

Until then, we can work around the issue by adding `--add-modules java.naming` to javac. Alternatively, we could have added another `requires` for `java.naming` in our module descriptor. As discussed previously, we prefer to avoid `requires` statements for indirect dependencies, hence the choice for `--add-modules` instead.

The application compiles successfully now. Running it still results in some errors.

Java Platform Dependencies and Automatic Modules

A `java.lang.NoClassDefFoundError` tells us we need to add `java.sql` to `--add-modules` for the java command. Why wasn't `java.sql` resolved without our manual intervention? Hibernate depends on `java.sql` internally. Because Hibernate is used as an automatic module, it doesn't have a module descriptor to require other (platform) modules. This problem is similar to the preceding problem with `java.naming`, but manifests itself differently. The `java.naming` example was a compile-time error because the Hibernate API that our code uses references a type from `java.naming`. In this case, Hibernate itself uses `java.sql` internally, but its types are not part of the Hibernate API that we compile against. Therefore, the error shows only at run-time.

With an extra `--add-modules java.sql`, we can move on to the next step.

Opening Packages for Reflection

We're getting close to successfully running the application, but rerunning the application still results in an error. This time the error is pretty straightforward:

```
Caused by: java.lang.IllegalAccessException:
class org.springframework.beans.BeanUtils cannot access class
  books.impl.service.HibernateBooksService (in module bookapp) because module
  bookapp does not export books.impl.service to unnamed module @5c45d770
```

Spring relies on reflection to instantiate classes. For this to work, we have to open implementation packages containing classes that Spring needs to instantiate. Hibernate, by the same token, also uses reflection to manipulate *entity classes*. Hibernate needs access to the Book interface and to the BookEntity implementation class.

For the API packages in the application, it makes sense to export them. Later, when splitting into more modules, these packages are most probably used by other modules as well. For implementation packages, we use opens instead. This way, the frameworks can do their reflection magic, while we still ensure encapsulation at build-time:

```
exports books.api.service;
exports books.api.entities;

opens books.impl.entities;
opens books.impl.service;
opens bookstore.impl.service;
```

In a larger application, it could be a good choice to use an open module at first instead of specifying individual packages to be open. After setting up our package opens/exports, we see another familiar error.

```
java.lang.NoClassDefFoundError: javax/xml/bind/JAXBException
```

One of our libraries is using JAXB (not our code), and in "Using JAXB and Other Java EE APIs" on page 162, you learned that java.xml.bind is not resolved by default. Simply adding the module to our --add-modules, like we did when running this example on the classpath, will help us out of this situation.

Almost done!

Unfortunately, the javassist library gives us a last obscure error when trying to run the application:

```
Caused by: java.lang.IllegalAccessError: superinterface check failed:
  class books.impl.entities.BookEntity_$$_jvstced_0 (in module bookapp)
  cannot access class javassist.util.proxy.ProxyObject
  (in unnamed module @0x546621c4) because module bookapp
  does not read unnamed module @0x546621c4
```

Fixing Illegal Access

Hibernate uses the javassist library to dynamically create subclasses of our entity classes. At run-time, our application code uses these subclasses instead of the original classes. Because our code runs from a module, the generated classes end up being part of the same bookapp module. The generated classes implement an interface (ProxyObject) from javassist. However, javassist is still on the classpath, which is unreachable from explicit modules. Therefore, the generated classes implement an interface that's not accessible for them at run-time. Although this is an obscure and hard-to-understand error, the fix is easy: move `javassist` from the classpath to the module path, so that it becomes an automatic module and can be accessed from other modules.

However, turning `javassist` into an automatic module introduces a new problem. Earlier you saw that `javassist` uses illegal deep reflection on JDK types. On the classpath, with its lenient `--illegal-access=permit` default, this was only giving us a warning. Because `javassist` is now an automatic module, the `--illegal-access` mechanism doesn't apply anymore. It affects only code on the classpath. This means we are now getting an error, which is essentially the same error that we would have seen if we had run the classpath example with `--illegal-access=deny`:

```
Caused by: java.lang.reflect.InaccessibleObjectException:
  Unable to make protected final java.lang.Class
  java.lang.ClassLoader.defineClass(...)
  throws java.lang.ClassFormatError accessible:
  module java.base does not "opens java.lang" to module javassist
```

We already know that we can work around this issue by adding `--add-opens java.base/java.lang=javassist` to the java command. Our final script to compile and run the application is shown in Example 9-5.

Example 9-5. run.sh (➥ chapter9/spring-hibernate)

```
CP=[list of JARs in lib]

javac -cp $CP \
    --module-path mods \
    --add-modules java.naming \
    -d out          \
    --module-source-path src \
    -m bookapp

cp $(find src -name '*.xml') out/bookapp

java -cp $CP \
    --module-path mods:out      \
    --add-modules java.xml.bind,java.sql \
    --add-opens java.base/java.lang=javassist \
    -m bookapp/main.Main
```

We've migrated the application by moving only the libraries to automatic modules that we really need. Alternatively, you could start migration by copying all JAR files to the module path. Although this generally makes it easier to quickly get an application running, it makes it harder to come up with a reasonable module descriptor for your application module. Because automatic modules set up implied readability to all other modules, it will hide missing `requires` in your own module. When upgrading automatic modules to explicit modules, things may break. It's important to get your module dependencies as well-defined as possible, so you should spend the time investigating this.

Refactor to Multiple Modules

Now that we have a working application, it would be nice to also split the codebase into smaller modules and embrace modularity in the design of the application. That's beyond the scope of this chapter, but the GitHub repository contains an implementation with multiple modules (➥ *chapter9/spring-hibernate-refactored*). Figure 9-4 provides a reasonable design for such an improved structure.

This design has trade-offs, and you should be aware of them. For example, you have a choice of whether to create a separate API module or to export the API from a module that also contains the implementation. We already discussed many of these choices in Chapter 5.

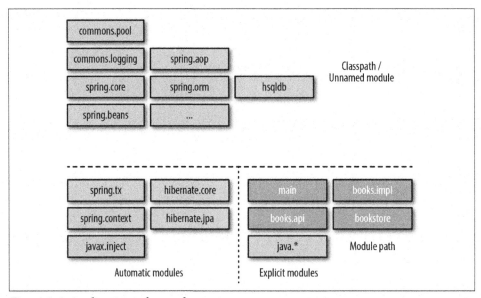

Figure 9-4. Application refactored

With this case study, you've seen all the tools and processes you need to migrate an existing classpath-based application to modules. Use jdeps to analyze your existing code and dependencies. Move libraries to the module path to turn them into automatic modules, allowing you to create a module descriptor for your application. When your application uses libraries that involve reflection, such as dependency injection, object-relational mapping, or serialization libraries, open packages and modules are the way to go.

Migrating an application to modules can expose violations of strong encapsulation, either in the application or its libraries. As we've seen, this can lead to sometimes baffling errors, although they can all be explained with enough knowledge of the module system. In this chapter, you've learned how to mitigate these issues. Life would be a lot better, though, if libraries already were proper Java 9 modules with explicit module descriptors. The next chapter shows how library maintainers can work toward Java 9 support.

CHAPTER 10

Library Migration

The previous chapters focused on migrating applications to the module system. Many of these lessons apply when migrating an existing library as well. Still, several issues affect library migration more than application migration. In this chapter, we identify those issues and their solutions.

The biggest difference between migrating a library and migrating an application is that libraries are used by many applications. These applications may run on different versions of Java, so libraries often need to work across a range of Java versions. It's not realistic to expect users of your library to switch to Java 9 at the same time your library switches. Fortunately, a combination of new features in Java 9 enables a seamless experience for both library maintainers and users.

The goal is to migrate an existing library in incremental steps to a modular library. You don't have to be the author of a popular open source project for this to be interesting. If you write code that is shared with other teams in a company, you're in the same boat.

A migration process for libraries consists of the following steps:

1. Ensure that the library can run as an automatic module on Java 9.

2. Compile the library with the Java 9 compiler (targeting your desired minimum Java version), without using new Java 9 features just yet.

3. Add a module descriptor and turn the library into an explicit module.

4. Optionally, refactor the structure of the library to increase encapsulation, identify APIs, and possibly split into multiple modules.

5. Start using Java 9 features in the library while maintaining backward compatibility with earlier versions of Java 9.

The second step is optional, but recommended. With the newly introduced `--release` flag, earlier versions of Java can be reliably targeted with the Java 9 compiler. In "Targeting Older Java Versions" on page 215, you'll see how to use this option. Throughout all steps, backward compatibility can be maintained with earlier versions of Java. For the last step, this may be especially surprising. It's made possible by a new feature, multi-release JARs, which we explore toward the end of this chapter.

Before Modularization

As a first step, you need to ensure that your library can be used as is with Java 9. Many applications will be using your library on the classpath, even on Java 9. Furthermore, library maintainers need to get their libraries in shape for use as automatic modules in applications. In many cases, no code changes are necessary. The only changes to make at this point are to prevent showstoppers, such as the use of encapsulated or removed types from the JDK.

Before making a library into a module (or collection of modules), you should take the same initial step as when migrating applications, as detailed in Chapter 7. Ensuring that the library runs on Java 9 means it should not use encapsulated types in the JDK. If it does use such types, library users are possibly faced with warnings, or exceptions (if they run with the recommended `--illegal-access=deny` setting). This forces them to use `--add-opens` or `--add-exports` flags. Even if you document this with your library, it's not a great user experience. Usually the library is just one of many in an application, so tracking down all the right command-line flags is painful for users. It's better to use jdeps to find uses of encapsulated APIs in the library and change them to the suggested replacement. Use `jdeps -jdkinternals`, as described in "Using jdeps to Find Removed or Encapsulated Types and Their Alternatives" on page 161, to quickly spot problems in this area. When these replacement APIs are only available starting with Java 9, you cannot directly use them while supporting earlier Java releases. In "Multi-Release JARs" on page 221, you'll see how multi-release JARs can solve this problem.

At this stage, we're not yet creating a module descriptor for the library. We can postpone thinking about what packages need to be exported or not. Also, any dependencies the library has on other libraries can be left implicit. Whether the library is put on the classpath, or on the module path as an automatic module, it can still access everything it needs without explicit dependencies.

After this step, the library can be used on Java 9. We're not using any new features from Java 9 in the library implementation yet. In fact, if there are no uses of encapsulated or removed APIs, there's no need to even recompile the library.

Choosing a Library Module Name

> There are only two hard things in Computer Science: cache invalidation and naming things.
>
> —Phil Karlton

It is important at this point to think about the *name* your module should have when it becomes a real module later. What is a good name for a library module? On the one hand, you want the name to be simple and memorable. On the other hand, we are talking about a widely reusable library, so the name must be unique. There can be only one module on the module path for any given name.

A long-standing tradition for making globally unique names in the Java world is to use the *reverse DNS* notation. When you have a library called `mylibrary`, its module name could be `com.mydomain.mylibrary`. Applying this naming convention to non-reusable application modules is unnecessary, but with libraries, the extra visual noise is warranted. Several open source Java libraries, for example, are named `spark`. If no precautions are taken by these library maintainers, they may end up claiming the same module name. That would mean applications could no longer use those libraries together in an application. Claiming a reverse DNS–based module name is the best way to prevent clashes.

 A good candidate for a module name is the longest common prefix of all packages in the module. Assuming reverse-DNS package names, this top-level package name is a natural module identifier. In Maven terms, this often means combining the *group ID* and *artifact ID* as module name.

Digits are allowed in module names. It may be tempting to add a version number in the module name (e.g., `com.mydomain.mylibrary2`). Don't do this. Versioning is a separate concern from identifying your library. A version can be set when creating the modular JAR (as discussed in "Versioned Modules" on page 106), but should never be part of the module name. Just because you upgrade your library with a major version doesn't mean the identification of your library should change. Some popular libraries already painted themselves into this corner a long time ago. The Apache `commons-lang` library, for example, decided on the `commons-lang3` name when moving from version 2 to 3. Currently, versions belong to the realm of build tools and artifact repositories, not the module system. An updated version of a library should not lead to changes in module descriptors.

You've learned that automatic modules derive their name from the JAR filename in Chapter 8. Unfortunately, the ultimate filename is often dictated by build tools or other processes that are out of the hands of library maintainers. Applications using the library as an automatic module then require your library through the derived name in their module descriptors. When your library switches to being an explicit module later, you're stuck with this derived name. That's a problem when the derived filename isn't quite correct or uniquely identifying. Or worse, when different people use different filenames for your library. Expecting every application that uses the library to later update their `requires` clauses to your new module name is unrealistic.

That puts library maintainers in an awkward position. Even though the library itself is not a module yet, it will be used as such through the automatic modules feature. And when applications start doing so, you're effectively stuck with an automatically derived module name that may or may not be what you want it to be. To solve this conundrum, an alternative way of *reserving* a module name is possible.

Start by adding an `Automatic-Module-Name: <module_name>` entry to a nonmodular JAR in its *META-INF/MANIFEST.MF*. When the JAR is used as automatic module, it will assume the name as defined in the manifest, instead of deriving it from the JAR filename. Library maintainers can now define the name that the library module should have, without creating a module descriptor yet. Simply adding the new entry with the correct module name to *MANIFEST.MF* and repackaging the library is enough. The jar command has an `-m <manifest_file>` option telling it to add entries from a given file to the generated *MANIFEST.MF* in the JAR (➥ *chapter10/modulename*):

```
jar -cfm mylibrary.jar src/META-INF/MANIFEST.MF -C out/ .
```

With this command, the entries from *src/META-INF/MANIFEST.MF* are added to the generated manifest in the output JAR.

With Maven, you can configure the JAR plug-in to add the manifest entry:

```
<plugin>
  <groupId>org.apache.maven.plugins</groupId>
  <artifactId>maven-jar-plugin</artifactId>
  <configuration>
    <archive>
      <manifestEntries>
        <Automatic-Module-Name>
          com.mydomain.mylibrary
        </Automatic-Module-Name>
      </manifestEntries>
    </archive>
  </configuration>
</plugin>
```

You'll read more about Maven support for the module system in Chapter 11.

Reserving a module name with `Automatic-Module-Name` in the manifest is something you should do as quickly as possible. Naming is hard, and picking a name should be done deliberately. However, after settling on a module name, reserving it with `Automatic-Module-Name` is straightforward. It is a low-effort, high-impact move: no code changes or recompilation necessary.

 Add `Automatic-Module-Name` to your library's manifest only if you verified that it works on JDK 9 as an automatic module. The existence of this manifest entry signals Java 9 compatibility. Any migration issues described in earlier chapters must be solved before promoting the use of your library as a module.

Why not create a module descriptor instead? There are several reasons.

First, it involves thinking about what packages to expose or not. You can export everything explicitly, as would happen implicitly when the library is used as an automatic module. However, sanctioning this behavior explicitly in your module descriptor is something you cannot easily take back later. People using your library as an automatic module know that access to all packages is a side effect of it being an automatic module, subject to change later.

Second, and more important, your library can have external dependencies itself. With a module descriptor, your library is no longer an automatic module on the module path. That means it won't automatically have a `requires` relation with all other modules and the classpath (unnamed module) anymore. All dependencies must be made explicit in the module descriptor. Those external dependencies may not yet be modularized themselves, which prevents your library from having a correct module descriptor. Never publish your library with a dependency on an automatic module if that dependency doesn't at least have the `Automatic-Module-Name` manifest entry yet. The name of such a dependency is unstable in that case, causing your module descriptor to be invalid when the dependency's (derived) module name changes

Last, a module descriptor must be compiled with the Java 9 compiler. These are all significant steps that take time to get right. Reserving the module name with a simple `Automatic-Module-Name` entry in the manifest before taking all these steps is sensible.

Creating a Module Descriptor

Now that the library is properly named and usable with Java 9, it's time to think about turning it into an explicit module. For now, we assume the library is a single JAR (*mylibrary.jar*) to be converted to a single module. Later, you may want to revisit the packaging of the library and split it up further.

In "Library Module Dependencies" on page 216, we'll look at more complex scenarios in which the library consists of multiple modules or has external dependencies.

You have two choices with regard to creating a module descriptor: create one from scratch, or use jdeps to generate one based on the current JAR. In any case, it's important that the module descriptor features the same module name as chosen earlier for the Automatic-Module-Name entry in the manifest. This makes the new module a drop-in replacement for the old version of the library when it was used as an automatic module. With a module descriptor in place, the manifest entry can be dropped.

Our example mylibrary (➡ *chapter10/generate_module_descriptor*) is fairly simple and consists of two classes in two packages. The central class MyLibrary contains the following code:

```
package com.javamodularity.mylibrary;

import com.javamodularity.mylibrary.internal.Util;

import java.sql.SQLException;
import java.sql.Driver;
import java.util.logging.Logger;

public class MyLibrary {

    private Util util = new Util();
    private Driver driver;

    public MyLibrary(Driver driver) throws SQLException {
      Logger logger = driver.getParentLogger();
      logger.info("Started MyLibrary");
    }

}
```

Functionally, it doesn't really matter what this code does; the important part is in the imports. When creating a module descriptor, we need to establish what other modules we require. Visual inspection shows the MyLibrary class uses types from java.sql and java.logging in the JDK. The ...internal.Util class comes from a different package in the same *mylibrary.jar*. Instead of trying to come up with the right requires clauses ourselves, we can use jdeps to list the dependencies for us. Besides listing the dependencies, jdeps can even generate an initial module descriptor:

```
jdeps --generate-module-info ./out mylibrary.jar
```

This results in a generated module descriptor in *out/mylibrary/module-info.java*:

```
module mylibrary {
    requires java.logging;
    requires transitive java.sql;
    exports com.javamodularity.mylibrary;
    exports com.javamodularity.mylibrary.internal;
}
```

jdeps analyzes the JAR file and reports dependencies to `java.logging` and `java.sql`. Interestingly, the former gets a `requires` clause, whereas the latter gets a `requires transitive` clause. That's because the `java.sql` types used in `MyLibrary` are part of the public, exported API. The `java.sql.Driver` type is used as an argument to the public constructor of `MyLibrary`. Types from `java.logging`, on the other hand, are used only in the implementation of `MyLibrary` and are not exposed to library users. By default, all packages are exported in the jdeps-generated module descriptor.

 When a library contains classes outside any package (in the *unnamed package*, colloquially known as the *default package*), jdeps produces an error. All classes in a module must be part of a named package. Even before modules, placing classes in the unnamed package was considered a bad practice—especially so for reusable libraries.

You may think this module descriptor provides the same behavior as when `mylibrary` is used as an automatic module. And that's largely the case. However, automatic modules are open modules as well. The generated module descriptor doesn't define an open module, nor does it open any packages. Users of the library will notice this only when doing deep reflection on types from `mylibrary`. When you expect users of your library to do this, you can generate an open module descriptor instead:

```
jdeps --generate-open-module ./out mylibrary.jar
```

This generates the following module descriptor:

```
open module mylibrary {
    requires java.logging;
    requires transitive java.sql;
}
```

All packages will be open because an open module is generated. No `exports` statements are generated by this option. If you add `exports` for all packages to this open module, its behavior is close to using the original JAR as an automatic module.

It's preferable to create a nonopen module, exporting only the minimum number of packages necessary. One of the main draws of turning a library into a module is to benefit from strong encapsulation, something an open module does not offer.

You should always view the generated module descriptor as just a starting point.

Exporting all packages rarely is the right thing to do. For the mylibrary example, it makes sense to remove exports com.javamodularity.mylibrary.internal. There is no need for users of mylibrary to depend on internal implementation details.

Furthermore, if your library uses reflection, jdeps won't find those dependencies. You need to add the right requires clauses for modules you reflectively load from yourself. These can be requires static if the dependency is optional, as discussed in "Compile-Time Dependencies" on page 100. If your library uses services, these uses clauses must be added manually as well. Any services that are provided (through files in *META-INF/services*) are automatically picked up by jdeps and turned into pro vides .. with clauses.

Finally, jdeps suggests a module name based on the filename, as with automatic modules. The caveats discussed in "Choosing a Library Module Name" on page 209 still apply. For libraries, it's better to create a fully qualified name by using reverse-DNS notation. In this example, com.javamodularity.mylibrary is the preferred module name. When the JAR you're generating the module descriptor from already contains an Automatic-Module-Name manifest entry, this name is suggested instead.

Updating a Library with a Module Descriptor

After creating or generating a module descriptor, we're left with a *module-info.java* that still needs to be compiled. Only Java 9 can compile *module-info.java*, but that does not mean you need to switch compilation to Java 9 for your whole project. In fact, it's possible to update the existing JAR (compiled with an earlier Java version) with just the compiled module descriptor. Let's see how that works for *mylibrary.jar*, where we take the generated *module-info.java* and add it:

```
mkdir mylibrary
cd mylibrary
jar -xf ../mylibrary.jar ❶
cd ..
javac -d mylibrary out/mylibrary/module-info.java ❷
jar -uf mylibrary.jar -C mylibrary module-info.class ❸
```

❶ Extract the class files into *./mylibrary*.

❷ Compile just module-info.java with the Java 9 compiler into the same directory as the extracted classes.

❸ Update the existing JAR file with the compiled `module-info.class`.

With these steps, you can create a modular JAR from a pre-Java 9 JAR. The module descriptor is compiled into the same directory as the extracted classes. This way, javac can see all the existing classes and packages that are mentioned in the module descriptor, so it won't produce errors. It's possible to do this without having access to the sources of the library. No recompilation of existing code is necessary—unless, of course, code needs to be changed, for example, to avoid use of encapsulated JDK APIs.

After these steps, the resulting JAR file can be used in various setups:

- On the classpath in pre-Java 9 versions
- On the module path in Java 9 and later
- On the classpath in Java 9

The compiled module descriptor is ignored when the JAR is put on the classpath in earlier Java versions. Only when the JAR is used on the module path with Java 9 or later does the module descriptor come into play.

Targeting Older Java Versions

What if you need to compile the library sources as well as the module descriptor? In many cases, you'll want to target a Java release before 9 with your library. You can achieve this in several ways. The first is to use two JDKs to compile the sources and the module descriptor separately.

Let's say we want `mylibrary` to be usable on Java 7 and later. In practice, this means the library source code can't use any language features introduced after Java 7, nor any APIs added after Java 7. By using two JDKs, we can ensure that our library sources don't depend on Java 7+ features, while still being able to compile the module descriptor:

```
jdk7/bin/javac -d mylibrary <all sources except module-info>
jdk9/bin/javac -d mylibrary src/module-info.java
```

Again, it's essential for both compilation runs to target the same output directory. The resulting classes can then be packaged into a modular JAR just as in the previous example. Managing multiple JDKs can be a bit cumbersome. A new feature, added in JDK 9, allows the use of the latest JDK to target an earlier version.

The `mylibrary` example can be compiled using the new `--release` flag with just JDK 9:

```
jdk9/bin/javac --release 7 -d mylibrary <all sources except module-info>
jdk9/bin/javac --release 9 -d mylibrary src/module-info.java
```

This new flag is guaranteed to support at least three major previous releases from the current JDK. In the case of JDK 9, this means you can compile toward JDK 6, 7, and 8. As an added bonus, you get to benefit from bug fixes and optimizations in the JDK 9 compiler even when your library itself targets earlier releases. If you need to support even earlier versions of Java, you can always fall back to using multiple JDKs.

The Release Flag

The `--release` flag was added through JEP 247 (*http://openjdk.java.net/jeps/247*). Before then, you could use `-source` and `-target` options. Those made sure that you didn't use language features from the wrong level (`-source`) and that the generated bytecode conforms to the right Java release (`-target`). However, these flags did not enforce the right usage of APIs for the target JDK. When compiling with JDK 8, you could specify `-source 1.7 -target 1.7` and still use Java 8 APIs in the code (though language features such as lambdas would be prohibited). Of course, the resulting bytecode doesn't run on JDK 7, because it doesn't ship the new Java 8 APIs. External tools such as *Animal Sniffer* (*http://www.mojohaus.org/animal-sniffer/*) had to be used to verify backward API compatibility. With `--release`, the right library level is enforced by the Java compiler as well—no need to install and manage multiple JDKs anymore.

Library Module Dependencies

So far, we've assumed that the library to be migrated doesn't have any dependencies beyond modules in the JDK. In practice, that's not always the case. There are two main reasons a library has dependencies:

1. The library consists of multiple, related JARs.
2. External libraries are used by the library.

In the first case, there are dependencies between JARs within the library. In the second case, the library needs other external JARs. Both scenarios are addressed next.

Internal Dependencies

We're going to explore the first scenario based on a library you've already seen in Chapter 8: Jackson. Jackson already consists of multiple JARs. The example was based on Jackson Databind, with two related Jackson JARs, as shown in Figure 10-1.

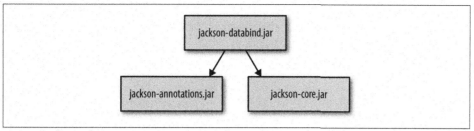

Figure 10-1. Three related Jackson JARs

Turning those JARs into modules is the obvious thing to do, thereby preserving the current boundaries. Luckily, jdeps can also create several module descriptors at once for related JAR files (➥ *chapter10/generate_module_descriptor_jackson*):

```
jdeps --generate-module-info ./out *.jar
```

This results in three generated module descriptors:

```
module jackson.annotations {
    exports com.fasterxml.jackson.annotation;
}

module jackson.core {
    exports com.fasterxml.jackson.core;
    // Exports of all other packages omitted for brevity.
    provides com.fasterxml.jackson.core.JsonFactory with
        com.fasterxml.jackson.core.JsonFactory;
}

module jackson.databind {
    requires transitive jackson.annotations;
    requires transitive jackson.core;
    requires java.desktop;
    requires java.logging;
    requires transitive java.sql;
    requires transitive java.xml;
    exports com.fasterxml.jackson.databind;
    // Exports of all other packages omitted for brevity.
    provides com.fasterxml.jackson.core.ObjectCodec with
        com.fasterxml.jackson.databind.ObjectMapper;
}
```

We can see in the last two module descriptors that jdeps also takes into account service providers. When the JAR contains service provider files (see "ServiceLoader Before Java 9" on page 64 for more information on this mechanism), they are translated into `provides .. with` clauses.

Services uses clauses, on the other hand, cannot be automatically generated by jdeps. These must be added manually based on `ServiceLoader` usage in the library.

The `jacksons.databind` descriptor requires the right platform modules based on the jdeps analysis. Furthermore, it requires the correct other Jackson library modules, whose descriptors are generated in the same run. Jackson's latent structure automatically becomes explicit in the generated module descriptors. Of course, the hard task of demarcating the actual API of the modules is left to the Jackson maintainers. Leaving all packages exported is definitely not desirable.

Jackson is an example of a library that was already modular in structure, consisting of several JARs. Other libraries have made different choices. For example, Google Guava has chosen to bundle all its functionality in a single JAR. Guava aggregates many independently useful parts, ranging from alternative collection implementations to an event bus. However, using it is currently an all-or-nothing choice. The main reason cited (*https://github.com/google/guava/issues/605*) by Guava maintainers for not modularizing the library is backward compatibility. Depending on Guava as a whole must be supported in future versions.

Creating an aggregator module that represents the whole library is one way to achieve this with the module system. In "Building a Facade over Modules" on page 90, we discussed this pattern in the abstract. For Guava, it might look like this:

```
module com.google.guava {
  requires transitive com.google.guava.collections;
  requires transitive com.google.guava.eventbus;
  requires transitive com.google.guava.io;
  // .. and so on
}
```

Each individual Guava module then exports the associated packages for that feature. Guava users can now require `com.google.guava` and transitively get all Guava modules, just as before. Implied readability ensures they can access all Guava types exported by the individual, smaller modules. Or, they can require only the individual modules necessary for the application. It's the familiar trade-off between ease of use at development time or a smaller resolved dependency graph leading to a lower footprint at run-time.

When your library consists of a single large JAR, consider splitting it up when modularizing. In many cases, the maintainability of the library increases, while at the same time users can be more specific about what APIs they want to depend on. Through an aggregator module, backward compatibility is offered for those who want to depend on everything in one go.

Especially if different independent parts of your API have different external dependencies, modularizing your library helps users. They can avoid unnecessary dependencies by requiring only the individual part of your API they need. Consequently, they're not burdened by dependencies thrusted upon them through parts of the API they don't use.

As a concrete example, recall the java.sql module and its dependency on java.xml (as discussed in "Implied Readability" on page 23). The only reason this dependency exists is the SQLXML interface. How many users of the java.sql module are using their database's XML feature? Probably not that many.

Still, all consumers of java.sql now get java.xml "for free" in their resolved module graph. If java.sql were to be split up in java.sql and java.sql.xml, users would have a choice. The latter module then contains the SQLXML interface, doing a requires transitive java.xml (and java.sql). In that case, java.sql itself doesn't need to require java.xml anymore. Users interested in the XML features can require java.sql.xml, whereas everyone else can require java.sql (without ending up with java.xml in the module graph).

Because this requires the breaking change of putting SQLXML in its own package (you can't split a package over multiple modules), this was not an option for the JDK. This pattern is easier to apply to APIs that are already in different packages. If you can pull it off, segregating your modules based on their external dependencies can enormously benefit the users of your library.

External Dependencies

Internal dependencies between libraries can be handled in module descriptors and are even taken care of by jdeps when generating preliminary module descriptors. What about dependencies on external libraries?

Ideally, your library has zero external dependencies (frameworks are a different story altogether). Alas, we don't live in an ideal world.

If those external libraries are explicit Java modules, the answer is quite simple: a `requires (transitive)` clause in the module descriptor of the library suffices.

What if the dependency is not modularized yet? It's tempting to think there's no problem, because any JAR can be used as an automatic module. While true, there's a subtle issue related to naming, which we touched upon already in "Choosing a Library Module Name" on page 209. For the `requires` clause in the library's module descriptor, we need a module name. However, the name of an automatic module depends on the JAR filename, which isn't completely under our control. The true module name could change later, leading to module-resolution problems in applications using our library and the (now) modularized version of the external dependency.

There is no foolproof solution to this issue. Adding a `requires` clause on an external dependency should be done only when you can be reasonably sure the module name is stable. One way to ensure this is to compel the maintainer of the external dependency to claim a module name with the `Automatic-Module-Name` header in the manifest. This, as you have seen, is a relatively small and low-risk change. Then, you can safely refer to the automatic module by this stable name. Alternatively, the external dependency can be asked to fully modularize, which is more work and harder to pull off. Any other approach potentially ends in failure due to an unstable module name.

Maven Central discourages publishing modules referring to automatic modules that don't have a stable name. Libraries should require only automatic modules that have an `Automatic-Module-Name` manifest entry.

One more trick is used by several libraries to manage external dependencies: *dependency shading*. The idea is to avoid external dependencies by inlining external code into the library. Simply put, the class files of the external dependency are copied into the library JAR. To prevent name clashes when the original external dependency would be on the classpath as well, the packages are renamed during the inlining process. For instance, classes from `org.apache.commons.lang3` would be shaded into com.javamodularity.mylibrary.org.apache.commons.lang3. All this is automated and happens at build-time by post-processing bytecode. This prevents the atrociously long package names from seeping into actual source code. Shading is still a viable option with modules. However, it is recommended only for dependencies that are internal to the library. Exporting a shaded package, or exposing a shaded type in an exported API, is not recommended.

After these steps, we have both the internal and external dependencies of the library under control. At this point, our library is a module or collection of modules, targeting the minimum version of Java we want to support. But wouldn't it be nice if the library implementation could use new Java features—while still being able to run it on our minimum supported Java version, that is?

Targeting Multiple Java Versions

One way to use new Java APIs in a library implementation without breaking backward compatibility is to use them optionally. Reflection can be used to locate new platform APIs if they are available, much like the scenario described in "Optional Dependencies" on page 99. Unfortunately, this leads to brittle and hard-to-maintain code. Also, this approach works only for using new platform APIs. Using new language features in the library implementation is still impossible. For example, using lambdas in a library while maintaining Java 7 compatibility is just not possible. The other alternative, maintaining and releasing multiple versions of the same library targeting different Java versions, is equally unattractive.

Multi-Release JARs

With Java 9, a new feature is introduced: multi-release JAR files. This feature allows different versions of the same class file to be packaged inside a single JAR. These different versions of the same class can be built against different major Java platform versions. At run-time, the JVM loads the most appropriate version of the class for the current environment.

It's important to note that this feature is independent of the module system, though it works nicely with modular JARs as well. With multi-release JARs, you can use current platform APIs and language features in your library the moment they are available. Users on older Java versions can still rely on the previous implementation from the same multi-release JAR.

A JAR is multi-release enabled when it conforms to a specific layout and its manifest contains a `Multi-Release: true` entry. New versions of a class need to be in the *META-INF/versions/<n>* directory, where *<n>* corresponds to a major Java platform version. It's not possible to version a class specifically for an intermediate minor or patch version.

As with all manifest entries, no leading or trailing spaces must exist around the `Multi-Release: true` entry. The key and value of the entry are not case-sensitive.

Here's an example of the contents of a multi-release JAR (➡ *chapter10/multirelease*):

```
mrlib.jar
├── META-INF
│   ├── MANIFEST.MF
│   └── versions
│       └── 9
│           └── mrlib
│               └── Helper.class
└── mrlib
    ├── Helper.class
    └── Main.class
```

It's a simple JAR with two top-level class files. The `Helper` class also has an alternative version that uses Java 9 features under *META-INF/versions/9*. The fully qualified name is exactly the same. From the perspective of the library users, there's only one released version of the library, represented by the JAR file. Internal use of the multi-release functionality should not violate that expectation. Therefore, all classes should have the exact same public signature in all versions. Note that the Java runtime does not check this, so the burden is on the developer and tooling to ensure that this is the case.

There are multiple valid reasons for creating a Java 9–specific version of `Helper`. To start, the original implementation of the class might use APIs that are removed or encapsulated in Java 9. The Java 9–specific `Helper` version can use replacement APIs introduced in Java 9 without disrupting the implementation used on earlier JDKs. Or the Java 9 version of `Helper` may use new features simply because they're faster or better.

Because the alternative class file is under the *META-INF* directory, it is ignored by earlier JDKs. However, when running on JDK 9, this class file is loaded instead of the top-level `Helper` class. This mechanism works both on the classpath and on the module path. All classloaders in JDK 9 have been made multi-release-JAR aware. Because multi-release JARs are introduced with JDK 9, only 9 and up can be used under the *versions* directory. Any earlier JDKs will see only the top-level classes.

You can easily create a multi-release JAR by compiling the different sources with different `--release` settings:

```
javac --release 7 -d mrlib/7 src/<all top-level sources>  ❶
javac --release 9 -d mrlib/9 src9/mrlib/Helper.java  ❷
jar -cfe mrlib.jar src/META-INF/MANIFEST.MF -C mrlib/7 .  ❸
jar -uf mrlib.jar --release 9 -C mrlib/9 .  ❹
```

❶ Compile all normal sources at the desired minimum release level.

❷ Compile the code only for Java 9 separately.

❸ Create a JAR file with the correct manifest and the top-level classes.

❹ Update the JAR file with the new `--release` flag, which places class files in the correct *META-INF/versions/9* directory.

In this case, the specific `Helper` version for Java 9 comes from its own *src9* directory. The resulting JAR works on Java 7 and up. Only when running on Java 9 is the specific `Helper` version compiled for Java 9 loaded.

 It's a good idea to minimize the number of versioned classes. Factoring out the differences into a few classes decreases the maintenance burden. Versioning almost all classes in a JAR is undesirable.

After Java 10 is released, we can extend the `mrlib` library with a specific `Helper` implementation for that Java version:

```
mrlib.jar
├── META-INF
│   └── versions
│       ├── 10
│       │   └── mrlib
│       │       └── Helper.class
│       └── 9
│           └── mrlib
│               └── Helper.class
├── mrlib
│   ├── Helper.class
│   └── Main.class
```

Running this multi-release JAR on Java 8 and below works the same as before, using the top-level classes. When running it on Java 9, the `Helper` from *versions/9* is used. However, when running it on Java 10, the most specific match for `Helper` from *versions/10* is loaded. The current JVM always loads the most recent version of a class, up to the version of the Java runtime itself. Resources abide by the same rules as classes. You can put specific resources for different JDK versions under *versions*, and they will be loaded in the same order of preference.

Any class appearing under *versions* must also appear at the top level. However, it's not required to have a specific implementation for each version. In the preceding example, it's perfectly fine to leave out `Helper` under *versions/9*. Running the library on

Java 9 then means it falls back to the top-level implementation, and the specific version is used only on Java 10 and later.

Modular Multi-Release JARs

Multi-release JARs can be modular as well. Adding a module descriptor at the top level is enough. As discussed earlier, *module-info.class* will be ignored when using the JAR on pre-Java 9 runtimes. It's also possible to put the module descriptor under *versions/9* and up instead.

That raises the question of whether it's possible to have different versions of *module-info.class*. Indeed, it is allowed to have versioned module descriptors—for example one under *versions/9* and one under *versions/10*. The allowed differences between module descriptors are minor. These differences should not lead to observable behavior differences across Java versions, much like the way different versions of normal classes must have the same signature.

In practice, the following rules apply for versioned module descriptors:

- Only nontransitive `requires` clauses on `java.*` and `jdk.*` modules may be different.
- Service `uses` clauses may be different regardless of the service type.

Neither the use of services nor the internal dependency on different platform modules leads to observable differences when the multi-release JAR is used on different JDKs. Any other changes to the module descriptor between versions are not allowed. If it is necessary to add (or remove) a `requires transitive` clause, the API of the module changes. This is beyond the scope of what multi-release JARs support. In that case, a new release of the whole library itself is in order.

If you are a library maintainer, you have your work cut out for you. Start by deciding on a module name and claiming it with `Automatic-Module-Name`. Now that your users can use your library as an automatic module, take the next step and truly modularize your library. Last, multi-release JARs lower the barrier for using Java 9 features in your library implementation while maintaining backward compatibility with earlier Java versions.

PART III

Modular Development Tooling

CHAPTER 11

Build Tools and IDEs

In this book, we have been working with java and javac directly on a command line. This is not how most applications are built today. Most projects are built using tools such as Maven or Gradle. These build tools can take care of concerns such as managing the classpath during compilation, dependency management, and building artifacts such as JAR files. On top of that, most developers use an IDE such as Eclipse, IntelliJ IDEA, or NetBeans. IDEs make development easier by providing features such as code completion, error highlighting, refactoring, and code navigation.

Both build tools and IDEs need to know what types are available in a given context. Tools typically interact with the classpath to accomplish this. This significantly changes with the introduction of the Java module system. The classpath is no longer the (only) mechanism that controls which types are available. Tools now have to consider the module path as well. Moreover, there might be a mix of explicit modules, the classpath, and automatic modules. At the time of writing, the tool ecosystem is still working hard on Java 9 support. This chapter introduces some of the available tools, and discusses how they support the Java module system or likely will in the near future.

Apache Maven

Building a single module project with Maven is trivial. We will go over the steps to do this now, but we will not present the code or configuration. An example is included in the GitHub repository if you want to try it out: ➡ *chapter11/single-module*.

Place *module-info.java* in the project's *src/main/java* directory, and Maven will set up the compiler correctly to use the module source path. Dependencies are always put on the module path, even when the dependency isn't modularized yet. This means dependencies that are not modules yet are always handled as automatic modules.

This is different from what we did in Chapter 8 and Chapter 9, where we used a mix of classpath and module path. Both approaches are fine, although putting everything on the module path might hide some future problems. Besides the fact that the output of the project is now a modular JAR, there's really not much else to see. Maven takes care of this nicely.

Although there's not a lot to see on the surface, a lot is happening internally. Apache Maven now has to take the rules of the Java module system into account. The most important changes made to Apache Maven for support of the Java module system are as follows:

- Uses the module path during compilation
- Supports a mix of explicit modules and automatic modules as dependencies

Interestingly enough, the list doesn't include anything about integrating the POM with *module-info.java*, although there is clearly a relationship between dependencies in a POM and `requires` in *module-info.java*. It's not as strange as it might first look. Think about it this way: Apache Maven configures only the module path and classpath. The Java compiler takes this input and uses it to compile sources (including *module-info.java*). Apache Maven replaces the shell scripts we have been using in this book; it doesn't replace the Java compiler. Clearly, we need both, but why doesn't Maven generate a *module-info.java* for us? This has a lot to do with naming of modules.

There are three names in play:

- The module's name defined in *module-info.java*
- The Maven project name defined in *pom.xml*
- The name of the JAR file generated by Maven

We will use the module name when we reference to the module from other *module-info.java* files—for example, to `require` the module. The Maven name is used when adding a dependency to the module on the Maven level, in *pom.xml*. Finally, the JAR file generated by the Maven build is what will be shipped for deployment.

In Maven, a module name, also known as the Maven *coordinate*, has three parts: `groupId` : `artifactId` : `version`. The `groupId` is used for namespacing. Many projects of multiple modules exist, and the `groupId` logically brings them together. Usually the `groupId` is the reverse domain name of the project. The `artifactId` is the name of the module. Unfortunately, different projects use different naming strategies. Sometimes the project name is included in the `artifactId`, sometimes not. Finally, a Maven module is versioned.

A module in the Java module system doesn't have a `groupId`, and doesn't use version information. For public modules, it is recommended to include the reverse domain name of the project in the module name. In any case, the Maven module name, the Java module system module name, and the Maven artifact name will likely be somewhat related, but not the same. Figure 11-1 describes this.

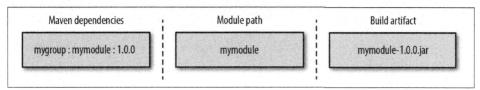

Figure 11-1. Artifact naming

Adding dependencies also requires a two-step approach. First, a dependency needs to be added to the Maven artifact that represents the module, using its Apache Maven *coordinates* in the form of `groupname:artifactname:version`. This isn't any different than it was for Apache Maven in a pre–Java module system world. Second, the dependency needs to be added as a `requires` statement in *module-info.java* to make the types exported by that module available to your code. If you didn't add the dependency in the POM file, the compiler would fail on the `requires` statement because the module couldn't be found. If you didn't add the dependency to *module-info.java*, the dependency would remain effectively unused.

The fact that we reference the dependency in two places also makes it possible that the name of a module isn't necessarily the same as the Apache Maven `group:arti fact:version` coordinate. A dependency may or may not be an explicit module. If no *module-info.class* is found, the dependency becomes an automatic module. This is transparent to the user: there is no difference in using an explicit module or automatic module from the perspective of an Apache Maven user.

We will look at a complete code example of a multimodule project in the next section.

Multimodule Projects

Before the Java module system, it was already common practice to create multimodule projects with Apache Maven. Even without the much stronger constraints that the Java module system brings, this is a great start for modular projects. Each module in a multimodule project has its own POM, a Maven-specific build descriptor in XML format. In the POM, the module's dependencies are configured. This includes dependencies to external libraries as well as dependencies to other modules in the project. Every type used in a module must be part of the module itself, the JDK, or an explicitly configured dependency. Conceptually, this is not very different from what you've seen with the Java module system.

Although multimodule projects are common with Apache Maven, you might wonder what a module exactly is in a pre–Java 9 world. The representation of a module is a JAR file, which is the common artifact produced by Apache Maven. At compile-time, Maven configures the classpath such that it contains only the JAR files that are configured as dependencies. This way, it can emulate similar behavior as what the Java module system enforces by using `requires` in a module descriptor.

Without the Java module system, Apache Maven doesn't support strong encapsulation of packages. If a dependency is configured to another module, every type in that module can be read.

EasyText with Apache Maven

This section walks through migrating EasyText to Maven, the example application that we introduced in Chapter 3. The code itself is unchanged and will not be listed here.

First of all, the EasyText directory structure is changed to conform with the standard Apache Maven directory structure. Each module has its own directory, with an *src/ main/java* directory that contains the module's source files (including *module-info.java*), and *pom.xml* at the root of the module. Also note the *pom.xml* at the root of the project. This is a *parent POM* that makes it possible to compile all the modules with a single command. Here's the directory structure:

```
├── algorithm.api
│   ├── pom.xml
│   └── src
│       └── main
│           └── java
├── algorithm.coleman
│   ├── pom.xml
│   └── src
│       └── main
│           └── java
├── algorithm.kincaid
│   ├── pom.xml
│   └── src
│       └── main
│           └── java
├── algorithm.naivesyllablecounter
│   ├── pom.xml
│   └── src
│       └── main
│           └── java
├── algorithm.nextgensyllablecounter
│   ├── pom.xml
│   └── src
│       └── main
│           └── java
```

```
├── cli
│   ├── pom.xml
│   └── src
│       └── main
│           ├── java
│           └── resources
├── gui
│   ├── pom.xml
│   └── src
│       └── main
│           └── java
└── pom.xml
```

The parent POM contains references to its subprojects, the actual modules. It also configures the compiler plug-in to use Java 9. Example 11-1 is a snippet with the most interesting parts of the *pom.xml* file.

Example 11-1. pom.xml (➥ chapter11/multi-module)

```
<modules>
  <module>algorithm.api</module>
  <module>algorithm.coleman</module>
  <module>algorithm.kincaid</module>
  <module>algorithm.naivesyllablecounter</module>
  <module>algorithm.nextgensyllablecounter</module>
  <module>gui</module>
  <module>cli</module>
</modules>

<build>
  <pluginManagement>
    <plugins>
      <plugin>
        <groupId>org.apache.maven.plugins</groupId>
        <artifactId>maven-compiler-plugin</artifactId>
        <version>3.6.1</version>
        <configuration>
          <release>9</release>
        </configuration>
      </plugin>
    </plugins>
  </pluginManagement>
</build>
```

Note that the `modules` section isn't new and isn't directly related to the Java module system. The modules themselves all have their own *pom.xml* file as well. In it, the module's Apache Maven coordinates are specified (group name, artifact name, and version), as well as its dependencies. Let's take a look at two of them, `easytext.algo rithm.api` and `easytext.algorithm.kincaid`. The API module doesn't have any dependencies, so its *pom.xml* is straightforward, as shown in Example 11-2.

Example 11-2. pom.xml (➡ chapter11/multi-module/algorithm.api)

```
<parent>
  <groupId>easytext</groupId>
  <artifactId>parent</artifactId>
  <version>1.0-SNAPSHOT</version>
</parent>

<artifactId>algorithm.api</artifactId>

<name>Algorithm API</name>
```

In its *module-info.java*, the module is defined as in Example 11-3.

Example 11-3. module-info.java (➡ chapter11/multi-module/algorithm.api)

```
module easytext.algorithm.api {

    exports javamodularity.easytext.algorithm.api;

}
```

Note that technically the group/artifact names are not tied to the module name speci-fied in the module's *module-info.java*. They could be completely different. In any case, just remember that when you're creating a dependency in a *pom.xml* file, you will need to use the Apache Maven coordinates. When you `require` a module in *module-info.java*, you use the name specified in the other module's *module-info.java*; the Apache Maven coordinates don't play any role on that level. Moreover, also notice that the directory name is not required to be the same as the module name.

Running a build will produce *target/algorithm.api-1.0-SNAPSHOT.jar*.

Now let's move on to a module that uses the `easytext.algorithm.api`. In this case, we will have to add a dependency in the module's *pom.xml*, and add a `requires` state-ment in its *module-info.java*, as shown in Example 11-4.

Example 11-4. pom.xml (➡ chapter11/multi-module/algorithm.kincaid)

```
<groupId>easytext</groupId>
<artifactId>algorithm.kincaid</artifactId>
<packaging>jar</packaging>
<version>1.0-SNAPSHOT</version>
<name>algorithm.kincaid</name>

<parent>
  <groupId>easytext</groupId>
  <artifactId>parent</artifactId>
  <version>1.0-SNAPSHOT</version>
</parent>
```

```
<dependencies>
  <dependency>
      <groupId>easytext</groupId>
      <artifactId>algorithm.api</artifactId>
      <version>${project.version}</version>
  </dependency>
</dependencies>
</project>
```

In *module-info.java*, we see the expected `requires`, as shown in Example 11-5.

Example 11-5. module-info.java (➡ chapter11/multi-module/algorithm.kincaid)

```
module easytext.algorithm.kincaid {

    requires easytext.algorithm.api;

    provides javamodularity.easytext.algorithm.api.Analyzer
        with javamodularity.easytext.algorithm.kincaid.KincaidAnalyzer;

    uses javamodularity.easytext.algorithm.api.SyllableCounter;
}
```

Removing either the dependency in *pom.xml* or the `requires` in *module-info.java* results in a compilation error. The exact reasons are subtly different. Removing the dependency from *pom.xml* results in the following error:

```
module not found: easytext.algorithm.api
```

Removing the `requires` statement results in the following error:

```
package javamodularity.easytext.algorithm.api is not visible
```

As discussed previously, Apache Maven configures only the module path. An Apache Maven dependency works at a different level than a `requires` statement in *module-info.java*.

If you've used Apache Maven before, the *pom.xml* files should look familiar. No new syntax or configuration is required in Apache Maven when it comes to working with the Java module system.

This example shows that a properly modularized Apache Maven application is easy to migrate to the Java module system. Essentially, the addition of *module-info.java* files is all that's required. In return, we get encapsulation and a much stronger run-time model.

Running a Modular Application with Apache Maven

We have our example project configured to be built by Apache Maven, but how do we run it? Maven is only a build tool and doesn't have a role at run-time. Maven builds the artifacts we want to run, but in the end we still have to configure the Java runtime to run with the correct module path and/or classpath.

Configuring the module path manually is a lot easier than the classpath, but it would still be duplicate work because the information is in the *pom.xml* files already. Maven has an **exec** plug-in that helps with this process. Remember that this configures only the module path; it doesn't have a run-time presence. The module path will be configured based on the dependencies listed in *pom.xml*. We need to configure the plug-in only with a module and main class to execute. Example 11-6 provides the configuration for the CLI module.

Example 11-6. pom.xml (➥ chapter11/multi-module/algorithm.cli)

```
<build>
  <plugins>
    <plugin>
      <groupId>org.codehaus.mojo</groupId>
      <artifactId>exec-maven-plugin</artifactId>
      <version>1.6.0</version>
      <executions>
        <execution>
          <goals>
            <goal>exec</goal>
          </goals>
        </execution>
      </executions>
      <configuration>
        <executable>${JAVA_HOME}/bin/java</executable>
        <arguments>
          <argument>--module-path</argument>
          <modulepath/>
          <argument>--module</argument>
          <argument>easytext.cli/javamodularity.easytext.cli.Main</argument>
          <argument>${easytext.file}</argument>
        </arguments>
      </configuration>
    </plugin>
  </plugins>
</build>
```

We can execute the plug-in by using the **exec** command to start the application:

```
mvn exec:exec
```

Gradle

At the time of writing, unfortunately, Gradle has no official Java module system support yet. Support is expected and will probably be similar to Maven's. When it comes to modularizing code, Gradle is already in excellent shape. Support for multimodule projects is good, which is a great start to prepare for the Java module system.

IDEs

IDEs such as IntelliJ, Eclipse, and NetBeans all have support for the Java module system, even before the official release of Java 9. The most important feature for an IDE to support the Java module system is understanding `requires` and `exports` in *module-info.java* files. These keywords control what types are available to a module, and an IDE should use this for syntax completion, pointing out errors, and suggestions for module dependencies. All three IDEs support this. This is closely related to the way Java modules map to *projects*, *workspaces*, and *modules* in IDEs. Each IDE has its own structure, and Java modules have to be mapped to this structure.

In Eclipse, each *project* represents a module, assuming it contains a *module-info.java*. As always, projects are grouped in a *workspace*. Both IntelliJ and NetBeans already had their own concept of a *module*, and this now maps directly to Java module system modules.

Editing of *module-info.java* files is also supported by all three IDEs. This includes error highlighting and syntax completion on module names. Some IDEs even support showing a visual module graph based on a module descriptor.

Although this should be mostly transparent to users, clearly some duplication exists in IDEs when it comes to managing project structure. The IDEs have their own internal representation of modules (or projects, in the case of Eclipse). In the past, this model could be synchronized with an external model such as Maven or Gradle. The Java module system model is now a third level of module representation. Although the tools will hide this fact, it can still become somewhat confusing when you dig deeper. Figure 11-2 explains how both Maven and *module-info.java* are used to configure a project within the IDE. The same will likely be true for Gradle in the future.

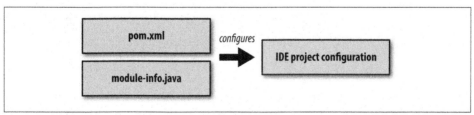

Figure 11-2. Configuring visibility in the IDE

In future releases of tools, we can expect to see much better support for refactoring, hints, and migration to modules.

CHAPTER 12

Testing Modules

Building modular codebases also involves testing. The Java community has always fostered a strong culture of automated testing. Unit tests play a large role in Java software development.

What effect does the module system have on existing testing practices? We want to be able to test code inside modules. In this chapter, we look at two common scenarios:

Blackbox testing

Test modules *from the outside*. Blackbox tests exercise the public API of a module, without knowledge of internals (hence, the *box* is opaque). The tests can test either a single module or several modules at once. As such, you can also characterize these tests as integration tests for modules.

Whitebox testing

Test modules *from the inside*. Instead of taking the outside view, whitebox tests assume knowledge of the internals of a module. These tests are typically unit tests, testing a single class or method in isolation.

Although other testing scenarios are possible, these two cover a wide range of existing practices. Blackbox tests are more restricted in what they can test, but are also more stable because they exercise public APIs. Conversely, whitebox tests can test internal details more easily, at the risk of needing more maintenance.

The focus of this chapter is to highlight the interplay between testing and the module system. It is expected that build tools and IDEs will take care of a lot of the details described in this chapter. Still, it's important to get a feeling for how testing scenarios play out with the module system in place.

For the remainder of this chapter, we assume the following module is under test:

```
easytext.syllablecounter
├── javamodularity
│     └── easytext
│           └── syllablecounter
│                 ├── SimpleSyllableCounter.java
│                 └── vowel
│                       └── VowelHelper.java
└── module-info.java
```

The module descriptor of `easytext.syllablecounter` is as follows:

```
module easytext.syllablecounter {
    exports javamodularity.easytext.syllablecounter;
}
```

The package containing `VowelHelper` is not exported, whereas `SimpleSyllable Counter` is in an exported package. Internally, `SimpleSyllableCounter` uses `Vowel Helper` to implement the syllable-counting algorithm. This distinction becomes important when moving from blackbox to whitebox testing.

In the following sections, we are going to look at what it takes to run both types of tests with modules.

Blackbox Tests

Let's say we want to test the `easytext.syllablecounter` module. Rather than unit testing all internal details, we want to test the functional behavior of the module's API. In this case, that means testing the public API as exposed by `SimpleSyllable Counter`. It has one public method, `countSyllables`.

The easiest way to do so is to create another module that requires `easytext.sylla blecounter`, as shown in Figure 12-1. It is also possible to just put the module and its tests on the classpath. We don't pursue this option here because we want the module to be tested as a module (i.e., including its module descriptor with `requires` and `uses` clauses), not just as some code on the classpath. In "Whitebox Tests" on page 243, where we look at testing the internals of modules, the classpath testing approach is shown.

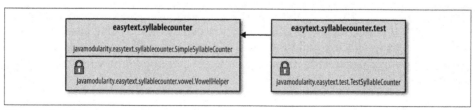

Figure 12-1. Testing module easytext.syllablecounter with a separate easytext.syllable-counter.test module

To start things slowly, we're going to create a test without a testing framework first. Later, we'll adapt the test to use JUnit, a popular unit-testing framework. Example 12-1 presents the code that performs the test, using standard Java asserts for verification purposes.

Example 12-1. Blackbox test for SimpleSyllableCounter (➡ chapter12/blackbox)

```
package javamodularity.easytext.test;

import javamodularity.easytext.syllablecounter.SimpleSyllableCounter;

public class TestSyllableCounter {

  public static void main(String... args) {
    SimpleSyllableCounter sc = new SimpleSyllableCounter();

    assert sc.countSyllables("Bike") == 1;
    assert sc.countSyllables("Motor") == 2;
    assert sc.countSyllables("Bicycle") == 3;

  }

}
```

This code is as simple as it can get: the `main` method instantiates the publicly exported `SimpleSyllableCounter` class and verifies its behavior by using asserts. The test class is placed in its own module with the following descriptor:

```
module easytext.syllablecounter.test {
  requires easytext.syllablecounter;
}
```

Then, it can be compiled and run as usual. We assume the module under test is already compiled in the *out* directory:

```
$ javac --module-path out \ ❶
--module-source-path src-test -d out-test -m easytext.syllablecounter.test
$ java -ea --module-path out:out-test \ ❷
-m easytext.syllablecounter.test/javamodularity.easytext.test.TestSyllableCounter ❸
Exception in thread "main" java.lang.AssertionError
  at easytext.syllablecounter.test/javamodularity.easytext.test.
    TestSyllableCounter.main(TestSyllableCounter.java:12)
```

❶ Compile the test with the module under test on the module path.

❷ Run with assertions enabled (`-ea`) and with both the module under test and the test module on the module path.

❸ Start the test module's class containing the `main` method.

An `AssertionError` is thrown, because the naive syllable–counting algorithm chokes on the word *Bicycle*. That's good, because it means we have a working blackbox test. Before we move on to introducing a test framework to run the test, let's reflect on this blackbox-testing approach.

Testing a module this way has several advantages but also some drawbacks. An advantage of doing blackbox testing is that you can test a module in its *natural habitat*. You're testing the module just as other modules would use it in the application. If, for example, the module under test would offer a service, this can be tested as well in this setup. Just add a `uses` constraint to the module descriptor of the test module, and load the service with `ServiceLoader` in the test.

On the other hand, testing a module this way means that only the exported parts can be tested directly. There's no way to directly test, for example, the encapsulated `Vowel Helper` class. Nor would any nonpublic parts of `SimpleSyllableCounter` be accessible.

 You could run the tests by using, for example, `--add-exports` or `--add-opens` flags to give the test module access to encapsulated parts.

Another limitation is that the test classes need to be in a different package than the classes under test. For unit tests in Java, it's customary to put test classes in a different source folder but under the same package name. The goal of this setup is to be able to test elements that are *package-private* (e.g., a class without the `public` modifier). In the classpath situation, this was no problem. The packages would, as it were, merge when running the tests. However, two modules containing the same package cannot be loaded in the boot layer (as discussed in "Classloading in Layers" on page 132).

Last, all dependencies of the module under test and the test module itself must be satisfied. If `easytext.syllablecounter` had other modules it required, those would need to be on the module path as well. Of course, it's possible to create *mock modules* in those situations. Instead of putting the actual module dependency on the module path, you can create a new module with the same name, containing just enough code to get the test running. Whether you want to do this depends on the scope of the test. Running it with actual modules makes it more of an integration test, whereas running the test with mock modules offers more isolation and control.

Blackbox Tests with JUnit

At this point, we can run test code against `easytext.syllablecounter` from a separate test module. Writing tests using plain asserts in a main method isn't really what you'd expect from tests in Java, though. To fix that, we're going to rewrite the test to use JUnit 4, as shown in Example 12-2.

Example 12-2. JUnit test for SimpleSyllableCounter (➥ chapter12/blackbox)

```
package javamodularity.easytext.test;

import org.junit.Test;
import javamodularity.easytext.syllablecounter.SimpleSyllableCounter;

import static org.junit.Assert.assertEquals;

public class JUnitTestSyllableCounter {

    private SimpleSyllableCounter counter = new SimpleSyllableCounter();

    @Test
    public void testSyllableCounter() {
        assertEquals(1, counter.countSyllables("Bike"));
        assertEquals(2, counter.countSyllables("Motor"));
        assertEquals(3, counter.countSyllables("Bicycle"));
    }

}
```

The test module now has a dependency on JUnit. At run-time, the JUnit test runner will reflectively load our test class to execute the unit-test methods. For this to work, the test package must be exported or opened. An open module suffices:

```
open module easytext.syllablecounter.junit {
  requires easytext.syllablecounter;
  requires junit;
}
```

Figure 12-2 shows the new situation, adding JUnit to the mix.

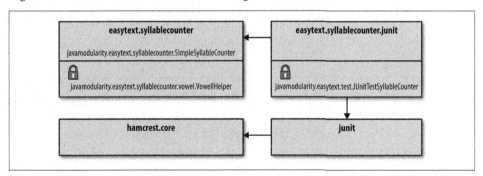

Figure 12-2. The easytext.syllablecounter.junit module depends on the (automatic) module junit

To make this work, we put the JUnit JAR (and its Hamcrest dependency) in a *lib* folder:

```
lib
├── hamcrest-core-1.3.jar
└── junit-4.12.jar
```

Then, JUnit can be used as an automatic module by putting the *lib* folder on the module path. The derived module names are junit and hamcrest.core.

As before, we assume the easytext.syllablecounter module is available in the *out* folder:

```
$ javac --module-path out:lib \  ❶
        --module-source-path src-test -d out-test -m easytext.syllablecounter.junit
$ java --module-path out:lib:out-test \
       -m junit/org.junit.runner.JUnitCore \  ❷
          javamodularity.easytext.test.JUnitTestSyllableCounter

JUnit version 4.12

.E
Time: 0,002
There was 1 failure:
1) initializationError(org.junit.runner.JUnitCommandLineParseResult)
java.lang.IllegalArgumentException: Could not find class
[javamodularity.easytext.test.JUnitTestSyllableCounter]
```

❶ Compile the test with the module under test and JUnit (as an automatic module) on the module path.

❷ Start the JUnitCore test runner from the JUnit (automatic) module.

Running the test is done using the JUnitCore runner class, part of JUnit. It's a simple console-based test runner, where we provide the classname of the test class as a command-line argument. Unfortunately, running the unit test ends in an unexpected exception, saying the JUnitTestSyllableCounter class can't be found by JUnit. Why can it not find the test class? We made the module open so that JUnit can access it at run-time, after all.

The problem is that the test module is never resolved. JUnit is used as the root module for starting the runner. Because it is an automatic module, the other automatic module (hamcrest.core) on the module path gets resolved as well. However, junit does not require easytext.syllablecounter.junit, the module containing our test. Only at run-time does JUnit try to load the test class from the test module using reflection. That doesn't work, because the easytext.syllablecounter.junit module is never resolved by the module system at startup, even though it is on the module path.

To resolve the test module as well, we can define an `--add-modules` statement when starting the test runner:

```
$ java --module-path out:lib:out-test \
       --add-modules easytext.syllablecounter.junit \
       -m junit/org.junit.runner.JUnitCore \
          javamodularity.easytext.test.JUnitTestSyllableCounter

JUnit version 4.12
.E
Time: 0,005
There was 1 failure:
1) testSyllableCounter(javamodularity.easytext.test.JUnitTestSyllableCounter)
java.lang.AssertionError: expected:<3> but was:<1>
```

Now we get a legitimate test failure, meaning JUnit was able to run our test class.

We've extended our blackbox test to use an external test framework. Because JUnit 4.12 is not modularized, it has to be used as an automatic module. Running the test through JUnit is possible only if the test module is resolved and our test class is accessible at run-time.

Whitebox Tests

Now, what if we want to test `VowelHelper` as well? It's a public, but nonexported class with a public method `isVowel` and a package-private method `getVowels`. Unit testing this class means crossing from blackbox testing to whitebox testing.

Access to the encapsulated `VowelHelper` class is necessary. Also, when we want to test package-private functionality, we need our test classes to be in the same package. How can we get these capabilities in a modular setup? Using `--add-exports` or `--add-opens` to expose types for testing works to a limited extent. If test classes need to be in the same package as the classes under test, a package clash between the test module and the module to be tested arises.

There are two major approaches to solving this problem. Which one will be the best in practice remains to be seen. Again, it's mostly up to the build tools and IDEs to lead the way here. We'll examine both approaches, to get a feeling for the underlying mechanisms at play:

- Using the classpath for tests
- Patching modules by injecting tests

The first approach is the most straightforward, because it mostly builds on what was always happening:

```
package javamodularity.easytext.syllablecounter.vowel;

import org.junit.Test;
import javamodularity.easytext.syllablecounter.vowel.VowelHelper;

import static org.junit.Assert.assertEquals;
import static org.junit.Assert.assertTrue;

public class JUnitTestVowelHelper {

    @Test
    public void testIsVowel() {
        assertTrue(VowelHelper.isVowel('e'));
    }

    @Test
    public void testGetVowels() {
        assertEquals(5, VowelHelper.getVowels().size());
    }

}
```

We can test encapsulated code in a compiled module by not treating it as a module at
test-time. Modules placed on the classpath behave as if they have no module descriptor in the first place. Furthermore, split packages between JARs on the classpath do
not pose any issues. If the test class is then compiled outside a module as well, things
work remarkably well:

```
$ javac -cp lib/junit-4.12.jar:out/easytext.syllablecounter \
        -d out-test $(find . -name '*.java')

$ java -cp lib/junit-4.12.jar:lib/hamcrest-core-1.3.jar:\
          out/easytext.syllablecounter:out-test \
        org.junit.runner.JUnitCore \
        javamodularity.easytext.syllablecounter.vowel.JUnitTestVowelHelper
JUnit version 4.12
..
Time: 0,004

OK (2 tests)
```

Of course, using the classpath means we don't benefit from automatic resolving of
modules. Dependencies declared in the module descriptor are not resolved, because a
module on the classpath behaves as a regular, nonmodular JAR. The classpath needs
to be constructed manually. Also, any service provides/uses clauses in the module
descriptor of the module under test are ignored. So, even though the classpath-based
testing approach works, it has several drawbacks. Ultimately, it seems better to test a
module as a module, and not as though it were a nonmodular JAR.

There's a way to keep the module structure intact, while at the same time creating a test class in the same package. Through a feature called *module patching*, new classes can be added to an existing module.

Creating a whitebox unit test within the same module and package works as follows. First, the test class needs to be compiled with the `--patch-module` flag:

```
$ javac --patch-module easytext.syllablecounter=src-test \ ❶
        --module-path lib:out \
        --add-modules junit \ ❷
        --add-reads easytext.syllablecounter=junit \ ❸
        -d out-test $(find src-test -name '*.java')
```

❶ The test sources are compiled *as if they were part* of the `easytext.syllable counter` module. There's no module descriptor for the test code.

❷ Because there's no test module descriptor to require `junit`, it must be added explicitly.

❸ With the test class added to `easytext.syllablecounter`, this module must now read `junit`. There's no `requires` clause in the original module descriptor for that, so `--add-reads` is necessary.

By patching a module, we can compile the unit-test class as part of the already compiled `easytext.syllablecounter` module. Because the test lives in the same package, it can invoke the package-private `getVowels` method.

Making the test class part of the `easytext.syllablecounter` module on the fly does pose some challenges. Steps must be taken to ensure that the module now reads `junit`. At run-time, `junit` must be able to access the test class in a nonexported package. That leads to the following, quite impressive, java invocation:

```
$ java --patch-module easytext.syllablecounter=out-test \ ❶
  --add-reads easytext.syllablecounter=junit \ ❷
  --add-opens \ ❸
  easytext.syllablecounter/javamodularity.easytext.syllablecounter.vowel=junit \
  --module-path lib:out \
  --add-modules easytext.syllablecounter \ ❹
  -m junit/org.junit.runner.JUnitCore \
      javamodularity.easytext.syllablecounter.vowel.JUnitTestVowelHelper

JUnit version 4.12
..
Time: 0,004

OK (2 tests)
```

❶ At run-time, the module must be patched with the compiled test class.

❷ As during compilation, the module needs to read junit, which is not expressed in the module descriptor.

❸ Because junit reflectively instantiates JUnitTestVowelHelper, its containing package needs to be opened or exported to junit.

❹ As before, junit is the initial module and doesn't require easytext.syllable counter, so it must be added explicitly.

Unlike with the compiler invocation, there is no need to have --add-modules junit. JUnit is used as root module to run, and is therefore already resolved.

In Figure 12-3, you can see the whole picture of what patching a module to run unit tests entails.

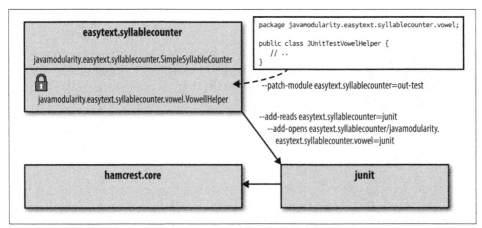

Figure 12-3. The JUnitTestVowelHelper class (in the same package as VowelHelper) is patched into the easytext.syllablecounter module

This second approach has quite a few moving parts. On the upside, all features of the module are taken into account at test-time as well. The module's dependencies are resolved, and uses/provides clauses are taken into account. On the downside, setting up all the correct command-line flags seems like a lot of wizardry. Even though we could explain why everything needs to be done this way, it's still a lot to take in.

In practice, setting up all the intricate details for unit-testing scenarios shouldn't be up to developers. Build tools and development environments offer their own test runners for most of the popular testing frameworks. These runners should take care of setting up the environment such that tests are automatically patched into modules.

Test Tooling

Test frameworks such as JUnit and TestNG are well supported by IDEs as well as build tools. Typically, they are used to write and run whitebox unit-tests. Most tools are currently taking the classpath route to run tests, even when code includes a module descriptor. This way, the module descriptor is basically ignored, as is strong encapsulation. Because of this, tests run the same way you're used to. This also keeps compatibility with existing project structures, where the application code and test code are in different folders but in the same package structure.

If code is relying on services using the new keywords in module descriptors, this will not automatically work on the classpath. Then, the blackbox testing scenario described in this chapter is more appropriate. There is no specific support for these scenarios in the current versions of test frameworks. It is to be expected that new tools, or support in existing tools, will be created to help with testing modules following the strategies in this chapter.

CHAPTER 13

Scaling Down with Custom Runtime Images

Now that you've seen all the tools and processes to work with modular applications, there's one more exciting opportunity to explore. In "Linking Modules" on page 41, you got a taste of creating runtime images tailored to a specific application. Only the modules required to run the application become part of the image. A minimal runtime image can be automatically generated with jlink by using explicit dependency information available in modules.

Creating a custom runtime image is beneficial for several reasons:

Ease of use
jlink delivers a self-contained distribution of your application and the JVM, ready to be shipped.

Reduced footprint
Only the modules that your application uses are linked into the runtime image.

Performance
A custom runtime potentially runs faster by virtue of link-time optimizations that are otherwise too costly or impossible.

Security
With only the minimum required platform modules in a custom runtime image, the attack surface decreases.

Even though creating a custom runtime image is an optional step, having a smaller binary distribution that runs faster is a compelling motivation—especially when applications target resource-constrained devices, such as embedded systems; or, when they run in the cloud, where everything is metered. Putting a custom runtime image into a Docker container is a good way to create resource-efficient cloud deployments.

 Other initiatives are improving Java's support for containers. For example, OpenJDK 9 now also offers an Alpine Linux port. Running the JDK or a custom runtime image on top of this minimalistic Linux distribution is another way to reduce the footprint of the deployment.

Another advantage of distributing the Java runtime with your application: there's no more mismatch between already installed Java versions and the version your application needs. Traditionally, either a Java Runtime Environment (JRE) or Java Development Kit (JDK) must be installed before running Java applications.

 The JRE is a subset of the JDK, designed to *run* Java applications rather than to *develop* Java applications. It has always been offered as a separate download geared toward end users.

A custom runtime image is fully self-contained. It bundles the application modules with the JVM and everything else it needs to execute your application. No other Java installation (JDK/JRE) is necessary. Distributing, for example, JavaFX-based desktop applications becomes easier this way. By creating a custom runtime image, you can offer a single download containing the application and the runtime environment. On the flip side, an image is not portable, because it targets a specific OS and architecture. In "Cross-Targeting Runtime Images" on page 262, we'll discuss how to create images for different target systems.

It's time to take a deep dive into what jlink is capable of. Before you look at the tool itself, we'll first discuss linking and how it opens up new possibilities for Java applications.

Static Versus Dynamic Linking

Creating a custom runtime image can also be characterized as a form of static linking for modules. *Linking* is the process of bringing together compiled artifacts into an efficiently executable form. Traditionally, Java has always employed *dynamic linking* at the class level. Classes are lazily loaded at run-time, and wired together dynamically where necessary at any point in time. The just-in-time (JIT) compiler of the virtual machine is then responsible for compilation to native code at run-time. During this process, the JVM applies optimizations to the resulting ensemble of classes. Although this model allows for great flexibility, optimizations that are straightforward in more static situations are harder (or even impossible) to apply in this dynamic landscape.

Other languages make different trade-offs. Go, for example, prefers to statically link all code into a single binary. In C++, you can choose to link statically or dynamically. With the introduction of the module system and jlink, we now have that choice in Java as well. Classes are still dynamically loaded and linked in custom runtime images. However, the available modules from which classes can be loaded can be statically predetermined.

An advantage of static linking is that it affords optimizations across the whole application ahead of time. Effectively, this means optimizations can be applied across class and module boundaries, taking into account the whole application. This is possible only because through the module system we have up-front knowledge about what the whole application actually entails. All modules are known, from the root module (the entry point of an application), to the libraries, all the way through to the required platform modules. A resolved module graph represents the whole application.

 Linking is not the same as ahead-of-time (AOT) compilation. A runtime image generated with jlink still consists of bytecode, not native code.

Examples of whole-program optimizations are dead-code elimination, constant folding, and inlining. It's beyond the scope of this book to describe these optimizations. Fortunately, much literature is available.[1]

The applicability and effectiveness of many of these optimizations hinges on the assumption that all relevant code is available at the same time. The linking phase is that time, and jlink is the tool to do so.

---

1 A good language-agnostic introduction can be found in "Whole-Program Optimization of Object-Oriented Languages" (*http://bit.ly/chambers-et-al*) by Craig Chambers et al.

Using jlink

Back in "Linking Modules" on page 41, we created a custom runtime image consisting of just a `helloworld` module and `java.base`. Toward the end of Chapter 3, we created a much more interesting application: EasyText, with its multiple analyses and CLI/GUI frontends. Just as a reminder, running the GUI frontend on top of a full JDK is achieved by setting up the right module path and starting the right module:

```
$ java -p mods -m easytext.gui
```

Assuming the *mods* directory contains the modular JARs for EasyText, this results in the situation depicted in Figure 13-1 at run-time.

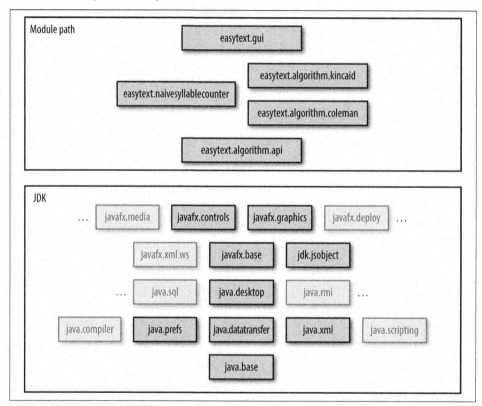

Figure 13-1. Modules resolved at run-time when running easytext.gui. Grayed-out modules are available in the JDK but not resolved.

At JVM startup, the module graph is constructed. Starting with the root module `easy text.gui`, all dependencies are recursively resolved. Both application modules and platform modules are part of the resolved module graph. However, as Figure 13-1 shows, many more platform modules are available in the JDK than strictly necessary for this application. The grayed-out modules are only the tip of the iceberg, because about 90 platform modules exist. Only nine of them are necessary to run easy text.gui with its JavaFX UI.

Let's get rid of this dead weight by creating a custom runtime image for EasyText. The first choice we must make is, what exactly should be part of the image? Just the GUI, just the CLI, or both? You could create multiple images targeting distinct groups of users of your application. There's no general right or wrong answer to this question. Linking is explicitly composing modules together into a coherent whole.

For now, let's settle on creating a runtime image just for the GUI version of EasyText. We invoke jlink with easytext.gui as the root module:

```
$ jlink --module-path mods/:$JAVA_HOME/jmods              \ ❶
        --add-modules easytext.gui                        \ ❷
        --add-modules easytext.algorithm.coleman          \
        --add-modules easytext.algorithm.kincaid          \
        --add-modules easytext.algorithm.naivesyllablecounter \
        --launcher easytext=easytext.gui                  \ ❸
        --output image ❹
```

❶ Set the module path where jlink can find modules, including platform modules in the JDK.

❷ Add root modules to be included in the runtime image. Besides easytext.gui, service provider modules are added as root modules as well.

❸ Define the name of a launcher script to be part of the runtime image, indicating the module it should run.

❹ Set the output directory where the image is generated into.

> The jlink tool lives in the *bin* directory of the JDK installation. It is not added to the system path by default, so in order to use it as shown in the preceding example, you must add it to the path first.

It's possible to provide multiple root modules separated by commas as well, instead of the multiple --add-modules used here.

The specified module path explicitly includes the JDK directory containing platform modules (*$JAVA_HOME/jmods*). This is different from what you've seen when using java and javac: there the platform modules are assumed to come from the same JDK you run java or javac from. In "Cross-Targeting Runtime Images" on page 262, you'll see why this is different for jlink.

As discussed in "Services and Linking" on page 75, service provider modules must be added as root modules as well. Resolving the module graph happens only through `requires` clauses; jlink does not follow `uses` and `provides` dependencies by default. In "Finding the Right Service Provider Modules" on page 256, we'll show you how to find the right service provider modules to add.

 You can add the `--bind-services` flag to jlink. This instructs jlink to take into account `uses`/`provides` as well when resolving modules. However, this also binds all services between platform modules. Because `java.base` already uses a lot of (optional) services, this quickly leads to a larger set of resolved modules than strictly necessary.

Each of these root modules is resolved, and these root modules along with their recursively resolved dependencies become part of the generated image in *./image*, as shown in Figure 13-2.

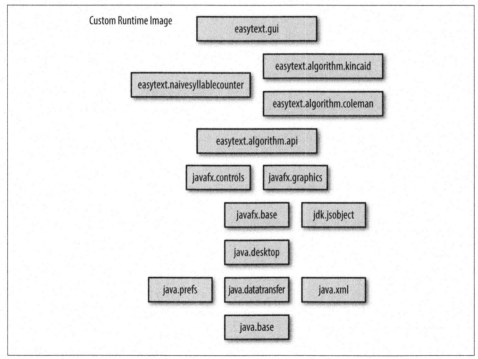

Figure 13-2. A custom runtime image contains only the modules necessary for the application

The generated image has the following directory layout, which is similar to the JDK:

```
image
├── bin
├── conf
├── include
├── legal
└── lib
```

In the *bin* directory of the generated runtime image, you'll find an *easytext* launcher script. It's created because of the `--launcher easytext=easytext.gui` flag. The first argument is the name of the launcher script, and the second argument is the module it starts. This script is an executable convenience wrapper that starts the JVM directly with **easytext.gui** as the initial module to run. You can directly execute it from the command line by invoking *image\bin\easytext*. On other platforms, similar scripts are generated (see "Cross-Targeting Runtime Images" on page 262 for how to target other platforms). Windows runtime images get batch files instead of shell scripts for Unix-like targets.

A launcher script can be created for modules containing a class with an entry point (static main method). That's the case if we create the **easytext.gui** modular JAR as follows:

```
jar --create                                    \
    --file mods/easytext.gui.jar                \
    --main-class=javamodularity.easytext.gui.Main \
    -C out/easytext.gui .
```

You can also build a runtime image from exploded modules. In that case, there's no main class attribute from the modular JAR, so it must be explicitly added to the jlink invocation:

```
--launcher easytext=easytext.gui/javamodularity.easytext.gui.Main
```

This approach also works if there are multiple classes with main methods in a modular JAR. Regardless of whether specific launcher scripts are created, you can always start the application by using the image's java command:

```
image/bin/java -m easytext.gui/javamodularity.easytext.gui.Main
```

There's no need to set the module path when running the java command from the runtime image. All necessary modules are already in the image through the linking process.

We can show that the runtime image indeed contains the bare minimum of modules by running the following:

```
$ image/bin/java --list-modules
easytext.algorithm.api@1.0
easytext.algorithm.coleman@1.0
easytext.algorithm.kincaid@1.0
```

```
easytext.algorithm.naivesyllablecounter@1.0
easytext.gui@1.0
java.base@9
java.datatransfer@9
java.desktop@9
java.prefs@9
java.xml@9
javafx.base@9
javafx.controls@9
javafx.graphics@9
jdk.jsobject@9
```

This corresponds to the modules shown in Figure 13-2.

The *bin* directory can contain other executables besides the launcher scripts discussed so far. In the EasyText GUI image, the *keytool* and *appletviewer* binaries are also added. The former is always present, because it originates from `java.base`. The latter is part of the image because the included `java.desktop` module exposes applet functionality. Because other well-known JDK command-line tools such as jar, rmic, and javaws all depend on modules that are not in this runtime image, jlink is smart enough to omit them.

Finding the Right Service Provider Modules

In the previous EasyText jlink example, we added several service provider modules as root modules. As mentioned earlier, it is possible to use the `--bind-services` option of jlink and let jlink resolve all service provider modules from the module path instead. While tempting, this quickly leads to an explosion of modules in the resulting image. Blindly adding all possible service providers for a given service type is rarely the right thing to do. It pays to think about what service providers are right for your application and add those as root modules yourself.

Fortunately, you can get help from jlink in selecting the right service provider modules by using the `--suggest-providers` option. In the following jlink invocation, we add only the `easytext.gui` module and ask for suggestions of provider modules for the `Analyzer` type:

```
$ jlink --module-path mods/:$JAVA_HOME/jmods \
        --add-modules easytext.gui \
        --suggest-providers javamodularity.easytext.algorithm.api.Analyzer

Suggested providers:
  module easytext.algorithm.coleman provides
        javamodularity.easytext.algorithm.api.Analyzer,
        used by easytext.cli,easytext.gui
  module easytext.algorithm.kincaid provides
        javamodularity.easytext.algorithm.api.Analyzer,
        used by easytext.cli,easytext.gui
```

You can then select one or more provider modules by adding them with `--add-modules <module>`. Of course, when these newly added modules have uses clauses themselves, another invocation of `--suggest-providers` is in order. For example, in EasyText, the `easytext.algorithm.kincaid` service provider module itself has a uses constraint on the `SyllableCounter` service type.

It's also possible to leave off the specific service type after `--suggest-providers` and get a complete overview. This includes service providers from platform modules as well, so the output can quickly get overwhelming.

Module Resolution During Linking

Although the module path and module resolution in jlink appear to behave similarly to other tools you've seen so far, important differences exist. One exception you've already seen is that platform modules need to be added explicitly to the module path.

Another important exception involves automatic modules. When you put a nonmodular JAR on the module path with java or javac, it is treated as valid module for all intents and purposes (see "Automatic Modules" on page 173). However, jlink does not recognize nonmodular JARs on the module path as automatic modules. Only when your application is fully modularized, including all libraries, can you use jlink.

The reason is automatic modules can read from the classpath, bypassing the module system's explicit dependencies. In a custom runtime image, there is no predefined classpath. Automatic modules in the resulting image could therefore cause run-time exceptions. When they rely on classes from the classpath that won't be there, the application blows up at run-time. Allowing this situation voids the reliable configuration guarantees of the module system.

Of course, when you're absolutely sure an automatic module is well behaved (i.e., it requires only other modules and nothing from the classpath), this situation is unfortunate. In that case, you can work around this limitation by turning the automatic module into an explicit module. You can use jdeps to generate the module descriptor (as discussed in "Creating a Module Descriptor" on page 211) and add it to the JAR. Now you have a module that can be put on jlink's module path. This is not an ideal situation; patching other people's code never is. Automatic modules are really a transitional feature to aid migration. When you run into this jlink limitation, it's a good time to contact the maintainer of the library in question to urge them to modularize it.

Last, the same caveats with respect to modules using reflection apply during linking, as with running modules on a full JDK. If a module uses reflection and does not list those dependencies in the module descriptor, the resolver cannot take this into account. Consequently, the module containing the code that is reflected upon may not be included in the image. To prevent this, add the modules manually with `--add-modules`, so they end up in the runtime image anyway.

jlink for Classpath-Based Applications

It seems as though jlink is usable only with fully modularized applications. That's true only in part. You can also use jlink to create custom images of the Java platform without involving any application modules. For example, you can run

```
jlink --module-path $JAVA_HOME/jmods --add-modules java.logging --output image
```

and get an image containing just the `java.logging` (and the mandatory `java.base`) module. That may seem only marginally useful, but this is where things get interesting. If you have an existing classpath-based application, there's no way to use jlink directly on application code to create a custom runtime image for that application. There are no module descriptors for jlink to resolve any modules.

However, what you can do is use a tool such as jdeps to find the minimal set of platform modules necessary to run the application. If you then construct an image containing just these modules, you can later start your classpath-based application on this image without issues.

That probably sounds a bit abstract, so let's look at a simple example. In "Using the Modular JDK Without Modules" on page 30, Example 2-5, we already had a simple `NotInModule` class that uses the `java.logging` platform module. We can inspect this class with jdeps to verify that is the only dependency:

```
$ jdeps out/NotInModule.class

NotInModule.class -> java.base
NotInModule.class -> java.logging
    <unnamed>                        -> java.lang             java.base
    <unnamed>                        -> java.util.logging     java.logging
```

For larger applications, you would analyze the JARs of the application and its libraries in the same manner. Now you know which platform modules are necessary to run the application. For our example, that's just `java.logging`. We already created the image containing only the `java.logging` module earlier in this section. By putting the `NotInModule` class on the classpath of the runtime image, we can run this classpath-based application on a stripped-down Java distribution:

```
image/bin/java -cp out NotInModule
```

The `NotInModule` class is on the classpath (assuming it's in the *out* directory), so it is in the unnamed module. The unnamed module reads all other modules, which, in the case of this custom runtime image, is the tiny set of two modules: `java.base` and `java.logging`. Through these steps, you can create custom runtime images even for classpath-based applications. Had EasyText been a classpath-based application, the same steps would result in an image containing the nine platform modules shown in Figure 13-1.

There are some caveats. When your application tries to load classes from modules that are not in the runtime image, NoClassDefFoundError is raised at run-time. This is similar to the situation where your classpath lacks a necessary JAR. It is up to you to list the right set of modules for jlink to put into the image. At link-time, jlink doesn't even see your application code, so it cannot help with module resolution as it can in the case of a fully modularized application. jdeps is helpful to get a first estimation of the required modules, but use of reflection in your application can, for example, not be detected by the static analysis of jlink. Testing your application on the resulting image is therefore important.

Furthermore, not all performance optimizations discussed in the subsequent sections are applicable to this classpath-based scenario. Many optimizations work because all code is available at link-time—which is not the case in the scenario we just discussed. The application code is never seen by the linker. In this scenario, jlink works only with the platform modules you add to the image explicitly, and their resolved platform module dependencies.

This use of jlink shows how the lines between the JDK and JRE have blurred in a modular world. Linking allows you to create a Java distribution with any desired set of platform modules. You're not confined to the options offered by the platform vendors.

Reducing Size

Now that we have the basic use of jlink covered, it's time to turn our attention to the optimizations we were promised. jlink uses a plug-in-based approach to support different optimizations. All flags introduced in this section and the next section are handled by jlink plug-ins. The aim is not to give an exhaustive overview of all plug-ins, but rather to highlight some plug-ins to illustrate the possibilities. The number of jlink plug-ins is expected to grow steadily over time, both by the JDK team and the community at large.

You can get an overview of all currently available plug-ins by running jlink --list-plugins. Some plug-ins are enabled by default; this is indicated in the output of this command. In this section, we'll look at plug-ins that can reduce the disk size of run-time images. The next section covers run-time performance improvements.

Creating a custom runtime image as we did for EasyText already reduces the size on disk relative to a full JDK by leaving out unnecessary platform modules. Still, there's more to be gained. You can use several flags to trim the image size even further.

The first one is --strip-debug. As the name implies, it removes native debug symbols and strips debug information from classes. For a production build, this is what you want. However, it is not enabled by default. Empirical evidence shows roughly a 10 percent reduction in image size with this flag enabled.

You can also compress the resulting image with the --compress=n flag. Currently, n can be 0, 1, or 2. It does two things on the highest setting. First, it creates a table of all string literals used in classes, sharing the representation across the whole application. Then, it applies a generic compression algorithm on the modules.

The next optimization affects the JVM that is put into the runtime image. With --vm=<vmtype>, different types of VMs can be selected. Valid options for vmtype are server, client, minimal, and all (which is the default). If a small footprint is your most important concern, choose the minimal option. It offers a VM with only a single garbage collector, one JIT compiler, and no serviceability or instrumentation support. At the moment, the minimal VM option is available only for Linux.

The last optimization concerns locales. Normally, the JDK ships with many locales to suit different date/time formats, currencies, and other locale-sensitive information. The default English locales are part of java.base, and so are always available. All other locales are part of the module jdk.localedata. Because this is a separate module, you can choose to add it to a runtime image or not. Services are used to expose the locale functionality from java.base and jdk.localedata. This means you must use --add-module jdk.localedata during linking if your application needs a non-English locale. Otherwise, locale-sensitive code simply falls back to the default English locale, because no other locales are available in the absence of jdk.locale data. Remember, service provider modules are not resolved automatically, unless --bind-services is used.

A similar situation arises when your application uses character sets that are not part of the default sets (i.e., US-ASCII, ISO-8859-1, UTF-8, UTF-16). Traditionally, these nondefault character sets were available through *charsets.jar* in the full JDK. With the modular JDK, add the jdk.charsets module to your image in order to use nondefault character sets.

However, jdk.locale is quite large. Adding this module easily increases the size on disk with about 15 megabytes. In many cases, you don't need *all* locales in the image. If that's the case, you can use the --include-locales flag of jlink. It takes a list of *language tags* as an argument (see the java.util.Locale JavaDoc for more information on valid language tags). The jlink plug-in then strips the jdk.locale module from all other locales. Only the resources for the specified locales will remain in the jdk.locale module that ends up in the image.

Improving Performance

The previous section presented a range of optimizations pertaining to the size of the image on disk. What's even more interesting is the ability of jlink to optimize runtime performance. Again, this is achieved by plug-ins, some of which are enabled by default. Keep in mind that jlink and its plug-ins are still at an early stage and mostly aimed at improving startup time of applications. Many of the plug-ins discussed in this section are still experimental in JDK 9. Most of the performance optimizations available require in-depth knowledge of how the JDK works.

A lot of the experimental plug-ins generate code at link-time to improve startup performance. One optimization that is enabled by default is the pre-creation of a platform module descriptor cache. The idea is that when building the image, you know exactly which platform modules are part of the module graph. By creating a combined representation of their module descriptors at link-time, the original module descriptors don't have to be parsed individually at run-time. This decreases the JVM startup time.

In addition, other plug-ins perform bytecode rewriting at link-time to achieve runtime performance gains. An example is the `--class-for-name` optimization. It rewrites instructions of the form `Class.forName("pkg.SomeClass")` to static references to that class, thus avoiding the overhead of reflectively searching for the class at run-time. Another example is a plug-in that pre-generates *method handles* invocation classes (extending `java.lang.invoke.MethodHandle`), which would otherwise be generated at run-time. While this may sound esoteric, the implementation of Java lambdas makes heavy use of the method handles machinery. By absorbing the cost of class generation at link-time, applications that use lambdas start faster. Unfortunately, using this plug-in currently requires highly specialized knowledge of the way method handles work.

As you can see, many plug-ins offer quite specialized performance-tuning scenarios. There are so many possible optimizations, a tool such as jlink is never *done*. Some optimizations are better suited to some applications than others. This is one of the prime reasons jlink features a plug-in-based architecture. You can even write your own jlink plug-ins, although the plug-in API itself is marked experimental in the Java 9 release.

Optimizations that have traditionally been too costly to perform just-in-time by the JVM are now viable at link-time. What's remarkable is that jlink can optimize code coming from any module, whether it's an application module, a library module you use, or a platform module. However, because jlink plug-ins allow arbitrary bytecode rewriting, their usefulness extends beyond performance enhancements. Many tools and frameworks currently use JVM agents to perform bytecode rewriting at run-time. Think of instrumentation agents or bytecode enhancing agents from Object-Relation

Mappers such as OpenJPA. In some cases, these transformations can be applied up front at link-time. A jlink plug-in can be a good alternative (or complement) to some of these JVM agent implementations.

Keep in mind, this is the territory of advanced libraries and tools. You are unlikely to write your own jlink plug-in as part of a typical application development process, just as you are unlikely to write your own JVM agent.

Cross-Targeting Runtime Images

A custom runtime image created by jlink runs on only a specific OS and architecture. This is similar to how JDK or JRE distributions differ for Windows, Linux, macOS, and so forth. They contain platform-specific native binaries necessary to run the JVM. You download a Java runtime for your specific OS, and on top of that you run your portable Java applications.

In the examples so far, we've built images by using jlink. jlink is part of the JDK (which is platform-specific), but it can create images for different platforms. Doing so is straightforward. Instead of adding the platform modules of the JDK currently running jlink to the module path, you point at the platform modules of the OS and architecture you want to target. Obtaining these alternative platform modules is as easy as downloading the JDK for that platform and extracting it.

Let's say we are running on macOS and want to create an image for Windows (32-bit). First, download the correct JDK for 32-bit Windows, and extract it into *~/jdk9-win-32*. Then, use the following jlink invocation:

```
$ jlink --module-path mods/:~/jdk9-win-32/jmods  ...
```

The resulting image contains your application modules from *mods* bundled with platform modules from the Windows 32-bit JDK. Additionally, the */bin* directory of the image contains Windows batch files instead of macOS scripts. All that's left to do now is distributing the image to the correct target!

Runtime images built with jlink don't update automatically. You are responsible for building updated runtime images when a new Java version is released. Ensure that you distribute only runtime images created from an up-to-date Java version to prevent security issues.

You have seen how jlink can create lean runtime images. When your application is modularized, using jlink is straightforward. Linking is an optional step, which can make a lot of sense when targeting resource-constrained environments.

CHAPTER 14

A Modular Future

We're nearing the end of our journey through the Java module system—starting from the modular JDK, all the way through creating your own modules and migrating existing code to modules. On the one hand, there's a lot of new functionality around modules to take in. On the other hand, Java modules simply encourage tried-and-true best practices around modular development.

Using modules for new code is recommended except for the smallest of applications. Applying strong encapsulation and managing explicit dependencies from the start lays a solid foundation for maintainable systems. It also unlocks new capabilities such as creating a custom runtime image with jlink.

Entering the modular future of Java requires adherence to the principles of modularity. When your existing applications have a modular design, the transition will be smooth. Many people already use multimodule Maven or Gradle builds for their applications. Often these existing module boundaries map naturally to Java modules. In some cases, the `ServiceLoader` mechanism offered by the JDK is a good alternative to using a full-blown dependency injection framework.

However, when your applications are anything but modular, the transition will be challenging.

You saw in earlier chapters that it is certainly possible to migrate existing applications to modules. When their design is lacking in modularity, though, you effectively take on two problems at the same time during migration. The first is untangling the architecture so that it conforms to the principles of modularity. The second is the actual migration to Java 9 and its module system.

Whether it is worth to take on this effort is a trade-off that cannot be captured in a general guideline. It depends on the scope of the system, expected lifetime, and many other context-dependent variables. Note that even the massive JDK succeeded in modularizing itself, although that took years of hard work. Clearly, where there's a will, there's a way. Whether the benefits outweigh the costs is the main question to be answered for existing codebases. There is no shame in leaving an application on the classpath.

In the remainder of this chapter, we take stock of the Java module system in the existing landscape of modular development approaches.

OSGi

Long before the Java module system, other module systems emerged. These existing systems offer application-level modularity only, whereas the Java module system also modularizes the platform itself. The oldest and most well-known existing module system is OSGi. It offers run-time modularity by running bundles (JARs with OSGi wiring metadata) in an OSGi container. Isolation between bundles is achieved by controlling visibility of classes through a clever arrangement of classloaders. Essentially, each bundle is loaded by its own, isolated classloader, delegating only to other classloaders based on the bundle's metadata. Isolation through classloaders happens only at run-time inside the OSGi container. At build-time, development tools such as Bndtools or Eclipse PDE must be used to enforce strong encapsulation and dependencies.

Does OSGi become obsolete with the introduction of the Java module system? Far from it. First of all, existing OSGi applications can keep running on Java 9 by using the classpath. When you have an OSGi-based system, there's no rush to make your bundles into Java modules. Also, the OSGi Alliance is doing preliminary work on interoperability between OSGi bundles and Java modules.

The question then becomes: when to use OSGi and when to use the Java module system for new systems? To answer that question, it's important to understand how OSGi and the Java module system differ.

There are some notable differences between OSGi and the Java module system:

Package dependencies

OSGi bundles express dependencies on packages, not directly on other bundles (though this is possible as well). The OSGi resolver wires together bundles based on the exported and imported packages given in the bundle metadata. This makes a bundle's name less important than a Java module name. Bundles export at the package level, just like Java modules.

Versioning

Unlike modules in Java, OSGi has versions for both bundles and packages. Dependencies can be expressed on exact versions or version ranges. Because each bundle is loaded in a separate classloader, multiple versions of a bundle can coexist, although this is not without caveats.

Dynamic loading

Bundles can be loaded, unloaded, started, and stopped inside an OSGi runtime. There are callbacks for these bundle life-cycle events, since bundles must cope with this dynamic environment. Java modules can be loaded at run-time in `Modu leLayers`, and be garbage collected later. In contrast with OSGi bundles, no explicit life-cycle callbacks are defined for Java modules, because a more static configuration is assumed.

Dynamic services

OSGi also defines a services mechanism with a central service registry. The API for OSGi services is richer than what is offered by Java's `ServiceLoader`. High-level frameworks (such as Declarative Services) are offered on top of basic OSGi services. OSGi services can come and go at run-time, not in the least because bundles offering them can come and go dynamically. Java services with `Service Loader` are wired once during module resolution. Only with `ModuleLayer` can new services be introduced at run-time. Unlike OSGi services, they do not support start and stop callbacks.

A repeating theme across these differences is that OSGi supports more-dynamic scenarios in its runtime. OSGi has more features in this regard than the Java module system. This is partly because OSGi's roots are in embedded systems. Zero downtime updates are possible because OSGi bundles can be hot-swapped. New hardware can be plugged in, and services supporting them can be dynamically started.

In enterprise software, this same paradigm can extend to other resources with dynamic availability at run-time. If you need these dynamics, OSGi is the way to go. OSGi's dynamic life cycle does add some complexity for developers. Part of this inherent complexity can be abstracted away during development by using higher-level frameworks such as Declarative Services. In practice, many applications (including those using OSGi) tend to wire together services at startup, without any dynamic changes afterward. In those cases, the Java module system offers enough functionality out of the box.

Tooling around OSGi has been a source of frustration to many developers. It just doesn't have the critical mass behind it to get full attention of the community and vendors, even after more than a decade. With modules being part of the Java platform, vendors are already creating tooling and support ahead of its release. Because the OSGi framework is in action only at run-time, tooling has to mimic its rules during development. Java's module system rules are enforced at all stages in a consistent manner, from development to run-time.

The Java module system also has features that are not in OSGi, mostly around migration to modules. There's no direct OSGi equivalent of automatic modules. Not all Java libraries offer (correct) OSGi metadata, meaning patches or pull requests are the only means of using those libraries with OSGi. Libraries sometimes also contain code that doesn't play nice with OSGi's isolated classloading setup. In the Java module system, classloading is implemented in a more backward-compatible manner. Because the Java module system doesn't use classloaders for isolation, it offers stronger encapsulation. A whole new mechanism based on accessibility and readability is enforced deep within the JVM.

Time will tell whether adoption of the Java module system will be higher. Because modules are now part of the Java platform itself, we fully expect the Java community to take modularization seriously.

Java EE

Modules are a Java SE feature. Many developers, however, develop Java EE applications. In Java EE, Web Archives (WARs) and Enterprise Archives (EARs) bundle JAR files with deployment descriptors. These Java EE applications are then deployed onto application servers.

How will Java EE evolve, given modules are now part of the Java platform? It's fair to assume that at some point the Java EE specification will embrace modules. At the moment, it's too early to tell what this will look like. The Java EE 8 release builds on Java SE 8. So modules and Java EE meet at the earliest in Java EE 9, for which no release date is set. Until this convergence, Java EE application servers can keep on using the classpath as before.

You already saw in "Container Architectures" on page 142 that in principle, the module system has features to support application containers such as Java EE application servers. What modular Java EE applications will look like remains to be seen. For applications, Java EE modularity could be a form of modular WAR or EAR files, or something completely new.

A good first step would be to publish the Java EE APIs as modules with standardized names. The official JAX-RS API (*https://github.com/jax-rs/api*) distribution already has a module descriptor. With modules, it becomes even more attractive to regard Java EE as a loosely related set of specifications. Maybe there's no need to wait for monolithic application servers to support a full suite of specifications at once. When you can require just the parts of Java EE you need, new doors open. Keep in mind, though, this is all speculation based on what could be, not what is.

Microservices

In the past few years, microservices have gained prominence as an architectural style. One of the cited benefits of microservices is that they enable modular development. By dividing a system into independently deployable and runnable parts, the system is modularized. Each microservice runs as an independent process. Multiple microservices can even be written in completely different technologies. They communicate over the network by using standard protocols such as HTTP and gRPC.

Indeed, this architectural style inherently enforces strong module boundaries. How do microservices fare on the other two principles of modularity, well-defined interfaces and explicit dependencies? Interfaces between microservices fall on a spectrum from rigidly defined in an Interface Definition Language (IDL) such as Protocol Buffers, RAML, or even WSDL/SOAP, to unspecified JSON over HTTP. Dependencies between microservices typically arise by dynamic discovery at run-time. Not many microservices stacks offer statically verifiable dependencies akin to `requires` in module descriptors.

In this book, you have seen that modularity can be achieved without resorting to process isolation. Using the Java module system, strong encapsulation and explicit dependencies between modules can be enforced by the Java compiler and JVM. Use of Java interfaces and services with their explicit `provides`/`uses` wiring in the module system completes this modular development approach. Viewed from this perspective, microservices are somewhat like modules with a network boundary in between. But these network boundaries turn a microservices system into a distributed system with all the associated drawbacks. When you choose microservices solely for their modularity characteristics, think twice. Using Java modules for your system brings similar (or even stronger) modularity benefits, without the operational complexity of a microservices architecture.

To be fair, there are many reasons why microservices can be a good choice, besides the argument for modularity. Think of independent updates and scaling of services, or when using different technology stacks per service really is beneficial. Then again, choosing between modules or microservices doesn't have to be either/or. Modules can create a strong internal structure for a microservice implementation, allowing it to scale beyond what you would typically ascribe to *micro*. It's quite sensible to initially develop a system with modules, while at a later stage extracting some of those modules into their own microservices when operational concerns demand it.

Next Steps

We've discussed several alternative approaches to modularization and how they relate to the Java module system. The hard part still lies in correctly decomposing the domain of your application, regardless of what technique you use to do so. Java modules are another powerful tool in the toolbox to create well-structured systems.

Is the current state of the module system perfect? Nothing is, and the module system is no exception. Adding a module system this late in the Java platform's life cycle inevitably led to compromises. Still, Java 9 lays a solid foundation to build upon. Sure, it would be great to address issues such as running multiple versions of a module at the same time besides what's currently possible with `ModuleLayer`. The fact that this is not currently supported on the module path doesn't mean it will never be. For other features, the same holds. The module system is not done and will almost certainly gain new powers in subsequent releases. For now, it is up to the Java ecosystem and tool vendors to support modular Java.

As the Java community starts to embrace the module system, more libraries will become available as modules. This makes it easier to embrace modules in your own applications, although we have seen that automatic modules are an acceptable interim solution. To get started, it makes sense to gain experience with the module system in a greenfield setting. Build a small application consisting of a handful of modules, like the EasyText application you've seen throughout this book. This gives you a good feel for what a cleanly modularized application looks like. With this experience under your belt, you can take on a more ambitious step, such as modularizing one of your existing applications.

Having a module system as part of the Java platform is a game-changer. No, this is not something that will happen overnight. It will take considerable time for the Java community to embrace the concepts of the Java module system. That's just the nature of the beast: modularity is not a quick fix or new feature you can slap onto existing codebases. Yet the advantages of modularity are evident. The renewed attention for modularity through microservices illustrates that most people intuitively grasp this. With the module system, Java developers gain new options for building maintainable large-scale systems.

You now have learned the concepts of the Java module system. More important, you know the principles behind modularity and how to apply them by using the module system. Now it's time to use this knowledge in practice. May your software have a modular future!

Index

O

object-relational mappers (ORMs)
 access to implementation classes, 116
open keyword (in module descriptor), 118
open modules and packages, 113, 118, 156
 dependency injection reliance on, 121
 in libray module descriptor generated by
  jdeps, 213
 open modules, 179
 open packages, 177-179
 opening application packages to the container, 147
 selectively opening packages from non-open
  modules, 119
opens clause, 119
 --add-opens command-line flag, 180
 addOpens method in Module, 126
 for packages needing instantiation or injection, 123
 for Spring/Hibernate implementation packages, 202
 java --add-opens command and, 120
 qualified, 120, 178
 qualified versus unqualified, 123
operating systems
 cross-targeting runtime images for, 262
 separators on module path, 40
optimizations, whole-program, from custom
 runtime images, 251
optional dependencies, 99-105
 implementing with services, 104-105
 modeling using compile-time dependencies,
  100
OSGi, 6, 264, 266
 differences between Java module system
  and, 265
 running multiple versions of modules concurrently, 109
outgoing dependencies, 17

P

-p (module-path) compiler flag, 38
package-info.java file, 35
packages, 5
 and accessibility in modular Java, 23
 exported and open, 120
 exporting all, in automatic modules, 174
 exporting from a module, 46
 exporting or opening, reflection and, 176

exposing encapsulated resources in, 113
modules requiring packaged types, 33
naming, 36
open, 118, 156
opening for reflection in Spring/Hibernate
 migration, 201
packaging modules, 37
resource encapsulation in, 113
run-time access to, in open modules, 180
split, 94, 189
 cleanly split package, 95
parent POM, 230
Parnas partitioning, 80
Parnas, D. L., 80
--patch-module flag, 245
patching modules, 245-247
performance optimizations
 for custom runtime images, 261
 from custom runtime images, 249
platform JARs, 7
platform modules, 12, 17, 48-54
 deep reflection applied to, warnings by
  JVM, 155
 dependencies graph, 17
 encapsulated types in, 31
 finding the right module, 48
 getting full list of, 19
 of OS and architecture you want to target,
  262
 --patch-module flag for, 247
 qualified exports in, 27
 resolving in containers, 148-149
 split packages and, 189
PlatformClassLoader, 134
plug-in architectures, 137-142
 container architectures versus, 142
 host application extended by plug-ins, 137
Plugin interface, 138
POM files, 6
pom.xml file, 230
 dependencies listed in, module path configuration and, 234
primordial classloader, 134
.properties file, 113
protected access modifier, 5
provider method, 66
 Analyzer implementation example, 67
 factory class containing, 67
provider services, life cycle, 66

About the Authors

Sander Mak is a Fellow at Luminis in the Netherlands, where he crafts modular and scalable software, most often on the JVM but with a touch of TypeScript where needed. He is an avid conference speaker and loves sharing knowledge through his blog at *http://branchandbound.net* and as a Pluralsight (*http://bit.ly/sander-ps*) instructor. You can follow him on Twitter at @sander_mak.

Paul Bakker is a senior software engineer at Netflix, on the Edge Developer Experience team, where he primarily works on tools to increase developer productivity within the company. Besides his love for writing code, he has a passion for sharing knowledge. This is his second book, after coauthoring *Modular Cloud Apps with OSGi* (O'Reilly). Paul also frequently speaks at conferences about modularity, container technology, and many other topics. He blogs at *http://paulbakker.io* and is active on Twitter as @pbakker.

Colophon

The animal on the cover of *Java 9 Modularity* is a black-tailed godwit (*Limosa limos*), a large wading bird, first described by Carl Linnaeus in 1758, that nests in Europe and Asia. Its breeding range stretches from Iceland to northern India. They are found in wetlands, estuaries, and lake edges.

Black-tailed godwits have long legs and a long bill that allow them to wade through their swampy habitat probing underwater for food. Their diet mainly consists of insects and aquatic plants. The eponymous black tail can be most easily seen when the bird is in flight. Black-tailed godwits are mostly monogamous breeders. Pairs reunite at breeding sites after which the female lays three to six eggs in a nest. Unpaired males fight for territory and put on displays to attract females.

The black-tailed godwit was once considered a delicacy in Europe, but its declining population has led European governments to put in place hunting restrictions (although a limited amount of hunting is still allowed in France). The black-tailed godwit is currently listed as near-threatened.

Many of the animals on O'Reilly covers are endangered; all of them are important to the world. To learn more about how you can help, go to *animals.oreilly.com*.

The cover image is from *Wood's Illustrated Natural History*. The cover fonts are URW Typewriter and Guardian Sans. The text font is Adobe Minion Pro; the heading font is Adobe Myriad Condensed; and the code font is Dalton Maag's Ubuntu Mono.

Learn from experts.
Find the answers you need.

Sign up for a **10-day free trial** to get **unlimited access** to all of the content on Safari, including Learning Paths, interactive tutorials, and curated playlists that draw from thousands of ebooks and training videos on a wide range of topics, including data, design, DevOps, management, business—and much more.

Start your free trial at:

oreilly.com/safari

(No credit card required.)

CPSIA information can be obtained
at www.ICGtesting.com
Printed in the USA
BVOW04s1753100917
494410BV00005BA/6/P